THOSE WERE THE DAYS

Through the Seasons

BY WENDELL TROGDON

INTRODUCTION BY MARTIN NORTHWAY

ILLUSTRATED BY GARY VARVEL

HIGHLANDER
PRESS

Highlander Press First Edition
Copyright © 1986 by Wendell Trogdon
All rights reserved under International and Pan-American
Copyright Conventions. Published in the United States by
The Highlander Press, Chicago, Illinois.
Local distribution by Wendell Trogdon,
Mooresville, Indiana

Library of Congress No. 86-081934
ISBN: 0–913617–02–X

Cover design and book design by Martin Northway
Typography by Ampersand Associates, Inc., Chicago

Dedication

For all the good people who were role models during our formative years. They were kind and gracious folks who lived uncomplicated lives and taught us the value of humor, honesty, integrity and self-contentment. It is in their memories this book is dedicated.

—*Wendell Trogdon*

Acknowledgments

So many people helped make this book possible, it is impossible to name each of them.

There was my wife, Fabian, who offered criticism and compliments. There were my brother, Wayne, my sisters, Nora, Nellie and Martha, and dozens of other men and women who filled in gaps in my own memory. There were people like Wayne Faubion, who shared his recollection of a rural baptism, and Bob Harbin, the son of a minister who recalled the day the furnace at church "exploded" in his face. And, of course, there were all the characters in these stories, who deserve to be memorialized for generations to come.

There were Gary Varvel, a generation younger than the author, who illustrated these stories, and Martin Northway, who wrote introductions for each chapter, designed the book, and dealt gently with an anxious writer.

And there were my colleagues at *The Indianapolis News*, where these stories first appeared. Their advice, opinions, encouragement and colleagueship are, and have been, much appreciated.

Contents

Introduction 1

The Seasons of Our Lives 3
To everything, including our lives, there was a season

The Depression Era 18
From eagles to turkeys, the Depression wasn't always "foul"

The Seasons of War 30
Hoosier courage in a nation's time of trouble

Local Color 39
People were at their best in the harvest season

Wood Stove Time 51
The light in the window was eternal spring

The Fifth Season 65
They didn't call it Hoosier hysteria for nothing

The Green Season 76
Hope, like farm and field, bloomed eternal

Lazy, Hazy, Crazy Days 101
What we really did during those summer vacations

Just Plain Folk 115
There was nothing ordinary about these people

Seasons of Change 145
The mixed blessings of change and progress

Index 167

Introduction

Those were the days! We all seemed closer to nature, and maybe to each other, than we do today. You felt the changing of the seasons deep in your bones. With no central heat or air conditioning, you savored the warm comfort of a wood stove deep in winter—you felt the delight of a summer dip down to your toes.

But you also felt something else if you were growing up in rural Indiana in the 1930s and '40s. Along with the recurring cycle of the seasons, you sensed the pace of relentless change—Depression, "progress," the approach of war. You enjoyed life, but you also knew the world would never be the same.

These are the days a former Southern Indiana farm boy writes about now with heart and humor—chapters gleaned from the best of Wendell Trogdon's popular weekly columns in *The Indianapolis News*.

The author grew up in Lawrence County with creek christenings and frog-hunting, harvest and mushroom-hunting, Jack Armstrong on the radio, and basketball games that sometimes barely broke into double digits. His stories are a wonder. They have the seasoned journalist's instinct for accuracy, and they get the cadences of rural and small-town life just right. The author has an ear for the distinctive "Hoosier language," too—an ability to recall the unique wry Indiana humor.

There's something else here as well. Wendell Trogdon's stories are permeated with the true agrarian's understanding awareness of the world around him. You will share the joy and feel the pain.

—*Martin Northway*

The Seasons of Our Lives

Explaining the wear and tear on his body, movie adventurer "Indiana" Jones quipped, "It's not the years but the mileage." He could just as well have been talking about the folks he left back home in Indiana in the 1930s, living out the seasons of their lives. In the annual passing of the seasons in nature they experienced an accelerated version of the birth, growth, aging, and death in their own lives.

It is remarkable that with all our technology and medical breakthroughs, there has been so little change in how we human beings grow and age. Youth still passes too quickly, we still wrinkle or gray or bald too fast, still gradually lose our vigor.

What is different today, perhaps, is that this natural process frightens us more than it did people who were closer to the land and nature. We lack the reassurance that came from being enclosed by nature and by the wisdom of older generations and the good will of young people close by.

There was plenty of patience, too, with the pains of growing up. Adults seemed stern sometimes, to indulge children less, but they were also wise enough not to expect youngsters to grow up all at once. So, they sneaked beer, went joy-riding, and got green in the face smoking corn silk, but these mistakes "took," and weren't often fatal. As a consequence, a mother's or dad's approval of one's coming of age meant a great deal, and gray hair wasn't considered an affliction but a symbol of respect justly earned by age.

Too bad we can't appreciate this process today like we applaud fine wine or vintage cars. We should enjoy the trip more while we're adding to the mileage!
—MN

On Being a Good Neighbor

Ben was a cantankerous fella. At least it seemed that way to a couple of spirited boys who were his neighbors.

Maybe it was because Ben was on the dark side of the 70s. He and his wife, Ellie, hadn't been around children much for years and had little experience in dealing with the complex minds of the young.

It wasn't that Ben was mean. He just wasn't too neighborly. When you were around, he made you feel like you'd be more comfortable elsewhere, but if the truth were known, he may have enjoyed the company.

Almost every Saturday morning when he knew a trip was to be made into Bedford, the county seat, Ben would visit the home of his two young neighbors and ask their father if he could ride into town with him. His request was always obliged, even though he'd get on the nerves of almost everyone who went along. He liked to talk, probably because the only other person he conversed with days on end was Ellie.

Before leaving one Saturday, one of the boys pulled out a pack of Dentyne chewing gum, ripped open an end, and said: "Like some, Ben?"

"Don't mind if I do," said Ben, taking the entire package. He didn't return it, and by the time they arrived in Bedford he had all five pieces in his mouth.

The only car Ben ever owned was a Model T. When he grew older he parked it in the barn and gave up driving. Probably the fastest he ever drove was 30 mph.

His Saturday chauffeur drove a four-year-old 1937 Buick that somehow had a speedometer needle stuck at forty when the car was standing still. The driver always knew that "one way to shut up old Ben" was to drive fast. One day when Ben got on his nerves he speeded up the Buick to 80, which meant the speed showing on the dash was 120.

"How do you like to travel at this speed, Ben?" he asked. Ben saw the speedometer, mumbled something about a crazy driver, and didn't say another word the rest of the way into town.

Like many farmers, Ben always burned the broom-sage off his pastures before the grass began to grow each spring. There always was a chance the fire would spread into woodland and into land on adjoining farms.

On one occasion before he set fire to the sage, he asked his two young neighbors if they'd help him. They reckoned as to how it was a chance to make some spending money, so they agreed.

Ben gave each of them a burlap bag,

showed them how to wet it in the soapstone-bottom creek and to beat out the fire if it began to spread into the rail fences or otherwise get out of bounds.

Ben lighted his first match, stuck it into a brown clump and stood back. The fire took off with the wind.

The two youngsters spent the next four hours fighting to keep the fire under control. About 6:00 p.m. the last flame on the outer edges of the fire was out and any danger was over.

They took what was left of the burlap bags to Ben, barely managing to walk or talk. Their mouths were as dry as Prohibition was supposed to have been.

"You fellas did a good job," said Ben. The boys smiled, somehow, probably because they expected a sizable payoff.

"Here's a quarter for each of you," he said, sounding like a big spender.

The boys inched the half-mile home, telling each other Dad would cuss old Ben out for being so miserly.

"We want you to tell Ben we ought to have more money. We fought that fire for four hours without letting up and all he gives us is two bits a piece."

Their dad looked at them and said: "Seems to me you fellas have forgotten Ben's our neighbor. We're supposed to help our neighbors when they need help. Now, you be thankful he gave you quarters. He didn't have to give you a thing."

The boys got the message. They never forgot old Ben. Or the high cost of being a good neighbor.

A Boy's Dream: A Genuine Air Rifle

It didn't take much to make farm youngsters around Heltonville happy. Hightop boots, high-back overalls and an air rifle were all they needed.

Especially an air rifle. It was a priority item in the late '30s and early '40s, one no boy from eight to eleven wanted to be without. It gave prestige to its owner, who was too old to be a child, too young to be a man.

And the most prestige came to those who carried a genuine air rifle, better known as a BB gun, with Red Ryder's signature burned into the stock. There were other makers of air rifles, but none of them could match the value placed on the Red Ryder models made at the Daisy Manufacturing Co. in Plymouth, Michigan.

Red Ryder was a cowboy who appeared daily in comic strips in newspapers in Bedford and hundreds of other cities. If that wasn't enough to make him popular, Ryder and his friend, Little Beaver, starred in movie serials made by Republic Pictures. One of the serials lasted for twelve weeks and by the time Ryder and Little Beaver had nabbed the cattle rustlers, Tad, Tyke, Pokey, Blinky and Bunky were taking on their mannerisms.

Tyke was the oldest. He already had an air rifle, but it wasn't a Red Ryder. The others didn't have rifles of any kind. That's why they conspired to formulate a plan so each of them could have one of the five models Daisy made, including the one with Ryder's name on them.

They were at Blinky's house one cold winter day when Tyke pulled a page out of his back pocket he'd torn from a Captain Marvel comic book. He unfolded the page and held it up for the others. It was an ad for the Red Ryder rifles. It called for the readers to **"Get This Cowboy Carbine With Your Christmas Money."**

Tad said, "I ain't got no Christmas money. Didn't get any and if I had, I'd have already spent it."

The others all said about the same thing. That didn't stop them from reading the ad. It had pictures of the different models. There was a "double-barrel repeater . . . 100-shot break action automatic, engraved jacket . . . just like dad's double-shot." It cost $5.00. There was a "pump repeater, 50-shot" for $4.50, a "Buck Jones special 60-shot with a compass and sun dial in the stock" for $3.50 and a "500-shot lightning loader carbine" for only $2.50.

Tad said maybe he'd rather have the Buck Jones special. "The compass and sun dial would sure be nice," he said.

Tyke said, "You don't need a compass. You can find your way home, and we don't need a sun dial 'cause who cares what time it is?"

Blinky said, "Yeah. We want the golden-banded 1,000-shot Red Ryder cowboy carbine," reading from the ad.

Tyke said, "And listen to this. It comes with 16-inch leather saddle thong," then continued reading, "has lightning-loader invention . . . you can pour in 1,000 shot in 20 seconds . . . carbine style forepiece and cocking lever. Adjustable double-notch reader sight. Red Ryder's picture, signature and horse 'Thunder' branded on pistol-grip stock.''

He stopped long enough for Bunky to ask, "Where can we get one?"

Tyke said, "It says here you can buy your Red Ryder carbine at the nearest hardware, sports goods or department store."

Bunky said, "That means we can't get one in Heltonville. There are no hardware, sports goods or department stores here."

Tyke said, "Well, it says here you can send $2.95 and the Daisy company will send you the rifle."

"Okay," Tad asked, "how we each going to get the $2.95?"

That's when the conspiracy started. Each of the five agreed to tell his parents the other four were getting the rifle and that he'd be the only one without one if they didn't let him have one, too.

Each of them wrote orders for the Red Ryder carbine and addressed the envelopes with indelible pencils before taking their pleas for the rifles home.

The scheme worked. Each of the boys convinced his parents to write checks for $2.95 for the rifles and to give him three pennies to leave in the mail box for the stamps.

The boys were at church the next Sunday when Pokey's dad walked up to Tad's father and said, "Wouldn't have given the boy money for that air rifle if I didn't know you were buyin' one for Tad."

Tad's father was perceptive. He looked at Tad, then at Pokey and said, "I think we've been snookered."

Tad and Pokey looked like they'd swallowed castor oil and headed inside the church to safety.

It was the last time the scheme worked. But the boys got their Red Ryders, which they cherished for years.

From Corn Silk to Long Green, Chig Smoked 'Em

By the time a farm boy was ten he thought he knew all there was to know about smoking. Chig was no exception.

A pack of Marvels could be bought in the fall of 1940 for eight cents at Dee Terrell's grocery in Norman or at Roberts' general store in Heltonville. Some smokers complained they were overpriced. Lucky Strike, Philip Morris and Chesterfields cost a dime.

Chig seldom had eight cents, almost never a dime. Once in a while an older friend would let him try a cigarette, but not often enough for him to become a nicotine addict.

Chig, however, overcame his shortage of money with an oversupply of imagination, an imagination that led him to experiment with every type of smoke he'd heard about and some he hadn't.

He and Billy had rolled corn silks, wrapped them in newspaper and taken a couple of draws before the fire singed their fingers. They soon learned, the trouble exceeded the thrill.

They had tried smoking grape vines. And wished they hadn't.

They reamed out corncobs, opened

a hole near an end and inserted a hollowed-out elderberry stem. They packed coffee grounds into the pipe, then puffed until they were blue of face and queasy of stomach. Corn silks didn't burn any more slowly in the pipe than in the newspaper.

They had tried to roll their own cigarettes from cans of Prince Albert with store-bought paper. Usually the tobacco would drop out when they ran their tongues along the glued edge. The men they'd bummed the tobacco from would laugh at them and offer them more tobacco from Velvet cans and Bull Durham sacks.

Once, Jimmy, a hired hand, pulled out a plug of Days Work chewing tobacco, opened his pocket knife and sliced off a chew. He handed it to Chig and said, "Chew once, spit twice and don't get the two commands mixed up." After two chews and four spits, both Chig and the tobacco hit the ground.

Chig thought he had mastered smoking when he was handed a mild cigar. He wetted the stogy with his lips, brushed a kitchen match across the seat of his overalls until it struck and puffed until the end grew red. He smoked about two inches off the end, before he tossed it away as his dad approached.

Chig learned a lot that summer, mainly because he chose to repeat his experiences to test their validity.

That's probably why he convinced Billy they ought to try some long green tobacco before Tom decided to harvest it that September. "Long green" was another name for burley tobacco Tom grew on his farm for his own use.

The tobacco had turned brown, but it hadn't yet cured. The leaves looked dry enough to burn. Chig broke off a big leaf, carried it to a secluded spot and divided it with Billy.

The boys rolled the crispy leaf in their hands and fashioned the crushed tobacco into cigarettes. They each took a few drags.

"Tastes bitter," said Billy.

Chig coughed a couple of times before saying, between gasps, "I think we should have let Tom cure it before we snitched it."

"I feel like I'm dying," Billy said.

Chig said, "Death can't come too soon for me."

They lived, but only after staggering home to beat the darkness. Both skipped supper that night.

Their mothers felt sorry for them. Their fathers suspected the cause of their distress.

The next day when the school bus slowed down to pick up Billy, someone yelled, "Looks like Tom is getting ready to cut his tobacco."

Chig gagged. Only the quick reflex of hand to mouth kept him from further embarrassment.

Through a Perilous Night

Nobody was certain the story was true, but most people who knew the characters involved figured it was something that would likely happen to them.

The characters were three boys who went everywhere together, be it to perpetrate a prank, do a good deed or visit a Holy Roller service just to see what it was like. They never hesitated to tell anyone at school who would listen what they'd been up to. That's why each of them became good storytellers.

They spun their best yarn the day after they'd driven up to Smithville to visit a friend.

Jake waited until most of the high school boys had sat down on the ledge and opened up their sack lunches. Then he said, "You guys oughta been with old Tyke, Tad and me last night."

Nobody said anything because they knew he'd go on with the story.

"We went up to Smithville for a couple hours. When we got ready to come back it was dark. Tyke hadn't driven his dad's 1939 Chevy more'n two miles when the lights went out."

Len, who knew how winding and narrow the county road south of Smithville was, said, "You cain't drive on that road without lights, 'specially as dark as it was last night."

Jake took a bite out of his peanut-butter-and-jelly sandwich and said, "Right, Len. That's why Tyke and me told Tad he'd have to walk to the nearest farmhouse and borrow a lantern."

Tad decided he ought to join in the conversation. "Ever hear anything as mean? Had to do some convincin' to get that farmer to let me have a lantern. Good thing I had a dollar to give him as a deposit."

Jake took over again: "Anyhow, we put Tad out on the hood of the car and he held the lantern with one hand and the fender with the other and kinda directed Tyke by wavin' the lantern to the right or left.

"Wouldn't have been much to it at all if it hadn't been drizzlin'," Tad said. "The rain was runnin' down my eyes and I didn't have a free hand to wipe it off."

Tyke explained, "Things went slow until we got down to the Salt Creek bottom north of Bartlettsville and we noticed the steam comin' up around Tad which kinda caused him to move around a bit.

"He finally yelled he was on a hot seat, which made me know somethin' was wrong. The car had run low on water.

"Dad usually has a gas can in the car and Tad took it and stumbled over to the creek."

"Stumbled, heck, I just stepped into it," said Tad. "Couldn't see nothin', but I got enough water in the can to pour in the radiator and make my seat a little cooler."

Tyke said, "We moved along at about five miles per hour until we got to the bridge over Henderson Creek. I had to back up twice or we'd of hit the side of it."

Jake said, "What really upset Tyke and me, though, was when Tad began to sing 'The Old Rugged Cross.' It was so bad as we crept past Jess' house his coon dogs started bayin'."

"Had to do something to take my

mind off the cold and rain and the goose bumps," Tad explained.

Tyke said, "We didn't get back to Heltonville 'til about midnight. My dad wanted to know why I was so late and I told him the dern lights went out.

"All dad said was, 'Guess that would have slowed you down some since there ain't no mechanic or fillin' stations 'tween here and Smithville.' I told him it did slow us up a mite."

Jake said, "Think I'll stay home tonight."

"Me, too," said Tyke.

"Thank God," said Tad, who was beginning to sneeze and wipe his nose.

True Brew Blues

By the time he was sixteen, Bud thought he had experienced more than most people who were twenty-five.

But he learned one night that wasn't necessarily so. He lived out on Goat Run. The road a few miles northwest of Heltonville was called that because it was more like an animal path than a highway. That doesn't have anything to do with this story, except that it shows the remoteness of the area where Bud grew up.

That may be one reason why Bud's dad made beer, "home brew" he called it, in the years right after World War II. Every once in a while Bud got to sip the samples his dad drew before bottling the brew for sale at his home. He didn't make deliveries, which meant he couldn't be nabbed for running illegal contraband.

Bud wasn't above trying to impress the other youths around Heltonville. He and a couple of friends were sitting in the restaurant one summer evening trying to think of something to do when Bud suggested a couple of bottles of his dad's brew might give his imagination a broader perspective.

"Oh, sure, and I suppose you got a tubful iced down back in the rumble seat of your Model A there," said Stinky.

"Nope, ain't got any with me," sighed Bud.

Raspy, who could always be counted on to offer suggestions, said, "Suppose your pa's got it all locked up down in the cellar?"

"It's down in the cellar, all right," said Bud, "but it ain't locked up."

The three looked at each other. Bud turned toward his car, telling Stinky and Raspy, "Hop in. We're gonna get us somethin' to drink."

About a half mile from his house, Bud turned off the lights on the car, let it coast another quarter mile or so, then steered it to the side of the road. "We'd better walk the rest of the way or Mom and Dad will hear the car and wake up," he said.

At the house, he led Raspy and Stinky down the steps to the cellar. He handed each of them three bottles and said, "Don't drop 'em or we'll all be in trouble."

Raspy and Stinky already knew what he was thinking but Bud said it anyhow. "If dad finds out about this he'll kill me and put out a reward for you two guys."

The boys made it back to the car, drove out to Gilgal Cemetery and drank the brew, even though it was warm.

After the first bottle, Stinky admitted it was the first time he'd ever tasted beer. Raspy and Bud acted like they'd been boozin' for years, but Stinky found out later that wasn't true.

Later that evening, they all got a bit sick. Somehow, Bud got the boys back into Heltonville and drove on home.

The next day, none of the three boys showed up at school. Stinky told his folks he "must have had a bad hamburger up at the restaurant." Raspy said he couldn't understand why he was sick.

Bud told his folks he had a splitting headache for some unknown reason. His dad said, "Wouldn't have anything to do with that home brew that's missin' from the cellar would it?"

Bud didn't feel like lying. "Could be, I reckon."

His mom muttered something to his dad. His dad managed a smile and said: "Son, you learned more last night than you would have learned at school today."

He turned to Bud's mom and said, "Reckon you don't have to worry anymore about Bud sneakin' out the brew for the boys."

Tested Boy, Found Man

For months, the twelve-year-old boy had been begging his dad to let him operate the big farm tractor when spring arrived.

Tad figured he could disk and plow as well as anyone and had everyone convinced except his father. Tad had done assorted jobs around the place since he was seven. He could handle the Farmall, even tripping the plow and making a turn at the end of the field at the same time.

His dad knew that, but his father also figured the youngster would appreciate the hours he would spend later on the tractor if he passed a little test first.

Only thing was, Tad didn't consider it a "little test." When the fields were dry enough to plow, his dad told him what he had in mind: "Son, you can take over the H," which is what he called the tractor, "as soon as you plow four acres back at the yon side

of the west field. With the horses and walking plow."

"Man, I have trouble just holdin' onto those horses, let alone a plow. And besides, you know how rocky that ground is you want me to plow."

"It's up to you, son. Either do it, or wait another summer to drive the tractor. The point on that plow is sharp, just waitin' to slice open that sod back there."

Tad recognized an upper hand when he saw it. Since his dad had it, he awoke at dawn the next day, harnessed Bird and Molly; hitched them to the doubletree on the plow, turned it on its side and headed for the field.

Fortunately, the team knew exactly what to do once it had made a round trip across the field and Tad had thrown up two furrows back to back. All Tad had to do thereafter was to keep the lines around his neck and a plow handle in each hand. And watch out for the rocks. Always the rocks.

Every once in a while, the plow

would hit a geode six inches in diameter and the plow would bounce out of the furrow and skip across the sod for a foot or so before Tad could get the point to "take" again.

The two hours passed almost as quickly as a fortnight. If things went well, he figured about 9:00 a.m., as he gave the horse a breather, he'd get the field plowed by July 4.

At noon, his dad asked, "How's it goin'?"

"Just rock'n' and a-rollin'," Tad said. He figured he could bluff his way through.

"Just remember, Son, let the horses and the plow do the work. Don't try to steer it."

By late afternoon, Tad was getting the hang of it. But that night he dreamed of walking in furrows across the U.S.A.

He finished the job at sundown the next day. He checked the scales in the granary and noticed his weight was down from 120 to 111. "Fightin' weight," he said to himself. "Fightin' weight to go against a plow."

His dad made a quick inspection of the plowing and gave Tad an "A-minus. You'd've got an A but you got in too big a hurry on a dead furrow." Tad knew a dead furrow was where two furrows met. "I danged near died in that dead furrow, Dad," Tad said.

"You've lived through it to be a man," his dad said. "You can plow the rest of the field with the tractor starting tomorrow."

Tad tried to give a friendly salute as a thank you. But his arm was too sore from holding onto the plow.

*Illustration by
Gary Varvel*

There's No Need
To See Red over
a Little Bit of Gray

Millie, like most farm wives, wasn't vain. She didn't have time to primp in front of the mirror, not with a houseful of kids and an assortment of chores.

That didn't mean she didn't care about her appearance. She always tried to look nice for her husband.

Millie and Zeke lived on a farm, near Heltonville in the 30s and 40s. They attended church events and made occasional trips into Bedford. Other than that, they seldom socialized.

Millie didn't pay much attention to fashions and beauty aids in the Sears, Spiegel and Montgomery Ward catalogues. Or to the commercials on the radio.

That's why she was unfamiliar with the name of a product guaranteed to restore gray hair to its original color.

Millie noticed a few strands of her brown hair had turned gray, but that didn't bother her. Most women her age had some gray hair. It was to be expected, she thought.

Her daughters were more familiar with cosmetics, artificial fingernails, bogus eyelashes and hair dyes. And they knew that some women who lived in town covered up the gray in their hair.

Millie was surprised when one of them asked, "Why don't you surprise Daddy by turning your hair back to the color it looked five or six years ago?"

Millie objected, but she was outnumbered. And she didn't like to argue with her kids.

She took a few worn dollar bills from the egg and cream money she kept in a jar in the three-cornered cupboard and told the girls, "Fill out the purchase form. We'll get a money order from the mailman and send for the stuff."

The product arrived in a few days and Millie let the girls work it into her hair, just like the directions said. In a week or two the gray was gone from her hair.

But Zeke hadn't noticed. Millie didn't like to call attention to herself. She waited several days until she could keep her secret no longer.

"Notice anything different about me?" she asked Zeke.

He looked at her for a while, then replied, "No. You look as pretty as ever."

Millie cried for the first time in years, sobbing that she had gone to a lot of trouble just to please him. She stayed miffed for a couple of days.

But she smiled after he came in one day with a clipping he found in an old *Farmers Guide*, a homespun publication that offered advice about the land and the people on it.

What he showed her was the answer in an advice column to a question about how to keep hair from turning gray. It read:

"Some people turn gray younger than others. Yet gray hair is usually a sign of advancing years. But why wish to stop gray hair? Gray hair always is becoming to the face it surrounds for it is the sign of advancing years of service. If one will accept gray hair, kindly, there will be the calm serene expression of a face to accompany it—a most pleasing person indeed."

Millie cried again. But this time the sobs came because she was happy.

The gray returned to her hair. This time to stay. And the jar of hair coloring went out of the house with the broken jars and empty cans.

A Man-Making Job

Nothing ever came easy for Joe. He had been a bit crippled most of his life, and that caused him to sort of drag his left foot as he walked. Added to that at times was a chronic case of rheumatism.

A lot of people would have given up farming and found an easier line of work. But not Joe. He'd just grit his teeth and dig into whatever job had to be done. He made up in perseverence what he lacked in agility.

Two nephews, Tyke and Tad, found out how much stamina he had back in the summer of '44. One was thirteen at the time, the other eleven. At their ages, they figured they could whip both Germany and Japan if the Marine Corps would let them join up. Instead, they took a job baling hay with Joe.

Joe didn't have one of those newfangled pickup hay balers that were driven through the field along hay rows, spitting out the bales behind. His was a stationary baler, set in place in the field. The farmers hauled in the hay and Joe fed it into the baler.

Tad, who was eleven, got the job of putting in the blocks which separated the bales, then punching the wires toward the other side where Tyke tied them. Tyke also had to tote the bales away from the back of the baler.

Both were new to the job and Joe fed the baler slowly enough for them to get the hang of it. After a couple of days the three learned to work well together.

Tyke and Tad soon learned that when you worked for Joe, you worked. He didn't tolerate any foolishness.

One day when the two got into a big argument over whether Bob Feller or Hal Newhouser was the better pitcher, Joe just shut down the baler and yelled loud enough to be heard on Goat Run, six miles away: "All right, all right. Shaad up. Like right now. Ya wanna argue do it on your own time, not mine.

"This little mischief means we're gonna work until 6:15 tonight 'stead of 6. Get the message, boys?"

He didn't wait for an answer. He started up the baler again.

Joe promised the farmers every bale would weigh between seventy and seventy-five pounds and he wouldn't tolerate anything less, even though Tyke told him he'd be mighty thankful if he could toss around fifty-pound bales instead of the heavier ones.

"I'd make more money that way," Joe said. "But it'd be dishonest and I ain't about to burn down yonder for what little extra it'd get me."

Every Saturday Joe would pay the boys the nine dollars they earned, sometimes adding an extra dollar.

By summer's end, they'd grown to respect Joe and for years they would cut down anyone who laughed at his slow shuffle and conservative ways.

They learned the stature of a man is measured more by his heart than by his looks. And that was worth more than all the money they made.

The People One Brushes Against in an Off-Limits Tavern

Bugsy had no business being in the tavern in Bedford that Saturday night. He was not yet eighteen.

He said later he would have preferred to have been down the street, sipping a cherry phosphate at Leonard's confectionary instead of drinking Champagne Velvet beer. But he didn't want to be labeled a chicken by the two older friends, who had persuaded him to enter the place.

"Pull up the collar around your neck, walk right behind us and act like you own the place. No one will question your age," Red told him.

Bob added, "And let me order."

World War II was still under way and neither the waitress nor the bartender paid much attention to the age of their customers.

Bugsy was still sipping his first beer when Red ordered a second round.

He peeled the label off the side of the bottle, rolled it into a wet wad and said, "Man, I'm sure glad the coach doesn't visit taverns."

He was talking about the basketball coach at Heltonville, who expected his players to follow the training regimen he had laid out.

Red said, "Hey! Quit worrying. Ain't nobody coming in here that we know."

Red couldn't have been more wrong. Before he began another sentence, the side door of the tavern opened and a man they each knew walked in. The man lived in Heltonville and was the superintendent of a conservative church, whose members were more temperate than the WCTU.

The superintendent didn't see Bugsy, Bob or Red in the booth as he turned and walked along the bar. He ordered two bottles of liquor and a case of beer. The bartender sacked the liquor, and said, "I'll get the beer for you at the side door."

The church superintendent turned, then gulped when he saw the three youths. His face turned as red as a Bedford Stonecutter pennant in the bar. He looked perplexed, embarrassed, like he had been caught lifting money from the collection plate.

He swallowed deeply a couple of times, then approached the booth, nervously. He greeted Bob, Red and Bugsy by their first names, then suggested, "Let's make a deal. I won't tell anyone I saw you here. If you won't say anything about me stopping in."

It was a classic case of blackmail.

Red usually wasn't cruel, but he looked up at the superintendent and said, without blinking, "We're not ashamed to be here. And if you want to tell our folks and our friends, go right ahead."

The superintendent was a man who usually got his way. He appeared surprised at Red's lack of respect. He looked humiliated, then said, "I'll be seeing you boys later," and walked out into what he must have thought to be a clouded future.

Bugsy looked at Red and said, "Now you've done it. By tomorrow everybody in Pleasant Run Township will know we were here."

Red mumbled a mild profanity and replied, "Forget it. He won't say any-

thing. He's too afraid we'll tell about him being here."

Bugsy said, "You going to tell anyone?"

Red shook his head. "Ain't none of my business if he wants to drink. Or if he wants to be hypocritical about it."

Red never said anything. Neither did Bob. Bugsy just told his best friend, who waited until no one would be hurt to relate the story.

If the superintendent ever told anyone, Bugsy, Red and Bob never heard about it.

Pride Goeth before the Fall as the Plate Gets Passed

Tad, Tyke, Dale and some of their friends were waiting for the church bell to ring that Easter Sunday when Timmy walked up.

Timmy was six, going on sixteen. He tried to act older than he was. Timmy was wearing a new gray suit his parents had bought for him in Bedford.

His attempt to appear important was betrayed by his look of discomfort. He twisted his neck back and forth to ease the snugness of a starched vest collar. He tugged at his vest to keep it from riding up over the belt loops on his pants.

Tad, Tyke and Dale were two or three years older than Timmy, and they had no qualms about teasing him. "Suit like that doesn't make you grow up any faster," Tyke said.

Timmy didn't let that bother him. He slid the index finger of his right hand into a little pocket on the right side of his vest and pulled out a nickel and a penny.

"This makes me look older, though," he said, holding up the coins. "Got my Sunday School money here, not in my sock or tied up in a handerchief where the other kids in

my class will have theirs."

The year was 1938, maybe 1939. The church was Mundell, a rural congregation southeast of Heltonville. Most youngsters were lucky to have a few coins, and their mothers made sure they kept them secure until the Sunday-school collection was taken.

Tyke and Tad agreed that Timmy was grown up if he could carry loose money around. Dale watched him run up the steps, then yelled, "keep your hand on your vest so the money won't bounce out." They didn't think much more about Timmy until church was dismissed.

Afterward, he walked by them without saying anything, which was unusual. Tyke called back and said, "Whatsamatter? You too big to talk to us, now?"

Timmy told them what had happened. Mildred Cummings had been making her rounds, stopping at the Sunday School classes Doris Bowman, Florence Anna Harrell and Laura Cummings taught.

Timmy explained, frowning, "The teacher passed around the basket. The girls managed to get their handkerchiefs untied and dropped their money in. The boys reached inside their socks or shoes and found their change."

He paused until Tyke told him to go on. "Well, I waited until they were through. Then I stood up, reached into my pocket like this, and the money flipped out onto the floor. It rolled into the furnace register," Timmy said.

"Everybody laughed at me," he said, looking like he might cry.

Tyke, Tad and Dale liked Timmy too much to laugh at him. They waited for him to continue.

"The teacher was all dressed up and didn't want to get down on her knees to get the money. She just told Mildred to leave with what money she had and that she'd have the menfolk dig out the money later."

Timmy looked as sad as a calf that had just been weaned.

"Forget it," Tyke said. "You can wear that suit next Sunday and be more careful with your money then."

Timmy managed to smile to show he may have been down, but not out.

"Couldn't loan me a few cents to practice on until then, could you?"

And It Rhymes With 'P,' Which Stands for Pool

If Chig's mother told him once she told him 100 times: **"Anything worth doing, Son, is worth doing well."** She might not have been so adamant if she had known he was going to apply that bit of advice to pool. She was like most mothers. She didn't think a pool room provided a good environment for a boy. She preferred he spend his free time at the library.

Chig didn't object to the library at the school in Heltonville or the one in Bedford. He just never seemed to find anyone he knew there.

He could find boys his age, though, at the Katis pool parlor in Bedford. It was home base for most teen-age youths from rural Lawrence County when they were in Bedford.

Not everyone played pool. Some of the freshmen and sophomores would sidle up to a pool game, lean against a post and watch the action while sipping one of John Katis' thick chocolate malts.

Few, though, could resist learning the game. Chig couldn't. He was about fourteen when he decided he was going to learn to play pool and play it well.

He decided to do so one Saturday in December 1944. The crops had been harvested and he knew his folks would be driving into Bedford to start Christmas shopping. In town, he said, "I'll find a ride home in time to help with the chores."

He almost ran to the pool parlor, traded a one-dollar bill for ten dimes and walked up to Dan, a sixteen-year-old, and said, "I'll pay for the games if you'll teach me how to play."

Dan nodded and said, "Your break."

Chig went to the rack, pulled out a cue stick, rolled it on the green table-covering, making sure it was straight, then chalked the tip. He powdered his hands. Up to that point he looked like a shark. Then he formed a "U" be-

tween his thumb and index finger and slid the cue stick back and forth a couple of times.

"Wait a minute, good buddy," Dan said. "That ain't no way to hold a cue stick."

Dan wrapped his index finger over his middle finger and slid the cue stick in the opening.

"Best players hold the stick like this," he said.

Chig and Dan played a half-dozen or so games of rotation. Dan won each of them. Chig managed to get a few more balls in the pockets each game.

Dan finally tired and said he had to leave. Chig got change for another dollar and found another player, then another. Each added to his knowledge of the game and helped him sharpen his skill, which was a pretty good investment for ten cents a game. He learned how to use the "farmer's guide," which is what players called the "crutch," to reach certain areas on the table. And he learned how to bank shots, play the caroms, kiss the cue ball off one ball onto another, play for the lie, run the rail.

He stopped only once during the day, and then only to drink a malt and eat a package of peanut butter crackers. He wouldn't have stopped at all if a couple of his friends hadn't agreed to save the table for him.

He finally caught a ride home about four o'clock, but not before announcing, "I'll be back next week to learn how to play snooker." Nobody doubted that he would be.

At home that night, his mother asked him where he had been all day. "Getting an education," he said.

His dad bit his tongue to keep from laughing, and quickly changed the subject for Chig's protection.

The Depression Era

The broad, open, often flat, expanses of northern Indiana do not prepare visitors for what begins about twenty miles south of Indianapolis—rolling farm, pasture, and wood land punctuated by craggy ridges and chattering streams that stretch clear to the Ohio River.

In this self-sufficient environment, the Great Depression passed almost unnoticed at first. The owner of an orchard and canning factory in Brown County reported, "When the stock market crashed . . . it made no more commotion . . . than if the King of Ethiopia had announced that he was about to take unto himself a new wife."

But eventually the economic realities of the outside world battered their way through the region's relative isolation. Restrictive regulations, the cannery owner claimed, shut down his and hundreds of similar rural and small-town enterprises. Banks closed, and loan money became scarce. Red dust at sunset was a bittersweet reminder that the Great Plains were blowing away.

The reaction of the upland Hoosiers was characteristic: they adjusted, they adapted, they made do, they took it all with sarcastic humor, they just plain took it. Life became a little harder for an already sturdy people. Though some of them may have raised a little livestock along with their debts, they were not sheep. Some jokingly referred to the symbolic eagle of the National Recovery Administration as the "blue buzzard," and they rebelled when President Roosevelt tried to switch Thanksgiving Day one week earlier to extend the holiday selling season.

The droll, no-nonsense Hoosiers knew then, as they still do, that it is hard to soar like an eagle when you fly with turkeys.   *—MN*

Even Dust Storm Had Some Good

It was in 1936, on one of those ideal fall days in Southern Indiana before the skies changed dramatically to a strange amber. Tad and the other first graders at Heltonville school were on the playground for afternoon recess when they first noticed the odd formation of clouds being pushed eastward by the wind. The sun had turned a darkened red.

They didn't know it at the time, but the clouds carried tons of dust churned up from the arid soil of Oklahoma and Kansas that had been left barren by months of dry weather.

The girls were the first to ask Miss Lively for an explanation of the sudden change. She told them to wait until after recess so she could explain the phenomenon to the entire class. She did so in a way even six-year-olds could understand, telling them what caused the dust storm, how it had driven farmers on the Plains to give up and move west, what they could expect when the clouds arrived over Heltonville.

Gordon asked her if it was some-

thing like the whirlwinds he had noticed at his farm home north of town. Miss Lively allowed as how he wasn't far off. The other youngsters also asked a lot of questions, but neither Miss Lively nor the students were prepared for what actually came.

By the time the last bell rang and the students hurried to their buses, the clouds had swept into town, bringing with them enough dust for them to taste it when they licked their lips. Some of the older students, who had seen some desert movies, were smart enough to tie handkerchiefs over their nostrils. Films of dirt had already covered the buses.

By the time Tad's bus reached the top of Groundhog Hill, the driver had turned on the wiper so he could keep the dirt off the windshield. The visibility was down to a few hundred feet, which meant Cecil couldn't see his house, a quarter-mile off the road, when he got off the bus.

Nothing had changed when the bus dropped Tad off at his home. The skies were still the same. He noticed the cows were already at the barn, thinking that it was time to be milked.

Tad blinked his eyes to wash away the grit as he walked up the hill to his house, wiping his new lunch box free of dust and brushing the dirt off his hair. When he walked into the house, he saw his mother was in one of her rare bad moods.

"Spent the whole day fall-house-cleaning," she said. "Washed the downstairs windows and just finished when the dust came in," she told Tad. "Guess I'll just have to do it all over again, if this dust storm ever passes."

That night at dinner, Tad said he could taste the dust in his beans, but his mom said that was because he had only dipped his hands in the washpan instead of cleaning his face good. His dad said, "If this don't stop soon we all may have to take a bath before Saturday night."

The storm passed all right, but not until it made things worse. A heavy shower during the night turned the dust to mud and splattered it against the windows and the weatherboarding of the house and spotted the family car with gobs of dark dirt.

The skies were mostly clear the next morning, and the sun came out warm enough to bake the dirt as it dried. Tad noticed the brown polka-dot designs on the yellow school bus as it came down the road. The driver had washed the windshield, but the side windows were still covered with so much mud that it was hard to see out of them.

At school, Miss Lively let the first graders talk about the experience, then asked if anyone could think of any useful purpose it served. Tad held up his hand immediately and Miss Lively nodded for him to speak out.

"Well, my mom was so disgusted about the dust, she didn't notice how dirty my clothes would have been anyhow. It was the first day since I've been in school she didn't scold me for looking like a tramp when I got home."

Miss Lively decided it was time to get on with her phonics lesson.

Feed Sacks Spun into Yarn

His mom and five neighbor women were seated around the quilting frame when Tad bounded into the house from the school bus on a cold March afternoon.

He poured himself a glass of milk, lifted a sugar cookie from the jar and turned on the battery-powered radio. It was still five minutes before Jack Armstrong, and he couldn't have heard the program over the six-way conversation in the next room, anyhow.

The women had about finished the quilt and were adding bits of bright-colored floss as decorations. They were talking about what they planned to do the next day.

"I'm going to rip apart all the cotton mash sacks I've been saving all winter. Figure I can make a couple dozen wash clothes and at least that many towels," Tad's mother said.

Flossie wanted to know, "What kind of mash do you buy?"

"Acme," Tad's mother said.

Flossie said, "Hardest kind of sack there is to remove the letter from," ending the sentence with a preposition.

That set off a discussion on how to remove the colored wording from feed sacks. Each of the women had a special formula for doing so.

Tad's mother, though, was not only the hostess, she was a voice of reason, explaining: "Since the letters aren't all the same inks or dyes, what will remove some kinds won't remove other kinds."

She went on to explain that she sometimes soaked the letters with kerosene, rolled up the sacks and left them for a day, then boiled them in hot suds in which she had put a little lye.

Flossie said she saturated the letters with turpentine, let it soak for a day, then washed as usual.

Millie said she could get the same results by boiling the sacks in lye water.

Maudie mentioned javelle water, then went on to tell how she made it by mixing sal soda and pearl ash, chloride of lime and rain water. Once the javelle water had set for a time in a corked bottle, she said, she'd rub it into the lettering on sacks, put them in clear water, add water and let soak. Then, she said, she washed the sacks like any other material.

They all agreed cotton feed sacks, once cleaned of the lettering, made good material for everything from bloomers to curtains.

The best towels, they said, came from old clover-seed sacks which were made of heavy, thick material.

"Never have figured out what to do with burlap sacks, though," Flossie said.

"Why don't you make your husband a pair of underdrawers?" Millie said. "That ought to put some life into the old codger."

The women laughed and Tad's mother suggested he ought to turn up the radio so he wouldn't miss his program.

A few months later Tad's mom brought home some factory-made towels from the J.C. Penney store in Bedford.

Tad tried them out. They were nice and smooth and soft, but they didn't dry the water from his face any better than the towels made from feed sacks.

'30s Nostalgia— Movies

There was nothing like Saturday night at the moving picture show back at Norman in the late 1930s.

The nation was slowly pulling itself out of the depths of the Great Depression. People had plenty of time to do anything they wanted, but not much money to do it with.

So for Saturday night in warm weather, C.E. Cummings, the town's biggest merchant, came up with a plan to bring people into the community. He succeeded so well, people showed up from almost every nearby Hoosier hamlet . . . Heltonville, Clearspring, Freetown, Kurtz, Zelma, Houston, Maumee and Hickory Grove.

It was a welcome deviation from chopping the sassafras shoots out of the corn, mending the crumbling barbed wire fence or hewing crossties.

C.E. started his weekly production well before dark. He would start by auctioning off almost anything anyone needed. The price was right . . . if you had the money.

While the old folks–anyone over twenty-two—nodded and rubbed shoulders and waited at the auction, the kids had time to spend their fifteen-cent allowance for the week.

With three Buffalo nickels you could buy an ice cream cone—stale cone, of course—a bottle of Nehi pop, warm, and a Kool candy bar.

These buys could be made on one of a half-dozen or so walks on the main drag, also known as Ind. 58, from Horace George's general store on the west to Dee Terrell's general store on the east. If you got tired of walking, you could watch Cecil change a tire on a Model A Ford or watch Ced cut hair.

The auction was conducted on a loading dock beside C.E.'s main store. He would figure it out so that everything he wanted to offer for sale could be sold just about the time it got dark.

That was the signal for the kids to get seated on crossties in the drive between the store and a neighboring building. If you didn't know what was going on, you'd think it odd that a bunch of youngsters would be sitting staring at the side of a barn. The adults would place their chairs and stools in what vacant spots they could find.

Meantime, one of C.E.'s employees would bring out the moving picture projector, and after some adjustments a white square would appear on the side of the barn. You always knew the picture was about to start because you'd see figures start to show up in reverse order. Some of the movies were so bad that the 5, 4, 3, 2, that preceded them was the highlight of the show.

But nobody blamed C.E. These were the best movies he could get. And besides, they weren't half as dull as having to shock wheat or carry water to the threshing crew.

When the movie was over and the lights came on, everybody present would stand and stretch and yawn and say how good the moving picture show had been. Then they would say goodbye to everyone else and head home.

Not many in Southern Indiana could wait until a week later to do it all over.

White Lightnin' Helps Make Ends Meet

Bunky and Tad never knew what they might discover when they tramped over the wooded hills and hollows east of Heltonville. The area was isolated and it was easy for them to imagine they were great explorers, going where no one had gone before.

They were wandering in their make-believe frontier one wintry Saturday in early 1939 when they walked into a small clearing surrounded by a thicket. Only a narrow lane, barely wide enough for a team and a wagon, broke the briers, brush and dried weeds that surrounded the spot.

In the center of the opening was a lean-to fashioned crudely from rough lumber. It covered an apparatus Bunky and Tad surmised was a still. It wasn't a bad supposition on their part, since each was only ten years old at the time.

Copper tubing ran through the apparatus to a big boiler. The boiler was empty, the fire out.

The boys found dozens of Mason jars, all empty. Tad kicked the dirt.

"What's the matter?" Bunky asked.

"Thought maybe we could have a snort of the rotgut," Tad said.

Bunky laughed, knowing Tad was kidding.

The boys looked around for a while, trying to figure out how the moonshine was made, before heading to Bunky's house to relate their findings to his father. They both tried to tell him about the still at the same

time. He finally said, "One at a time, one at a time. Now, exactly where were you?"

Bunky gave the location.

His dad said, "That's Jimmy's still. Chances are he's taking some time off. He may be marketing his product, or just loafing after selling a batch."

They never suspected Jimmy was a bootlegger. He was a kindly man, always friendly. Bunky's dad noticed their amazement.

"Jimmy makes white lightnin' to help make ends meet. Any profit he makes goes to make things more comfortable for his family. You may not like his means, but the end result is good," he said.

They talked for a while about the end of Prohibition and the fact moonshine production had continued. "The stuff is in demand," Bunky's father said, "because it's cheaper than legal liquor since there is no tax on it. That's why the revenue agents are always looking to bust up the stills." And he added that some of the buyers were so used to the moonshine that nothing else tasted right.

The boys wanted to know if Bunky's dad had ever come across a still.

"You bet I have. And I tell you boys, it's a good thing that was Jimmy's still and not somebody else's."

Bunky wanted to know what he meant.

"I was out looking at some timber I was thinking of buying down on Back Creek one time when I came across a still. It had a boiler that must.have held seventy-five gallons. It was eerie.

I felt like a dozen pairs of eyes were watching me. If I had turned around I probably would have seen the barrels of a dozen shotguns."

Bunky and Tad waited in suspense for Bunky's dad to continue.

"I knew I might be in trouble. The fire at the still was still burning. I turned, picked up a few pieces of wood and piled them on the fire."

Tad asked respectfully, "Didn't that mean you were helping make illegal whiskey?"

"Sure it did, Tad. It meant I was an accomplice, an accessory to the fact. It also meant that I couldn't testify in court against the operators of the still without them saying I was involved, too."

He paused to laugh. "But it also meant, the guys who owned them eyes that had been watching me let me walk away. It was probably one of the smartest things I ever done. Some intruders have been shot at for less."

He didn't act like he was kidding.

A few weeks later, Jimmy was arrested, convicted and sentenced to 180 days in prison.

Illustration by Gary Varvel

Cecil's Perfect Lunch

Nobody packed a better lunch than Cecil's mom. Most of the other students at Heltonville looked on with envy when Cecil opened his lunch pail at the noon recess. Some of them didn't start eating their own lunches until he had removed the sandwiches and cookies, opened the thermos and poured a cup of cocoa.

Cecil was in the lower grades at Heltonville in the late 1930s, a time before school cafeterias. The rural area was still recovering from the Great Depression, and the students brought their sparse lunches in an assortment of containers.

Bob brought his lunch in a newspaper held together by rubber bands one day, string the next. Gordy carried his in a round tin bucket, with an inset at the top for Jello or pudding. Some of the girls brought their lunches in brown sacks salvaged after the contents from the general store had been emptied. Billy had a flat rectangular tin box with a handle on the side and some drawings on the outside.

The boys ate what their mothers had prepared, which usually was a peanut butter, jelly or apple-butter sandwich and two or three homemade sugar cookies. Before Christmas, the cookies were made from dough cut out in the shapes of Christmas trees, stars, Santa Claus and other holiday motifs. The boys thought the shapes looked sissified, so they cupped the cookies in their hands so the others couldn't see them.

The girls sometimes traded items from their lunches. One day, Missy, who lived on a farm, wasn't impressed with a fresh tenderloin sandwich her mother had fixed after the family had butchered. And Millie, who lived in town, was tired of her mincemeat sandwich. Missy asked Millie, "What's mincemeat?" Millie said it was a bunch of stuff with meat mixed in. The girls traded sandwiches, each thinking she was getting something special.

But back to Cecil. He carried the same kind of lunchbox to school as the men carried to work at the limestone mill. It had a handle on top. A big thermos was inside the lid, and a space big enough for a half-dozen sandwiches was on the bottom.

Cecil always had a big meat, as well as peanut butter, sandwich, pudding or fruit and graham-cracker cookies. His mom made the cookies by putting thick layers of white icing between the graham crackers.

It was obvious how good those cookies were. Cecil always smiled, but he had an even bigger look of happiness when he savored them. Maybe that's why someone snitched one a few days before Christmas. The thief probably figured Cecil had so many other things to eat he wouldn't miss a graham-cracker cookie.

But Cecil knew he had been victimized. He reported the theft to Miss Hunter, who sympathized with him. But she was a teacher, not a detective. She suggested, "Maybe whoever took it was hungrier than you are. It was probably a bigger treat for him than it was for you."

Cecil said, "If I knew who took it, I'd have my mom to fix an extra one tomorrow."

He never found out. But he kept a much closer eye on his graham-cracker cookies after that.

Roosevelt Was the Thanksgiving Turkey

A lot of farmers around Heltonville were upset in 1939 when President Franklin Roosevelt decided to change the day Thanksgiving was observed. Zeke was one of them. He had grown disturbed over the years at Roosevelt's social-engineering programs.

The President, in an executive order, claimed merchants would sell more Christmas merchandise if there was an extra week between Thanksgiving and December 25. The decision by the President to change Thanksgiving from the fourth Thursday was the last straw for Zeke.

The change caused him to issue a decree himself: "This family will observe the holiday on the fourth Thursday, FDR be damned."

His wife, Millie, said that was O.K. with her. "It's as easy to fix turkey one day as it is another," she replied.

Their kids weren't that agreeable. Tad, one of their sons, said, "We'll be out of school the third Thursday. But we won't be the Thursday after that. How are we going to enjoy a big turkey if we have to wait until we get home from school, then have to worry about going to class the next day?"

Zeke replied, "Maybe that'll keep you from overeating."

His smile didn't keep Tad from complaining. Or his brother, Tyke. Or their sisters.

"What are we going to call the two days we're out of school if we can't call 'em Thanksgiving holidays?" Tyke asked.

His dad grinned, "You and Tad and me can call them corn-shucking days. We still got a field to get in before the snow flies."

The boys argued that no one else would be observing Thanksgiving a week later than Roosevelt wanted. But Zeke said, "I don't think we'll be alone." He mentioned some other farmers who planned to make the same protest against the President.

But even he was surprised when he read a story the next day in the *Bedford Daily Mail*. There in type was a story about Sheriff Lincoln "Curly" Dunbar, who also was irate because Roosevelt had changed the date to observe Thanksgiving. Dunbar announced he wasn't going along with the President. "I'll have none of it," he had told a reporter. He ordered prisoners to be fed their holiday feast on the fourth Thursday, not the third.

Zeke wasted no time showing the story to Tad and Tyke.

They shucked corn and settled for ham and beans on the third Thursday. But they enjoyed the turkey a week later.

So did the prisoners at the Lawrence County Jail.

Postscript: Two years later Congress agreed with Zeke and Sheriff Dunbar. It ordered that, henceforth, Thanksgiving be observed on the fourth Thursday.

Contoured Fields Put on More than a Pretty Face

Zeke just snorted when his wife pointed toward a farm on the rolling hills east of Bedford and asked: "Doesn't that look pretty?"

What she pointed to was a field that was being strip-farmed, "contoured" some said. It was one of the early experiments in contour farming undertaken in Lawrence County in the late 1930s.

The field had been laid out in patterns that followed the slopes. A 150-yard-wide strip halfway up the hillside was in alfalfa. Its dark-green cover was in sharp contrast to the red clay soil up on the slopes. Corn had just been planted in a 100-yard ribbon there.

Below the alfalfa, at the base of the slope, was a strip of growing wheat.

"Won't that be something when the wheat turns ripe and golden, the alfalfa blooms and the corn tassels?" Zeke's wife continued.

Zeke had listened to her carry on long enough. He took charge of the conversation then. Chig, a neighbor boy who had made the trip to town with them, sat in the back seat and listened, knowing better than to try to interrupt a tornado.

"Contour farming is some silly damned thing some professors at Purdue and some fancy-dressed fellers in Washington thought up to spend taxpayers' money," Zeke said, his face reddening as he gripped the steering wheel of his 1935 Terraplane.

The road back toward Heltonville was narrow and winding, but Zeke kept looking back at Chig to make sure he was listening, too.

"President Roosevelt's buddies figured they can save the country from another dust storm if they pay farmers to use contours and build grass strips," Zeke said.

He waited for his wife or Chig to say something, then went on: "All that stuff takes too damned much time. Good farmers plant in straight rows, not silly wavy lines."

Chig finally spoke up. "Pa says he may take part in the Leatherwood project."

The project involved about seventy-five farmers along the meandering seventeen-mile course Leatherwood Creek took from its mouth at White River to Zelma. The farmers involved used erosion control methods in an effort to keep topsoil from washing into the creek and heading for New Orleans.

"That ain't for me," Zeke said. "I paid for my ground and I got sense enough to take care of it through crop rotation and other means. Don't need none of them fancy programs the committeemen from the Agricultural Adjustment Act keep trying to sell me on."

Chig talked to his father that night about contour farming. His dad explained, "The furrows and rows run across the slope of the land. Rainfall collects in the troughs and soaks in instead of running off with a gush, taking the topsoil with it."

A couple of weeks later, Chig listened while his dad and Zeke talked.

"You know," Zeke said, "I may do some strip-farming next year. Them heavy rains night before last washed

big gullies in my corn field. I went to Bedford the next day and couldn't see much erosion at all in them fields that had been contoured."

Chig turned his head to keep from laughing.

A Child's Memories of Slot Machines and Tourist Cabins

Concrete was barely dry on new U.S. 50 between Bedford and Brownstown in the 1930s when work started on tourist cabins.

The cabins were small frame buildings with barely enough room for a bed, a dresser and a couple of chairs. A few were made of logs. The material was cheap, the architecture simple.

Most of the cabins sat back off the road behind a store where the manager kept the records and the registry book. The store offered an assortment of items that allowed hungry guests to fix quick snacks.

Tad and Tyke were maybe six or seven when they stopped for the first time at Jack Brown's tourist cabins in the Fairview community about eight miles east of Bedford.

They nosed around the store while their dad paid for a loaf of bread and talked to the clerk.

"What's that?" Tad asked, looking up at a machine that had a big handle on the right side and a picture of a cherry, a lemon and another cherry in a little window.

Tyke shook his head. Tad waited until his dad had quit talking, tugged at the hammer slot on his overalls and pointed to the machine.

His dad said, "Glad to see you've changed your mind."

Zeke said, "Hell, I'm tired of making life an upstream paddle."

His dad, who attended church regularly, whispered, "I'll tell you after a while." He waited until another customer diverted the attention of the clerk and said softly, "That's a slot machine, a device for gambling."

He called it a one-armed bandit and said, "Let me show you how it takes your money." He wrestled a nickel out of his pocket, dropped it in the slot and pulled the handle. The pictures spun rapidly until each wheel stopped and three clusters of cherries showed. A few nickles dropped clinking from the machine.

Tad's father looked embarrassed. He scooped up the coins, quickly jabbed them into his pocket and said, "It's time for us to get home."

He felt more inclined to talk in the car. He explained he had been lucky to win, that the odds were against the players, that "only fools would play slot machines."

When they returned to the farm east of Heltonville, the boys kept quiet. There was no point in telling their mother that their father had been a "fool."

In the next few years they learned more about tourist cabins and the roadhouses that sprang up near them. The roadhouses permitted drinking and dancing and a good time. And the nearby tourist cabins were convenient for couples who wanted to do more than drink and dance.

They heard this story, retold in James Guthrie's "History of Lawrence County, 1917–1941":

Customer: "How much for one of your cabins?"

Clerk: "Two bits an hour."

Customer: "How much for all night?"

Clerk: "Dunno. Nobody ever stayed all night before."

And they finally figured out why some customers insisted on parking their cars behind the cabins, hidden from the road. They didn't want anyone to know where they were.

Most of the roadhouses closed in the early 1940s and the tourist cabins were outdated by motels. Some of the stores remained open for a few more years, but the slot machines disappeared, removed by sheriffs and prosecutors or hidden behind locked doors.

And a colorful era in American history gradually died.

The Lesson Enclosed in a Wheaties Box

Youngsters around Heltonville would have eaten Wheaties even if the box tops were of no value. The cereal from General Mills was the "Breakfast of Champions." And what was good enough for Jack Armstrong, the all-American boy, was good enough for Blinky, Bunky, Tad, Tyke and the other boys who lived on farms east of town around 1940.

They could be found any afternoon at 4:30 huddled around the radios in their homes for the latest episode in the life of Jack Armstrong. The program was an escape from the monotony of long hours at school and the long days of winter.

Their mothers didn't object. They themselves were hooked on their own soap operas, programs like "Mary Foster, the Editor's Daughter" and "Lorenzo Jones."

Armstrong ate Wheaties, the young listeners were told, and so did athletes who wanted to be champions.

The cereal was good, especially with sugar and cream fresh from the milk separator. And the boxes were colorful and informative. And they offered, from time to time, special prizes—prizes like compasses, magic rings and pedometers.

Bunky got the compass, which took two box tops and a quarter. Blinky got a magic ring, which impressed the girls in Esther Hunter's third grade class.

Tad had saved three box tops, using his pocket knife to cut the last one off the Wheaties while the box was more than half-full. When his mother scolded him, he told her, "Takes three box tops and a quarter to get this pedometer." He pointed out the pedometer on the side of the Wheaties box. "Just like Jack Armstrong wears," he said.

His mother read the description. "Fits on hip . . . measures each step taken . . . records the miles the wearer walks." She helped Tad tape a quarter to one of the box tops and made sure he addressed the letter correctly and included all the information needed on the order blank. She pointed out

the small print: "Allow 21 days for delivery."

After about ten days, Tad started running into the house from the school bus each night asking, "Is it here yet?"

It arrived after about the eighteenth day, wrapped in brown paper with Tad's name on the front. It was the first time he'd ever received a package in the mail. He opened it slowly and carefully, knowing intuitively that this moment of suspenseful expectation would never be equaled again.

The pedometer looked just like the one on the Wheaties box. It was shiny and bright. And it was Tad's alone.

He stuck it on the right pocket against his hip and sat down to listen to Jack Armstrong. Every few minutes he'd pull it off and look it over.

He wore it to do chores that night, then walked over to show it to Blinky. When he got home, he'd walked more than one and a half miles.

After each recess and lunch the next day at school, he'd check the pedometer and tell anyone who would listen what the mileage was. By the end of the day it showed he'd walked three and a half miles, which he said was a lot.

His mom and dad just smiled.

The pedometer showed over three and a half miles one night when his dad asked if he would walk down to Saul's place and give him a message.

"That must be more than a mile each way," Tad protested.

His dad said, "It'll give you a chance to measure the exact distance with your pedometer, then."

When Tad returned, he looked at the pedometer and said, "It was one and a half miles down there. I've walked more than seven miles today. Bet that must be some kind of record."

His mother thought it might be time to teach him a lesson. "Mind if I wear your pedometer Monday? It'll give me a chance to see how far a farm wife walks on wash day," she said. Tad agreed, figuring she'd walk maybe a mile.

They were eating supper that night when his mother remembered to check the pedometer. It showed she had walked just over eight miles.

Tad looked bewildered. "Did you walk to a church meeting or something?" he asked.

She shook her head.

Tad said, "How did you walk that much, then?"

"It wasn't easy," she said. "Fed the chickens, gathered the eggs, helped with the milkin', carried in water, washed the clothes, carried in wood, cleaned the house, helped your dad do some work in the barn, looked for a sick calf . . . ."

Tad got the message. He looked at the pedometer.

Sometimes it taught a boy you can go a long way without ever leaving home.

The Seasons of War

No one was ever tempted to describe the Second World War as the "good" war." The only thing good that can be said about it is that it pulled America out of the Depression; it began brutally, was pursued insanely by our enemies, and ended tragically.

Like the Depression, the war came from out of the distance to Southern Indiana. It began on the radio and in the newspapers, and it did not seem real until young men began disappearing to basic-training camps and overseas, some of them returning to their native soil in pine boxes.

The people of Indiana have never liked war, but they have always fought. Generally, once provoked enough, they have battled as if they believed they could end the fighting with one ferocious blow. Their ancestors, the ragtailed army of George Rogers Clark, endured starvation and tramped through biting wet and cold to deliver a knockout punch to the British at Vincennes. Later, Hoosier bayonets at the Battle of Fallen Timbers brought a summary end to an Indian war, and during the War Between the States Indiana soldiers and militia helped chase Confederate General John Hunt Morgan and his "terrible men" from the state.

How is it Hoosiers can hate war so much and, apparently, be so good at it? War does not sit well with people who love farm and field, but true appreciation of the pastoral life does help spark men to defend it; it also helps breed the kinds of qualities that reinforce a nation to resist its enemies.

In war, Hoosiers have always given their best, in big and small ways, and because they did so forty years ago we are all free to enjoy our way of life today.
—MN

The Year the World Turned Around

It was there in almost every issue of the *Saturday Evening Post*, that full-page ad for a new 1939 Studebaker Champion. Full price, $795, the color advertisement said.

The car was small in size, sleek in design, nothing like the dust-covered rattletraps and puddle jumpers the farm boys around Heltonville drove.

The car was a bargain at $795, or would have been if they had that kind of money. But $795 would have been a fortune, especially to youths who seldom could find full-time jobs, even though President Franklin Roosevelt said the Great Depression had bottomed out. When they did find work on farms in the area they received no more than $1.50 a day for their labor.

That meant about all they could do was read the ads from top to bottom and side to side and dream about what it would be like to tool the Studebaker into Norman and Heltonville on Saturday nights and invite the girls to go for a drive.

The Champion was Studebaker's attempt to produce a low-cost custom car that combined appearance, safety and economy of operation. The South

Bend firm spent $1.25 million to advertise the car which was shown for the first time in May at Southern Indiana dealerships.

G.E. didn't waste any time in seeing the Champions, once they arrived at the Studebaker dealer in Bedford. He paid little attention to the new deluxe models that came out about the same time, or even to the four-door Champion. Instead, he'd walk around the Champion coupe and the two-door sedan, eyeing every contour of their bodies like maybe he was sizing up high school cheerleaders.

The dealer saw his interest and suggested maybe now was the time to buy. "Like to," G.E. said, "but I ain't got the money, and I don't know where I can get it."

"Your dad's got good credit. Maybe he'd sign your note."

G.E. shook his head. "Wouldn't ask him to do that, since I don't have a regular job and couldn't guarantee him I could pay for it."

G.E. hadn't counted on the Germans starting World War II later that September with an invasion of Poland. That prodded America on the road to rearmament and brought the Charlestown Powder Plant into existence.

The powder plant needed manpower, a lot of it, quickly, and G.E. joined the growing number of Lawrence County residents who joined that work force. He and his coworkers had two choices, live in whatever housing they could find near Charlestown, or drive the 135-mile round trip each day.

They voted to commute when G.E. said he could finally afford a Studebaker Champion, a decision that didn't set too well with his dad. "Car's too small for you to be takin' yourself and

four riders that far every day. Won't hold up and you'll be stashed in there like sardines," said his father.

He was wasting his time. G.E. had waited too long to buy the Champion.

He took good care of the car despite working ten hours a day and being on the road three hours more. He'd wash the car at the creek a couple of times a week, changing oil every two weeks and getting a tuneup every month or so.

If his riders ever felt cramped in the car they never complained. In fact, they were glad of it, until the last trip G.E. made on the Charlestown-to-Heltonville run. That trip ended on Ind. 252 near Dudleytown when G.E. tried to go through a one-lane bridge the same time a truck decided to enter from the opposite direction.

G.E. said he was blinded by the setting sun. Nobody doubted him, especially the people who knew how much he cared for the car.

No matter! The truck won. The Champion was demolished. Except for bruises, Butch and his passengers were not hurt.

G.E. didn't have much time to mourn the loss of the car. A few days later he got his notice that Uncle Sam wanted him to serve his country.

A day or two before G.E. was to report for duty, he and his dad settled up with the insurance company and paid off the balance due on what Butch owed on the car.

That night, G.E. told his dad he thought he might try to become a pilot in the Air Corps.

"Might be all right, Son, if you don't try to fly low through a narrow bridge."

G.E. just laughed and said, "As far as I know, Studebaker doesn't sell the Army any Champion planes. If it does, you may see me try."

The Autumn
We Geared for War

The nation was in transition in the fall of 1940. Even a farm boy of ten, insulated from much of the outside world, could tell that more was changing than the season.

Action in Washington was causing Americans to think more about military mobilization than the Great Depression that had gone on for eleven years. Men were moving from public works projects to the manufacture of armaments.

The country was not officially at war, but no one expected peace to last, not with Germany rampaging through Europe. Not with Japan taking over Indochina.

Some of the older boys were talking about trading their CCC outfits for Army uniforms. Older men, still scrimping to make ends meet, talked less about feeding their families and more about the ominous news from across "the big ponds."

Tad followed the news in the papers and knew that on September 16 President Franklin Roosevelt had signed a "military conscription" act Congress had haggled over for weeks. His father told him, "Military conscription is just a fancy name for the draft. Young men from twenty-one to thirty-six have to register for military service in a couple of weeks."

Tad learned that two draft boards at Bedford would classify the men into different categories from 1-A to 4-F. Men who were classified 1-A were immediately available for the draft. They could start thinking about fighting instead of farming, his dad said. The 4-Fs would be considered unfit for military duty because of physical, mental or moral reasons.

Some young men took the uncertainty out of their future and volunteered. One walked into the draft board office carrying a shotgun and said he was ready to serve.

Tad noted other changes, too.

A few weeks after Roosevelt ordered the draft, the Navy Department awarded contracts for six million dollars for powder-storage facilities near Burns City in nearby Martin County. The expenditure was raised to fifteen million dollars within days. Another big contract, this one for twenty-six million dollars, was issued for a powder plant at Charlestown, about sixty miles southeast of Bedford.

Few men remained idle. Some farmers let their teenage sons take over the fields while they worked at the ammunition depots. The boys became men, almost overnight.

Farmers who had cut back production to obtain help through the Agricultural Administration Act once again talked about planting from fencerow to fencerow.

Men and women whose days already were filled with work used the evenings to take welding courses, attend national defense schools and learn Civil Defense procedures.

The country, which had seemed mired in the depths of the Depression months before, hummed with activity. Gears, long-idle, shook loose cobwebs and began to turn, reviving the nation's industrial might in the preparation for war. The Depression was ended, the economic collapse forgotten.

But it was not a happy time. The war clouds were without silver linings.

Gripes about Chores Are Unworthy as War Begins

Chig never forgot the last time he had to polish the stove. It was a Saturday in December. Chig had helped his Dad work around the barn that morning, doing chores that made a ten-year-old seem like a man. The temperature was in the forties around Heltonville, but freezing temperatures were forecast for that night.

At noon, his mother observed, "We can get by without any fire this afternoon. With Christmas coming, this would be a good time to put polish on the stove and the stove pipes." Actually it was more of a command than an observation.

"Chig can do that for you," his dad volunteered.

Chig's sisters sniggered, knowing how much Chig hated housework.

His mother noticed the snickers. "And while Chig's doing that, you girls can clean the chimneys and fill the lamps with coal oil," she said.

The chimneys she mentioned had nothing to do with the stove. They were the flues on the lamps, which provided the only indoor light in the house.

The girls didn't care for chimney-cleaning any more than Chig liked to polish the stove. They looked as unhappy as Chig, who mumbled something about being too old for sissy jobs.

He waited until the fire died down to clean the potbellied stove and the pipes with kerosene-soaked rags. Still griping, he applied the polish with a brush, trying to keep the thin liquid from running off the pipes onto the old carpeting on the living room floor. Despite his grumbling, he worked more quietly than his sisters did.

They argued over the best way to clean the chimneys. One said it ought to be done with soapsuds and water. The other wanted to use old newspapers. Their mother said she didn't care which, "just get the job done and do it quietly."

Their father agreed that would be a good idea. "I want to hear the news before I go back outside." He turned on the radio, powered by a dry-cell battery, and found WHAS in Louisville. The news wasn't good, especially from the Pacific: *"All nonessential civilians ordered from Manila . . . Great Britain recalls all fighting men to their posts in Singapore . . . Tokyo recalls two military attaches from its embassy in Washington . . . An uneasy peace hangs over the Pacific as the United States waits for Japan to make its choice between conciliation or further attempts at conquest in the Far East."*

Chig's dad didn't say anything. He turned off the radio, put his coat and hat on and walked out, head down.

Chig finished coating the stove with polish, mumbling less than before. His sisters talked more softly as they worked.

A fire was rekindled in the stove and the lamps lighted as the sun went down. The radio was turned on again. The news was the same as it had been earlier, causing Chig's mother to ask: "What's going to happen?"

His dad shook his head. "Don't know," he replied.

The next day was December 7, 1941. The Japanese attacked Pearl Harbor. World War II was under way.

Chig's disgust with menial chores suddenly seemed insignificant. He regretted he had complained about little things, like polishing the stove.

But he wasn't assigned the job again. Boys like Chig had to take on farm work done by hired hands who left to carry out the business of winning a war.

Three-Pair Limit Didn't Faze the Fellows

Miss Clark was reading the morning paper when her freshman English students entered the classroom. She appeared to be in shock when she looked up.

Some of the students thought she might have read about the death of a friend. Others thought the news from the war front had taken a bad turn.

It was February 8, 1943, and what Miss Clark had just read was a story reporting that shoe-rationing was to start the next day. She shared the news with the class.

Without any advance warning, James Byrne, the Economic Stabilization director, had ordered that each American would be limited to three pairs of shoes per year. He had issued the decree, Miss Clark read from the paper, "to make certain that the American people will continue to have all the shoes they need."

The War Production Board had estimated shoe leather and reclaimed rubber would be available for only 335,000,000 pairs of civilian footwear. That was 105,000,000 fewer pairs than were made in 1942, Miss Clark explained, condensing the information as she read.

Miss Clark was not as fashion-conscious as some of the teachers, but she cared about her appearance and always made sure her shoes looked new.

The freshmen girls were at an age when they wanted to appear older so the junior and senior boys would pay attention to them. They were just beginning to look ahead to the days when they could wear high heels.

Miss Clark often used the news of the day to encourage discussion and to help students see how it related to them.

It was obvious from the response that the girls were more concerned than the boys about shoes. The girls asked for more information. Some of them groaned when Miss Clark read that gold and silver and all two-tone shoes were out for the duration, that colors would be limited to white, black, town brown and Army russet.

And some of them also sighed when she continued: "Women's heels will be limited to not more than $2\frac{5}{8}$ inches and platforms . . . those extra thick soles some women fancy . . . are forbidden."

But some of the girls didn't react at all. They were from big families who couldn't afford three pairs of shoes each year for each child, regardless of the style.

As usual, Gordy was the first boy to speak. He said, "I don't get but one pair of shoes a year. And that's right before school starts."

The other boys unconsciously looked toward his feet. Gordy had on the pair he had worn since Labor Day. The sole on the left shoe had come unglued and he held it on with a thin piece of wire twisted on the side.

That didn't bother Gordy. Not much did.

A few of the boys wore the same shoes to school they wore to the barn, scraping off whatever accumulated on the bottoms before boarding the school bus. The other boys tugged gum boots over their shoes when the weather was bad. Only a few of them had more than two pairs of shoes.

Chuckie, who liked sweets, left a standing offer with anyone in class to trade his shoe-rationing coupon for a pound of sugar. Miss Clark, figuring she ought to teach a few minutes of English, cut off the conversation about that time.

But the subject came up again the next morning, when Miss Clark asked if anyone had anything to say before she turned to her lesson outline.

Gordy said, "I do. I mentioned shoe-rationing to my folks last night at supper. Told them that we each were entitled to three pairs of shoes a year."

When he paused, Miss Clark said, "So?"

Gordy went on, "So, Mom told Dad, 'Looks like you're going to have to go to the bank and borrow enough money for us to buy two more pair than usual for each of the kids.'"

Everyone laughed. But no one complained about shoe-rationing again.

When the Green Went to War

Hardy dropped out of school on his way to adulthood. His dad thought he was lazy. His mother thought he was misunderstood. His teachers didn't know what to think.

Hardy was as intelligent as any other teenager around Heltonville. Boredom, more than anything, led him to quit school in 1942.

If the classroom was boring, his detour to the future didn't take him directly to excitement.

Having just turned seventeen, he had trouble finding employment even though World War II was under way and men were leaving daily for military service.

His time was filled by picking up a few odd jobs and a few bad habits.

One of the habits he acquired was smoking. He tried Marvels, Old Golds, Phillip Morris, Kools, Camels, Chesterfields and Wings. Once in a while, he tried, without success, to roll his own from a Bull Durham bag.

He finally settled on Lucky Strike.

Hardy was a few years older than Tad, Tyke, Bogey and Pokey, but that didn't stop him from sharing his thoughts and experiences with them. He never divvied up his cigarettes, though, partly because he wanted to keep them for himself, partly because he knew the boys wanted to be athletes. But he smoked a lot when they were around.

"This 'LS/MFT' on the package," he told them, "stands for 'Lucky Strike means fine tobacco.'"

The Luckies came in dark green

packages at first. Tyke noticed a change in the packs later. The area around the red bullseye on the package was no longer green. It was white.

Tyke wanted to know what happened to the green.

Hardy had an answer. "The materials used to make the green are needed for the war effort," he said, adding, "The base for the gold panel on the original package was copper powder. The green coloring contained chromium."

There were no chemistry classes at Heltonville, so Tad didn't know what that meant. "How's that used in the war effort?" he asked.

Hardy didn't seem to know for certain. "Guess it's used for dye for Army uniforms, paint for tanks and whatever," he said, twisting out a butt beneath the sole of his high-top boot. He walked off. The boys debated whether to believe what he said.

A few weeks later Tad and Tyke were listening to the radio when they heard a commercial. It rang out loud and clear. "Lucky Strike green has gone to war," an announcer sang, jingle-like.

The boys looked at each other. "Hardy was right," Tad said.

When they saw Pokey and Bogey at school the next day, they repeated the slogan, "Lucky Strike green has gone to war."

Pokey said, "It's not the only thing that's gone to war. Hardy's gone, too! His parents signed his papers yesterday and he's headed for the Navy."

None of the boys ever forgot Lucky Strike green, or Hardy.

Christmas Surprise Was Especially Sweet of Millie

No one liked sweets better than Zeke. He coated almost everything with sugar. Sometimes he sprinkled sugar on sugar·on sugar.

The sugar didn't seem to hurt Zeke. He looked rugged and strong, more like he lived on a diet of raw meat and thistles than on sweets. He had muscles on muscles on muscles that appeared rock-like under his weather-worn skin.

Zeke was as American as anyone, but despite his patriotism he almost cried on May 5, 1942. That was the day the Office of Price Administration required Americans to register for sugar-rationing.

Zeke, who farmed near Heltonville, could suffer limitations on how much gasoline and how many pairs of shoes he was allowed. He could even cut back on how much coffee he bought. But he wasn't sure whether he could live on the one pound of sugar he was allotted every two weeks.

"I use that much sugar every fourteen days in my coffee," he complained to his wife, Millie.

Not much bothered Millie. She promised to help him adjust to the change brought on by World War II.

In the weeks ahead, she bought corn sugar, Karo syrup and even artificial sweeteners. Zeke learned to use them, but he never enjoyed the flavor.

"Oatmeal doesn't taste right with syrup on it," he complained almost every morning.

He missed the biscuits he once coated with butter, covered with sugar and swamped in whole milk.

And the artificial sweetener did little to help the taste of Zeke's coffee, which was about forty percent cream.

Millie just smiled at Zeke's complaints, giving no clue to the fact she was scrimping, saving and hoarding sugar in a place back in the three-cornered cupboard where Zeke would never look.

She kept her secret until Christmas morning.

Zeke did the chores on the farm early that day and returned to the house for breakfast. He, Millie and their youngsters would open the gifts after the meal, which Millie had planned as carefully as she did a dinner for the minister.

She poured Zeke his coffee, then asked him to close his eyes. When he opened them, he saw a sugar bowl. It was nearly full.

"It's a Christmas treat," Millie said. "You can use the sugar on your cereal, in your coffee and on your biscuits. And the kids can use it on their cereal, too." She watched, pleased at the pleasure she had given them.

She brought out cake and pie later in the day. Zeke took his with two spoonfuls of sugar.

He and the youngsters enjoyed the treats, but not as much as Millie enjoyed being able to serve them.

She didn't have to remind them there would be sugarless days ahead, that the war was far from over, that friends and neighbors would die in battles yet to be fought, that rationing was, after all, only an inconvenience.

They knew that. But they knew she had made Christmas '42 a day they would remember longer than the shortages of all the other days that had passed and were still to come.

Boys Didn't Realize What the A-Bomb Meant

It seemed bewildering, almost incomprehensible, at the time. But it would be an evening that would remain vivid for a lifetime.

Frank and Jake were stretched out on their bunks, talking about how hard they'd worked that day, when Tad and Tommy climbed through the door.

Tad and Tommy dumped what they'd bought in downtown Tipton on their cluttered beds, which were in a grain bin being used temporarily as a dormitory. The four boys, all fifteen

and sixteen, had been in Tipton for three weeks, detasseling corn for the Pioneer Seed Co. They would be returning downstate to their homes one hundred miles away in Heltonville soon.

Jake picked up the newspaper Tad had bought and started to turn to the sports pages. The headline on page 1 stopped him: **"Atomic bomb dropped on Japan."**

It was August 6, 1945. Jake read the lead: "American airmen dropped an atomic bomb, equivalent to 20,000 pounds of TNT, on Japan today."

Frank whistled, trying to accentuate the damage.

Jake continued, "The seaport city of Hiroshima was heavily damaged and casualties were reported heavy."

Tommy asked, "What's an atomic bomb?"

Jake searched the story for the answer. "It says here it's a devastating force containing the harnessed basic power of the universe."

None of the four knew exactly what that meant. Neither physics nor chemistry was taught at Heltonville.

"Maybe Japan will surrender quicker than we thought," Tommy said, hopefully.

Jake eyed the paper again. "You may be right." He read another paragraph: "War Secretary Henry Stimson said the bomb will prove a tremendous aid in shortening the war."

Frank said, "If we're lucky, it'll be over before we get drafted."

None of the other three wanted to be heroes, either, they concurred.

Jake quoted a couple of comments from President Harry Truman: "Even more powerful bombs are in development.

"We shall completely destroy Japan's power to make war."

Had the boys been older and wiser, they would have known the order to drop the bomb wasn't an easy one for Truman. A clue was hidden in a sentence that explained, "The decision to drop the bomb came after Japan rejected an ultimatum to surrender."

There were other stories on the page. One estimated how many American lives could be saved if the bomb caused Japan to surrender. Another outlined the island-by-island progression the U.S. forces would have to take en route to Japan if surrender didn't come.

Not much was said about the bomb the next day when the boys boarded the school bus to take them to the fields.

Their .thoughts turned to other things, work, softball games in the evening, movies in town at night. They didn't learn until they arrived home that another atomic bomb had been dropped, that one on Nagasaki.

A few days later Japan surrendered, unconditionally. The allied world rejoiced in celebration.

Tad and the others were back in Heltonville when victory over Japan came. Everyone was excited except Clem, who had more common sense than he did book learning. He was as patriotic as anyone.

He showed concern, though, when he said, "Truman had no choice, I guess, but it seems like a high price to pay for peace. We may not know how high that price was for years to come," he said.

The "it" was the bomb.

Frank, Jake, Tommy and Tad were too young at the time to share his apprehension.

Local Color

If you want to fall in love with Southern Indiana, visit it during October. The harvest season is a harvest of color as well. Some visitors actually make an annual ritual of returning, making elaborate plans for touring and boarding.

Although to the casual tourist (Hoosiers call them "rubberneckers") all Indiana autumns may seem the same, natives know that each fall is like a snowflake—the same in certain ways, and yet distinctively different. During some years, a long late-summer dry spell mutes the color of the trees, but in others there is an awesome range and brilliance of hues.

There are other, subtler differences. To appreciate them, one must not simply observe fall, but live inside it. This takes some time. Sights, sounds, and smells await you. Try, for example, sitting with author Wendell Trogdon and experiencing the warmth of a farm clearing on an Indian summer day; breathe in the smell of drying corn and sniff the pleasant, sweet decaying-leaf aroma of the surrounding woods.

This prepares you to see rural people in a new light. The men at Lloyd White's sawmill, working in shirtsleeves against their cold-weather deadline, seem one with the animals gathering in food for the winter. Nature's frequent interruptions of the harvest make you appreciate the rough and ready people who remain in tune with nature, working hard when conditions are favorable, and pausing to reflect or socialize when the weather is bad. Autumn, then, becomes shaded eyes scanning the horizon, a finger testing the fickle wind, a calloused hand extended in friendship.

It is a time to learn, and re-learn, the lesson that "local color" doesn't just mean trees.   —*MN*

Lessons of Summer Yield to Lessons of the Classroom

Summer was giving way to autumn and an uneasiness gnawed at the reservoir of happiness built up during a four-month vacation. It had been a good summer for a boy of twelve, a time to work, a time to play and a time to observe the drama of life around him.

Chig seemed born to roam free on the farm east of Heltonville that summer in the '40s. It would take effort to relax, after being harnessed again to a desk in the classroom. Even if there had been no calendar, no one to tell him, he would have known the summer of his content was about to end. The grass in the pasture had turned brown. It no longer felt fresh, soft and cool beneath his bare feet. Now the blades cracked, then crumbled as he walked.

The water in the swimming hole was no longer inviting. A thin layer covered the pool and the weeds draped from the banks onto the water.

The corn, planted in dust in May, had grown skyward, the tassels had pollinated the silk, ears had formed and the milk had dried in the grains.

The blades that once were dark green were turning brown and hardening into razor-like sharpness.

The barn was filled to the rafters with hay that had been hauled in from fields once blanketed with red blooms of clover.

The wheat, which had once cast an amber wave over the big field back of the barn, had been harvested. The crop was stored in the granary, waiting for the price to rise. The straw stack that had glistened in the July sun was gradually turning dull in color.

The leaves on the softwood trees were changing, appearing as if an artist had begun to coat them in raw sienna. Occasionally, a few yellowed leaves were shaken loose by the breezes that preceded the late summer showers.

The garden had all but surrendered to the weeds, except for the patch that had been seeded in turnips. Only the tomatoes were left to be picked.

The lawn had given up, too, yielding to the relentless spread of crabgrass. The yard no longer needed mowing every five days.

If Chig had had a vote, he would have opted to cut the grass rather than return to school. He had always before adjusted easily to his classes, but this year was different. He was entering the seventh grade. That meant he would be in an assembly with students through high school, not just in a classroom with twenty-five other students. He would be subjected to the inspection of a hundred pairs of older, wiser eyes each morning before the assembly was sent on its way to classes.

Chig tried to keep school out of his thoughts over the Labor Day weekend. But they crept in so often he finally gave up and let them occupy his concerns, totally.

He did his chores the next morning, slipped on a new denim shirt, the cotton clinging softly to his tanned arms. He pulled on his new bib overalls, stiff and still unwashed. He tugged on a new pair of shoes, laced the rawhide and stood up to face the mirror. Only the toughness of the rubber kept the comb from breaking as he pulled it through matted hair.

He walked down the stairs, the overall legs swishing, seeming to count each step he took. The shoes creaked, pinching toes that sought their share of space. He grabbed his sack lunch, bade goodbye to his mother and walked down the hill toward the bus.

It was time, despite his uneasiness, to get on with the business of life, to get an education, to learn lessons he could apply when vacation came again eight months later.

Teacher, It Was Like This

Each fall, some teachers have their pupils stand before the class and tell "the most exciting thing I did this summer." It happens at the start of each school year.

Pupils who've had summers that only money can buy don't mind. They have had a number of experiences. It's the kids from poorer families who have little to talk about.

Such was the case at Heltonville grade school. Except the boys in the

class realized this and conspired to teach the teacher a lesson. It's likely she never forgot it.

"Johnny, would you like to be the first to tell about your summer?" she asked one student.

Johnny lived on one of the less prosperous farms in Pleasant Run Township, but he was part of the conspiracy.

"We didn't do much this summer," he began. "Probably the highlight came when, well you see we don't have our own bull. Dad said one morning Old Bessie was in heat and it was time to take her over to Jake's bull."

Johnny kept a straight face, but a few of his friends in the back row had to stifle snickers.

Johnny continued, "Dad asked if I'd like to go along. I followed behind as he led the old milker down the gravel road. Jake knew we was a-comin' and opened the gate just wide enough for Dad to lead the cow through.

"The bull was up on the hill. He pawed his left foot two or three times and came a-runnin' and jumpin'."

Johnny started to continue, but the teacher jumped up suddenly and said, "Ah, well, Johnny, we must move on. Martha, you're next."

The girls weren't in on the conspiracy, so Martha told a story about going down to Louisville shopping with her parents.

"Fine, fine," said the teacher, nodding to Billy to come forward. Billy was kind of shy, but he was game. He told a story about chasing rats out of the corn crib. This made the teacher look under her chair every now and then to see that no varmints were in the classroom.

Little Margie went next and told about visiting the museum in Chicago.

Jackie, one of the meaner fellas in town, was up next. He started to tell what he saw his sister and her boyfriend do one night, but the teacher gave a loud "harrump" and said, "You can sit down, Jackie. Like right now."

Her face was beginning to get redder.

Sarah told about visiting St. Louis and Hannibal, "where our friend Mark Twain lived."

It was now time for Chuckie, the son of one of the farmers in the area. "We all drove to Washington, D.C., this summer," he began. "That was all right, but the most exciting thing was on the way back.

"We stopped for gasoline and something to eat on U.S. 50 in West Virginia. My brother and me were looking around the place and saw this thing with an arm on the side and some fruit showing up at the top.

"There was a place for a nickel to drop in. I let a nickel fall, pulled that arm with my right arm and all of a sudden those fruits started rolling around at the top and when they stopped a whole handful of nickels came out.

"That was fun, until Dad saw what we had done. He preached a sermon for a while, then got madder and madder and started using swear words like . . ."

"Chuuckieee," shouted the teacher. "That's enough, class. Open your geography books and read the first three pages. We'll talk about what you've read later."

The teacher remained at the school for years, but she never again asked the students to describe their summers.

Buying Melons Was Really Thumpin' Special

A journey to buy watermelons was more than a forty-mile round trip. It was a pilgrimage, an adventure in geography, a lesson in financial negotiations, a study in human nature.

A lot of people around Heltonville made the trip to buy melons at least once each year. Some, like Tad's father, made the trip two or three times between mid-August and early September. Tad and Tyke never failed to ride with him if they were home. They thought he needed their help. He thought they needed his attention.

He preferred to buy the melons in the White River bottoms between Medora and Vallonia. "Best melons you can buy anywhere," he told them. "There's no better place to grow them than in the warm sand. We can't grow good ones because the clay is too hard. It's not the right kind of soil."

He drove south to U.S. 50 and turned east. He never failed to turn the ignition off whatever car he was driving and let it coast down the Medora Knobs hill to the Ind. 235 junction. He believed in conserving fuel. "A penny saved in gas is a penny more we have to spend on melons," he always said.

He drove south toward Medora, slowing the car at each farm where watermelons were stacked along the road. "Never buy melons in the hot

*Illustration by
Gary Varvel*

sun. Wait until you can do it in the shade," he said.

Sometimes he'd stop at Bundy Brothers elevators in Medora to check on the price of wheat and corn. Then he continued the drive, through the covered bridge over the river, on toward Vallonia.

A mile or so from the river, he turned south. "Always know where to turn by the round barns," he said. Two big round barns were nearby. That led him to discuss the relative merits of round and conventional barns.

The first place he stopped was a house surrounded by an iron-rail fence. The watermelons, some striped, some solid green, were stacked neatly in the shade between the fence and the road. The melons were priced by size. The muskmelons were in bushel baskets. A farm wagon loaded with melons was parked nearby.

Tad's father asked the price for one melon, then for a dozen. If he didn't like the quotation, he made a counter offer. If the melon-grower refused, Tad and Tyke headed for the car, knowing they'd drive on to the next farm.

They always waved at the man who had rejected the offer. He'd wave back. There were no hard feelings. It was just business.

It didn't take more than two or three stops for them to get the number of melons they wanted for the price they wanted to pay. The melons were loaded in the car, some in the trunk, some in the back seat.

Back home, they'd unload the melons and place them in the spring-house to cool. The taste would be savored later.

Their mother never failed to ask if they had learned anything on the trip. The boys usually shook their heads.

Tyke surprised her once, though, when he replied, "We learned a new art." She wondered what art had to do with buying melons. "The art of buying and selling." Tyke said.

The Real Champ of Corn-Shucking

Everyone who was there said they had never seen anything like it before. And they would never see anything like it again. It was a one-time affair, never repeated.

Tad wasn't there. He was in Miss Hunter's third-grade class at Helton-ville. But being only eight years old, he didn't question what adults said.

What he heard was a description of a contest held near Mitchell one October day in 1938 to decide the best corn husker in Lawrence County.

Tad had a good source of information about the event. His dad was among the competitors.

The contest had evolved from verbal boasts made a year earlier among three Bedford men, Dr. A.E. Newland, banker Ralph Moore and School Superintendent H.H. Mourer. They settled their dispute about who could shuck the most corn in the field, then decided a county tournament would generate some excitement.

Each township conducted contests to pick their representatives. Tad's father was the Pleasant Run champion and he competed that day against winners from the other eight townships. The newspapers had promoted the contest for days, announcing new details with each edition, facts like Gov. Clifford Townsend agreeing to attend.

Tad was more interested in his father than in the governor. He figured no one could beat his father. That's why he did all the chores he could when he arrived home from school that day. He had at least twenty questions that night when his dad finally arrived.

"Let me start at the beginning," his dad said, "so I won't forget anything. If I do, you can read about it in the *Bedford Daily Mail* tomorrow."

He described the farm and the crowd and the carnival atmosphere, and said Townsend and Rep. E.B. Crowe had engaged in a contest of their own.

"Who won?" Tad asked.

His dad replied, "Nobody said. Being politicians, neither one wanted to be embarrassed by the piddling amount they shucked."

The next event, he said, was the contest between Dr. Newland, Moore and Mourer and three Mitchell businessmen men, Ike Walton, Paul Chase and Harry Matthews.

He didn't wait for Tad to ask who won. "Chase won the businessman's contest. He shucked 7.89 bushels in eighty minutes, which explains why those six men work in town instead of on farms." Tad figured he could shuck almost that much.

His dad still hadn't said how he did.

"When that was all over," his father continued, "the officials lined up all of us at the start of rows. The governor fired a shot and we started. I never heard so many ears bang off bankboards in my life. Everybody started off fast, but then some of them faded after a few minutes."

Tad could stand it no longer. "Well, how much did you win by?"

His dad said, unashamedly, "I didn't win. Finished third. Harry Burton won. He shucked 17.47 bushels in 80 minutes, just a peck or two more than me."

Tad wondered if Burton had cheated. His dad laughed and said, "No, he didn't cheat. But I wore gloves and the men who finished ahead of me didn't."

Tad knew a person could shuck more without gloves on. "Bet you could have won if you'd taken your gloves off," he said.

His dad said, "Maybe! Maybe! At least I got an excuse for finishing third, plus a good pair of hands that haven't been cut to pieces by the blade on the corn." He turned his hands over so Tad could see.

"I never liked the limelight, anyhow. I bet tomorrow when nobody's looking I shuck more corn than Harry Burton, if he can shuck at all the way his hands were cut up."

Tad believed him.

Armistice Rites Surpass Lesson

E.O. Winklepleck waited until after lunch to tell his fifth grade students there would be no classes that afternoon. The boys cheered. The girls smiled approvingly.

"The principal has asked all the grades to join the junior high and high school students in the gym for a special Armistice Day program," he announced.

It was Friday, and November 11, 1940, wasn't until the following Monday, but school would be closed then for the holidays. Most of Mr. Winklepleck's students knew Armistice Day was a time to observe the end of World War I, a war fought to end all wars. That war hadn't ended all wars, but the sacrifice the Americans made in Europe was worth remembering, the teacher said.

The students walked from the classroom and down two flights of wooden stairs that creaked from years of use, and marched into the gym. Canvas covered the basketball floor and folding chairs had been placed in front of the stage. The older students sat in the back, some on the three rows of bleachers at the side of the gym.

The jabbering stopped when principal Loren Raines walked to the center of the stage. He said a few words about the occasion, then nodded to Mrs. Faubion, the music teacher. That was a signal for her to turn to the glee club, which sang a World War I song about "we're going over and we're not coming back 'til it's over over there."

One of the high school students then read the proclamation issued 32 years earlier by Marshal Ferdinand Foch, allied commander. It declared hostilities were to end at 11:00 a.m. on November 11, 1918.

The glee club sang "It's a Long Way to Tipperary," a tune made popular by allied forces in World War I.

One of the high school girls read a poem about Flanders Field, where some of the 50,510 Americans who died in battle were buried. Other students recited other information about the war.

Once the program was over, the students returned to their classrooms and Mr. Winklepleck said the program was better than any history lesson he could have taught that afternoon.

At supper that night, Pokey told his parents about the program and asked, "Anyone around here fight in the war?"

His dad named several men, citing one who was wounded by shrapnel, another who experienced mustard gas in battle, another who had recovered from shell shock.

"How come none of them ever say anything about it?" Pokey asked.

"Real heroes don't talk about their bravery," his dad said. "The biggest talk comes from men who didn't make it to the front until the fighting was over," he added, only half in jest.

It wasn't until years later that Bogey read in a historical report his father had served on the county draft board. His dad seldom talked about himself much. And besides, he probably just wanted to forget he had any part in having to send off to war men who were just a few years younger than he had been.

Armistice Day has been known as Veterans Day since 1954.

Some Folks Just Can't "Leaf" It Be

Clem and Hank couldn't see any point in driving up to Brown County to see the fall foliage, but their wives, being strong-willed farm women, usually got their way.

There was one time when Clem and Hank wished they'd been more assertive. That day in 1940 turned out not to be one of the better times of their lives.

Clem and Hank were outside Mundell Church, southeast of Heltonville, talking like they usually did after services, when their wives approached with the decision. They made it sound like a Sunday afternoon drive up to Nashville would be almost as exciting as a visit to the World's Fair.

"Besides, ain't gonna cost nothing except for a little gas," Clem's wife said.

"Ain't the cost," Clem said. "We got all the scenery 'round here I care to see."

Clem was right, of course. And Hank agreed. "God's country is right here in front of you, women, and you want to go galavanting up to Brown County."

Clem and Hank had just as well been talking to a couple of fence posts that had been set in concrete. The women didn't hear a word they said.

"We'll meet up at C.E. Cummings store in Norman at 1:15 p.m.!" Hank's wife said firmly and finally, with no opening for.renegotiation.

"The kids will all appreciate it. You'll see," Clem's wife added, as if that'd bring some satisfaction to the men.

Both families dined quickly on food that was already prepared to be warmed up, and drove up in front of C.E.'s place about the same time. Clem was driving his 1935 Pontiac painted with the red dust of a gravel road. One of the boys was in the front seat between Clem and his wife. The other three kids were in the back. Hank drove a 1936 Chevrolet. His kids were grown, except for the two boys and one girl in the back seat.

They drove east out of Norman through some of the best scenery in Southern Indiana, a spectacular kaleidoscope of colors painted with the leaves of sassafras, maple, beech, ash, gum, oak and others. Clem used his limited vocabulary to express the wonders of Jackson County, but his wife only shrugged, like she was waiting for something special in Brown County.

The two-car caravan turned north where Ind. 58 and Ind. 135 merge and proceeded uneventfully through Freetown and up past Story before traffic began to back up. By the time they got to the Ind. 135-Ind. 46 junction, it was almost bumper to bumper.

"We should have gone to New York City, if we'd wanted to see wall-to-wall cars," Clem said tauntingly as he drove west. His wife ignored him.

The procession moved along at 15–20 miles an hour until it reached the east entrance to Brown County State Park. Clem and Hank turned left, figuring the best place to see the leaves would be in the park.

That was before they learned every other Hoosier who owned a car had the same idea. They had gone no more than a couple of miles in the park when traffic stalled as visitors aban-

doned their cars to look out across the vistas. It was slow going from that point on.

Clem suggested—make that ordered—his wife and youngsters, "Get out and walk ahead and see what you can see." Hank stayed with his car, too, while his wife and kids craned their necks.

The jam cleared slowly and Clem caught up with his family just about the time his radiator began to steam. He used some words to express himself which he hadn't learned at church that morning, fitting in a report that he had the car ready for winter and the "damned alcohol has done boiled out."

He turned off the engine and coasted down a hill until he saw some water in the creek. To fill the radiator took several trips with the gallon bucket he kept in the car. It didn't help any to have all those other cars blowing their horns and yelling at him.

It was almost sundown when Clem and Hank managed to exit the park at the west entrance onto Ind. 46 again. They turned west, deciding it probably would be as quick to return through Bloomington.

The traffic finally cleared out when they turned south on South Walnut at Bloomington to Ind. 37, but it was long after dark when they got home. The cows and livestock were waiting. Clem had to do the chores by lantern light, which was bad enough when he was in a good mood.

Clem was still smarting the next morning when his wife walked out onto the porch, stood beside him, looked out across the hills and said,

*Illustration by
Gary Varvel*

"My what a beautiful spot we have here, Pa."

"Why in the hell didn't you realize that yesterday?" Clem said. He stood there awhile. Then he put his right arm around her waist and took a long look, letting her know it was a new day and a time to let bygones be bygones.

Around Halloween, Boys Will Be Boys

A visit to Lester's barber shop wasn't exactly like going to a church revival, but you could hear a lot of testifying there. Especially a few days before Halloween. A dozen men and boys filled the two benches in the shop down by the railroad in Heltonville on a late October Saturday in the early 1940s.

Clem waited for a lull in the debate over the basketball team to notice: "Looks like someone already soaped your windows, Lester."

Soap markings, three inches wide, ran vertically, horizontally and diagonally on each of the six-by-six panes. Lester glanced at the windows with a look of disgust and returned, without comment, to snipping.

One of the older men said, "Soap ain't so bad. It'll wash off. And, besides, it looks like them windows needed to be scrubbed, anyhow."

Everybody laughed, except Lester. But no one offered to take a towel and hot water and do the windows. Instead, the men turned to the Halloweens of their youths and began a round of confessionals. One man told of soaping the Chicago, Milwaukee & St. Paul tracks on the hill east of town. "We spread on so much of that homemade lye soap that locomotive just spun its wheels until it burned off the stuff."

Another man listed all the outhouses he'd overturned. Someone else said, "That ain't nothing. We turned over one with the owner inside."

Some of the boys mentioned that the Roosevelt toilets built during the Depression had concrete footings and were hard to overturn. "Take a rope or chain and pull 'em over with a tractor," one of the men advised, not thinking his comment might be put to use.

Lester finally finished with a customer. He looked at a kibitzer who was about forty-five and said, "Tell 'em about what you helped do back in 1917."

The man cleared his throat of Red Man, hitting the spitoon with a plunk. He recalled graphically how he and some friends, who were sixteen and seventeen at the time, disassembled a one-horse cart and lifted it piece by piece to the top of the Ragsdale & Alexander store.

"We had a heck of a time, but we managed to put the thing back together on the roof. Folks said it was the best trick they'd ever seen."

Lester agreed, adding, "And there hasn't been anything like it since."

That caused the men to ask the boys what they had planned.

Pokey said, "Can't top that. Besides, I've quit. Last year I soaped my teacher's windows. The next day she told me she knew it was me. Said she

recognized my handwriting."

Bogey said, "I'm not doing anything either. We did some stuff at the school last year. We were so excited about what we were doing, we forgot a teacher lived within hearing distance."

Tad said he used so much wire to fasten a gate the farmer had to use wire cutters to get it open. "He knew it was me. Said he recognized how I tied wires from when I worked on his baler last summer."

An adult said, "Guess you'll have to go up to Norman to pull off your stunts if you don't want to get caught."

"We tried that," Bogey replied, "but it's no fun pullin' stuff on people you don't know."

Tad said, "We've still got a few days to think of something. We may decide to come up with some pranks yet."

Another customer eased out of the barber chair about that time. He looked at the boys and said, "I'm sure you will."

The other men, having once been boys themselves, nodded in agreement.

Lessons Learned from the Passing of the Seasons

Shorty downshifted the bus and made a right turn at the Baptist church onto Groundhog Road. He eased across the ford in Leatherwood Creek, drove a few hundred feet, stopped and removed an ax he kept aboard the bus. He walked to the back of the bus and pounded out a geode that had been trapped between the dual tires when he crossed the creek.

This was nothing new for his twenty-five passengers, who were students at the school in Heltonville. The geode rocks often became wedged between the wheels. The delay didn't bother Chig. He used the time to look back at the golden richness of the leaves on the trees on the hills in town.

Shorty returned to the bus and Chig continued to look out the window as Billy talked to him. The trees and

brush were shedding their foliage, reluctantly it seemed, surrendering one leaf at a time.

Leaves on the hardwood trees were multicolored, and Chig mentally recorded the different hues . . . red, rust, crimson, yellow, yellow green, purple . . . as the bus passed the Butler place and stopped at the Miller farm. The corn in the fields had turned brown, awaiting the picker.

The bus turned east at the electric transformer, where Groundhog Road joined with Clearspring Road, which some folks called Powerline Road.

Chig counted the milkweed along the fence rows and noticed the reds in the leaves on briars and on sumac. The walnut trees along the road stood nude, already stripped of their leaves.

The bus passed George Sherrill's farm and Grover Hunter's fields. Chig used the windows on the bus to frame the landscaped picture nature had painted. At Stanley Hunter's place, the maple trees that had dripped sugar water in the spring seemed content, waving their yellow and red leaves as if to nod a greeting as the bus passed.

The bus stirred clouds of dust as it rounded the ninety-degree turn at Charlie Mark's house. Chig remembered the summer past when the pawpaws grew and the berries ripened. Summer, he thought, was midlife, a time between the youthful spring and the aging autumn.

A few hundred feet past Mundell Church, Shorty turned north up a lane toward the houses where Fern, Dale and Ruby lived. The sassafras was red in the woods, but the white blossoms were all but gone from the buckwheat.

Chig continued to watch as the bus continued east past the farms Harry Nichols, George Hunter and Clarence Harrell owned. The two streams on Clarence's bottom pasture were dry, exposing the soapstone beds that were covered only with the leaves that had fallen. Cattle, their backs showing the growing thickness of a winter blanket of hair, grazed on the short grass.

At the top of the hill, Shorty turned left on a road that would take him to Ind. 58, the last leg of the route to Norman.

Chig bounded off the bus and saw his neighbor Ben walking in a field dotted with corn shocks. He walked toward Ben, a boy in the springtime of his life, eager to talk with a man in the fall of his. It was easy for Chig to visit with Ben. Ben, like autumn, had learned the limits of life. He, like the passing seasons, had mellowed with time, learning a wisdom that comes only with approaching age.

As he often did, he shared his thoughts with Chig, explaining in short, simple sentences the meaning of the seasons and their relationship to men and boys, of birth, life and death.

As they usually did, Chig's parents asked him that night what he had learned that day. Chig shrugged. The lessons of an autumn day were too meaningful for the boy to share so soon, even with his parents.

Wood Stove Time

Jan Wills, a Chicago artist who resettled in Indiana, has painted a poignant evocation of a rural Indiana winter entitled "The Light in the Kitchen." It is a picture of a farm field under a bleak sky, corn stubble in the foreground, snow in tired furrows, and in the distance a warm light coming from the windows of a farm house.

To an outsider, winter in the country can seem a dreary time of cold and death, but it is important not to overlook the light in the window. In rural Indiana, winter is a time to rest from the labors of the warmer seasons, a season of planning and rejuvenation that begins with the excitement of the Christmas season, keeps busy with knitting, sewing, woodcutting, listening to the radio, and poring over seed catalogues, endures through the days of cabin fever, and ends with maple-sugaring, high school basketball sectional tournaments, and finally the first burst of jonquils, daffodils, and tulips, the harbingers of spring.

These, then, are the word-pictures that Wendell Trogdon paints of winter in the 1930s and '40s: pictures of cold mornings warmed by hot biscuits and gravy and simmering tenderloin strips, months of drawing on the bounty of the harvest laid away in a root cellar, and quiet pleasures like selecting, cutting, and trimming the Christmas cedar tree with its crochet-like branches. Not just a time of making do, but of every day living the lesson that in lack there is plenty, that less *can* be more.

That the light in the window is eternal spring.   —*MN*

The Cellar Farm Supermarket

Alex never saw any wine in cellars on farms. At least he didn't in the God-fearing rural areas around Heltonville in the late 1930s.

What he did see was a virtual storehouse of fruit, vegetables and canned goods that would last an average family for years. Row on row of Mason and Ball jars filled with corn, peas, beans, apples, cherries, jams, jellies, preserves, tomatoes, pears, peaches, juices . . . . Potatoes were in bushel baskets or in bins. So were turnips, apples, pears . . . anything that could be stored for long periods of time.

There was a place for everything and everything had to be in place. A cellar was a supermarket with items neatly arranged. But there were no prices stamped on the goods and no checkout lines.

Not all cellars were alike. Some were under houses, some under outbuildings, some mere dugouts with roofs over them. But they all kept the food warm enough not to freeze in winter and cool enough not to spoil in summer.

Mrs. Julian's cellar was under the house, the shelves stretching for forty feet. Only one daughter lived with her, but folks said there was enough food in the cellar to feed a CCC camp for years.

Mrs. Julian, however, liked to have her other children and her grandkids in for Sunday dinner and she wanted to make sure there would always be enough food available for them.

"Besides," she once told Alex, who was one of her many grandchildren, "you never know when we might have a famine, or a bad drought or some other disaster."

There were droughts, but they never prevented her from restocking the cellar with everything used the previous winter.

Alex's folks lived in a big farm house that didn't have a cellar underneath. The cellar was a basement under a frame building, about one hundred feet away from the house. The family called it the cellarhouse.

A big heavy door, two inches thick, covered the steps down into the cellar. Shelves lined the four walls. The "house" over the cellar was used to store the lawnmower, garden tools and old newspapers.

Alex was usually out helping his pa with the chores, sledding, or playing basketball in the barnloft when his ma needed something from the cellar. Except once.

He had just come in one day when his ma asked him to bring "a quart of raspberries, a quart of green beans and six big potatoes from the cellar."

Alex was back in a flash. "Snow's drifted against the cellar door and I cain't git it open," he said.

"Take a shovel and throw away the snow," his mother said, gently.

Alex did as he was told. But he decided to browse through some of the old newspapers when he did get the door open. A half hour or so later, he returned to the house and told his ma he had forgotten what she wanted.

"Son, you're the most forgetful boy I've ever known."

Alex said, "No, I ain't. I remember I just read in an old *Bedford Times* out in the cellarhouse that Norval Tanksley scored 13 points when Heltonville beat Needmore last year."

Alex returned to the cellar. This time he brought his ma the potatoes and the can of green beans.

"Where're the raspberries?" she asked.

"Fell on the ice, and the bottle smashed," he said.

"Didn't do that 'cause you hate raspberries, did you, Son?" she said.

"Nope," Alex said.

"Well, get out there and clean up the mess. *After* you've brought me an unbroken jar of raspberries."

Alex did as he was told.

After that, his ma usually went to the cellar herself when she needed something.

A few years later, Alex's parents built a new house with a cellar in the basement. The old cellarhouse was torn down and the hole that remained was filled.

Alex never liked the new cellar. There were no newspapers in it to read.

"Sprucing" Up for the Holidays

Two boys, hunched down in their plaid mackinaw jackets, shuffled their boots in the skift of snow that covered the tracks through the wooded pasture. The stillness of the winter day was broken by their tuneless attempts to hum "The Trail of the Lonesome Pine." It was an appropriate song, and they had memorized the words listening to a record on the Victrola.

They were in search of a Christmas tree. There were no pines on the farm near Heltonville, but there were cedar trees, and one of them would do just as well.

Tad, nine, carried a carpenter's saw. Tyke, eleven, held a piece of baling wire tied to a three-by-eight-foot sheet of galvanized roofing that left a corrugated trail in the snow. They crossed a small stream on its thick ice cover, then started appraising the cedars as they headed up the next hill.

They examined a number of trees before Tad pointed to one and yelled, "That's it." Tyke looked, then searched his memory for the worst profanity he could remember. He used it, then screamed, "That's the ugliest tree I've ever seen."

Tad eased himself between Tyke and the tree. "Hey, you'll hurt its feelings," he kidded.

The tree had a listless color, neither dark green nor dark brown. It was about six feet tall, lopsided and scraggy. A big hole was where some branches should have been. Tyke wondered why Tad had chosen that tree.

"Everybody and everything needs to be wanted, 'specially at Christmas time," Tad said.

Tyke walked around the tree, sized it up from all angles, then said, "Start sawin'. One tree is as good as another, I guess."

Once the tree was down, Tad laid it on the makeshift sled and tied it with binder twine. The boys talked about decorating the tree on the way back to the house. It wasn't a job they cared to do. Their sisters could do that chore.

Tyke nailed a wooden stand onto the tree, carried it inside and placed it in front of a window, then announced: "We have here a refugee from the Ugly Forest. It ain't pretty, but it's a friend of Tad's."

Tad smiled and said, "We've done our job. Me and Tyke are going out to the barn and shoot some baskets."

They waited in the barn until they thought the tree had been decorated, then dared return to the house.

Tad was pleased with what he saw. Tyke was surprised. The tree was no longer ugly. The house had no electricity, but flashing lights would have ruined the effect, anyhow. Circling the tree were strands of popcorn and cranberries, paper angels, and cookies shaped like Santa. Bells hung from the branches, and so did paper icicles and sycamore balls wrapped in tinfoil. A big star, cut from cardboard and wrapped in the tinfoil, topped the tree.

The tree that had looked sad in the bareness of the pasture appeared happy in its new attire. But not as happy as Tad, who looked at the tree a long time before going into another room and listening once again to "The Trail of the Lonesome Pine."

Christmas Chores Aren't Like Work

Farm chores had to be done on Christmas just like any other day, but it was the one time of the year when chores seemed more like pleasure than work.

Maybe it was the spirit of the season. Or maybe it was because youngsters like Tad, Tyke, Pokey, Billy and Bob knew they wouldn't be able to open all their gifts until the chores were done. Or maybe it was the extra care their parents demanded they give the livestock, chickens and other farm animals on Christmas Day.

Most of the families who lived around Heltonville observed similar rituals each Christmas in the late 1930s and early 1940s. Toddlers who still believed in Santa could bound out of bed early and open all their gifts. They weren't old enough to do outside work anyhow. Youngsters who were older usually were allowed to open one present before their fathers announced: "Let's wait to see what else we have until after we finish our chores." And their mothers would add, "While you boys are out doing your work, I'll do mine." Everybody knew she already had lighted the kindling in the wood range to fix the biggest breakfast of the year.

Tad had been big enough to help with the chores for several years before Christmas in 1939. The work had become routine with him until that day.

He was buttoning up his mackinaw jacket when his dad said they could do the chores together instead of separately as they usually did. When Tad looked puzzled, his dad explained: "This is a special day to be together. And I want to make sure the animals know it's Christmas, too."

They walked to the barn where Tad gave each of the draft horses three ears of corn and two scoops of oats, just like he always did. His dad pitched him a few more ears. "Give each of them two extra ears and another scoop of oats. It's Christmas."

He told Tad to feed the milk cows an extra scoop of ground feed and more bran than usual. "While I do the milkin', you throw down an extra helping of alfalfa for the beef cows, then give them a real treat," pointing to the ground feed they usually didn't get.

When Tad was finished, his dad. said, "Just as well jump in the stalls and curry the horses. They got a right to look good on a holiday."

The horses, Bird and Molly, seemed to appreciate the attention.

Later, when Tad and his father were in the milk house separating the cream, his dad said, "Let's take a couple of buckets of milk out to the hogs. We've got more than we need at the house."

Tad dumped a three-gallon bucket of the "de-creamed" milk into the hog trough and jumped back as the pigs ran up. He didn't have to be told to give the hogs an extra amount of corn, or extra dips of supplement.

"You're getting in the Christmas spirit," his dad told him.

At the chicken house, they put enough mash into the self-feeders to do the hens the entire day, made sure they had plenty of water and gave

them a bucket of scraps Tad's mother had filled the day before when she prepared part of the Christmas dinner.

As they walked to the back door of the house, Tad's mother handed him a bucket of warm milk. "Take this out to the kittens in the woodhouse." It wasn't the normal fare for the cats, who usually didn't get that much attention.

Tad's father gave his German shepherd a bone with some ham still on it. The dog looked as if he knew it was a special holiday.

Tad was pulling off his boots on the back porch when he looked at his dad and asked: "How come we treated the animals special? They don't know Christmas from any other day."

His dad put his arm around him and said, "They may not. But we do. And that's a lot more important."

Tad enjoyed his breakfast and his presents that day more than he ever had before, and when the light of the day turned to dusk, he was ready to do the evening chores.

A Customer Gives a Clerk a Lesson

Maggie had just turned sixteen when she went to work off the farm for the first time.

It was a new experience for her and for her folks, who had lived and worked all their lives on the farm outside Heltonville. They'd tried to talk her out of taking the part-time job, telling her she'd have to drive the ten miles into Bedford by herself each day she worked.

But she had enough convincing reasons to get her way. There was a war, there was a shortage of employees and anyone who could work should. Maggie was hired by the J.C. Penney store on the southeast corner of Courthouse Square in Bedford as an extra clerk for the Christmas season.

It was 1943 and, despite the grimness of the war in the south of Europe and in the South Pacific, most folks were determined to make Christmas as joyful as possible. Penney's was a popular place for shoppers seeking items of clothing to give as gifts.

Maggie's job was to help customers find what they wanted, make out sales tickets, accept the money, put both the ticket and the cash in a little box and send it on an electric route to the cashier's office on an upper floor. She wrapped the items while she waited for the change to return, chatting with the customers when time allowed.

She did her job well, trying to show those who looked like they had money the costlier item, those who appeared less well off merchandise that was less costly.

They seemed to appreciate it. All of them, that is, except Sharm, who came into the store the third day Maggie worked. It was the Saturday after Thanksgiving.

Sharm lived close to Maggie's parents. He never seemed to have much money and folks said he had to scrape up every cent he had just to feed his family and keep from losing the farm.

He told Maggie he wanted to buy trousers for his two sons for Christmas, gave her the sizes and followed her as she walked to the racks of pants. She pulled out the cheapest pairs the store had. Sharm shook his head. "What else you got?" he asked.

She showed him trousers that cost a couple dollars more each. He shook his head again, and again when she showed him still another pair that wasn't top-drawer. Finally, she went to the most expensive trousers in the store.

Sharm felt the material. "You got these in my boys' sizes, biggest boy in blue, smaller one in brown?"

Maggie found the sizes and the colors. She took the wrinkled twenty-dollar bill Sharm handed her, made out the sales ticket, which came to $17.96, and waited for the change.

While she did so, Sharm looked her in the eye and said softly, "Did you learn anything from this transaction?"

Maggie said, her face turning red, "Yes, I learned not to pre-judge what people might want."

Sharm smiled, then said, "To be a good salesperson you should show the most expensive items first. A customer can always ask for something cheaper. If they don't, you've sold the best. If they do, you can always move on down the line."

"The other way, they might buy the cheapest item right off the bat."

Maggie said, "Thanks."

Sharm touched her arm and said, "No charge," then walked out with his package.

Ice Cream Was Worth the Pain

It is January 1939, rural Lawrence County. Six inches of fresh snow have just fallen.

It is an era before bureaucrats find jobs for themselves warning other Americans about hazards to their health.

The threat of radioactive elements, contaminants, acid rain and PCBs will not come until years later.

Calories are not counted, and the only time people weigh themselves is on the big scales at the grain elevator or the penny scales in front of the Merit Shoe Store on the Square in Bedford.

Youngsters are encouraged to eat what they want, when they want. That doesn't take much encouragement.

One of the things they want to eat in January is ice cream made from snow. For youngsters like Pokey, ice cream is a rare treat. Most of them live in houses without electricity and refrigeration, and most of the ice cream they have comes when they visit the general store in Heltonville or Norman.

The recipe for homemade ice cream has been handed down from generation to generation. Pokey, who is nine, has memorized the formula for the ice cream, waiting for the snow to stop. By learning the recipe, he knows he can fix bowl after bowl of ice cream from the snow himself, without waiting for his mom or sisters to make it for him.

The recipe is simple: snow, covered with granulated sugar, flavored with a few drops of vanilla extract, topped with milk or cream. Pokey prefers the thick rich cream, fresh from the separator after the morning milking.

Once the snow stops, he carefully places a pitcher of cream next to the sugar bowl on the big, round kitchen table. He stands on a chair to reach the vanilla extract on the top shelf of the cupboard. Then he reaches for a dish his mother uses for mashed potatoes to feed a family of six.

Without stopping to put on his sock cap or Mackinaw jacket and mittens, he runs out into the snow, looking for a spot where no dog has stopped, no kitten has strayed and no chicken has landed. He finds pure unadulterated snow, as white as the minister's starched shirt.

He dips his hands into the snow and scoops out about four handfuls. It is enough to fill the dish. He runs back in, sets the dish on the table, spreads about four tablespoons of sugar over it, adds enough vanilla for flavoring, then pours on the right amount of cream to make the snow taste good without causing it to become soupy.

He begins to eat it, slowly at first, then with bigger heaps on the spoon, narrowing the distance between bites. The dish is empty in minutes.

If one dish was so tasty, a second will be twice as good, Pokey figures. He goes back outside, fills up the dish a second time and repeats the process.

This time he starts eating fast, finishing more slowly.

He waits about a half-hour for his third helping. This time he fills the dish only about a third-full. When he finishes, the sun has set behind the woods to the west, and it is time for Pokey to join his dad at the barn to help with the milking.

Pokey doesn't look too well, but he says, "I'm all right," when his dad asks if anything is wrong. Pokey looks even worse when he sees the thick, rich cream come out of the upper spout on the cream separator.

Back at the house, the two wash their hands. Supper is ready.

Pokey announces, "I'm not hungry. I'm going to go in and rest on the sofa."

His mother says, "We're having your favorite meat. Strips of tenderloin from the hog we butchered yesterday."

Pokey admits he has had too much ice cream.

"You've been waiting for months for tenderloin," his mom says.

Pokey replies over his shoulder as he heads for the living room, "The tenderloin will keep. The snow won't."

Then he plops onto the sofa, knowing the misery he's in was worth it.

Bob and His Furnace Were Well-Sooted

Bob was the son of a preacher, which meant he got into as much mischief as anyone else. Bob's dad was the minister at the Methodist church in Heltonville in the early 1940s.

Like most small churches, it had no janitor, and the pastor and the congregation performed any maintenance and cleaning that was done.

The minister never worried about who would fire the furnace each Sunday morning. Bob needed the responsibility, his dad decided. And if the church wasn't warm enough when the bell rang out across town, Bob would get the blame.

Bob wasn't afraid of work. He had hoed weeds out of corn the previous summer for fifty cents a day and cleaned bricks at the school for a penny each. But he didn't want to spend any more time at labor than any other teenager.

That may be why he was a bit careless when building a fire at the church one Sunday. He laid in some paper and kindling, tossed in a few lumps of coal, lighted a match and waited. The flames flickered briefly, then died down. Smoke replaced the flames, and the coal smoldered without igniting.

Bob didn't wait for natural combustion. He reached for a bottle of kerosene and splashed some of the

*Illustration by
Gary Varvel*

contents into the stove. Nothing happened. Bob became impatient. Exasperated, he stuck his head near the door of the furnace to look in.

Whhooooff!

The kerosene ignited into a burst of flames. The hot blast burned out the inside of the pipes, sending soot adrift over the entire sanctuary. It drifted onto the pews, sprinkling carbon on almost every seat.

Bob was too surprised to think about himself. He thought more about how he could get the mess cleaned up before the congregation arrived.

He did the best he could, as quickly as he could. When he finished he hurried home to change his clothes.

His parents were dressed in their Sunday clothes and waiting when he finally made it home. They seemed to ask in unison, "What took you so long?"

Bob wasn't about to admit anything. "Nothing particular," he replied, a bit sheepishly. "Why are you asking?"

His parents didn't answer that question. One of them suggested, "Go look in the mirror."

Bob looked at himself. He was covered with soot. His face was black. His eyebrows were burned. His hair was singed. His secret now belonged to the world.

Somehow, he managed to make himself look as clean and as presentable as the preacher's son was supposed to look.

If anyone complained about soot on the seats, Bob didn't hear him. The members were, perhaps, too comfortable in the warmth from the furnace.

Cold-Natured Chig

Not much bothered Chig, especially cold weather. He could credit his environment for that.

Take one winter day in January 1938. Chig awoke, warm beneath a stack of comforters, poked at the ice that had formed on the window panes next to his bed, bounded onto the cold floor and jumped into his overalls.

He could see his breath as he ran down the stairs. A fire roared in the potbellied stove, the only heat except the kitchen range in the big farmhouse that had no insulation or storm windows.

Chig warmed himself with cocoa, sipped between gulps of biscuits and gravy and fresh tenderloin strips. He pulled a sock cap over his ears, nestled into a warm jacket and headed out to do the chores.

The mercury in the thermometer outside stood at five-below, but the barn had been warmed by the cattle overnight. Chig made a game out of his work, his daydreams limited to his own imagination.

It was still dark when he finished, so he had plenty of time to get ready for school in Heltonville. He tugged on his coat, yanked his gloves in place, picked up his books and headed for the door.

His older sister wasn't as eager to face the cold. "It's still ten minutes before the bus will be here," she told him.

Chig had seen some men down at the road. He was eager to learn what they were doing.

Some of the men were at work. Others were crowded around a fifty-five-gallon drum, absorbing the heat from a fire inside the barrel. Two of them moved away from the drum so Chig could ease in.

"Whatcha doin'?" he asked.

A man who appeared to be the boss said, "We're a W.P.A. crew. We're cleaning out the ditches so the water won't run across the road. Ain't easy with the ground frozen, but we can manage."

Chig learned later that W.P.A. meant Works Progress Administration, an agency that provided jobs for the unemployed during the Depression.

He talked with the men until the school bus arrived. He found a seat on the bus next to the driver. He knew it was warmer next to the kerosene heater that Shorty, the driver, kept up front.

"What's that for?" he asked, pointing to a spinning fan fastened on the dash.

"That's to keep the frost off the inside of the windshield. Otherwise, I'd spend all my time keeping ice from forming," Shorty explained.

Chig looked back once in a while during the seven-mile trip at his sister, whose teeth were chattering. She was trying to carry on a conversation with some other girls, but their words seemed to hang like icicles from their mouths.

"Serves her well," he thought. She had told him earlier that the front row seats were for "children."

At school, Miss Hunter, the teacher, gave students the option of staying in at recess or going outdoors. Chig and a couple of his friends chose to go outside. They knew the janitor would let them warm next to the giant furnace just before the recess was over. Miss Hunter mentioned how comfortable they looked when they returned from their romp outside in the arctic air.

Chig noticed more of the other students tried to sit closer to the front of the bus that afternoon on the way home. His sister and her friends were among them.

At home, he made a few trips down the hill on a sheet of galvanized roofing he used for a sled. The thrill exceeded the chill.

That night, his sister complained, "I can't wait for summer."

About that time Chig's mom handed him a flatiron she had warmed and wrapped in newspapers and told him to put it at the foot of the bed to keep his feet warm. Chig took it, looked at his sister and said, "Summer's not nearly as much fun as winter." He turned and raced up to his room, outrunning his sister's remarks to the contrary.

Measles Makes Even School Look Inviting

Measles was an equal opportunity disease. Anyone who wasn't immune could catch it.

Danny, an only child of reasonably well-to-do parents, caught it. So did Gordy, one of six youngsters in a family that barely eked out an existence. In fact, it was easier to catch measles than it was a basketball, especially if you were a second grader.

Measles was a perennial visitor to Heltonville in the 1930s, but it didn't stop long at the school or too many homes until the winter of 1937–38. That winter was different. The measles attacked the lower grades, then spread, slowly at first, from one youngster to another. As the days passed, the outbreak raced throughout the school, then became an epidemic.

Teachers like Miss Mark, who taught the second grade, and Miss Hunter, who taught the third, knew the symptoms and could spot the infectious disease immediately. A red eruption on the skin was unmistakable. But sometimes they knew the virus was present as soon as a student complained of high fever.

The teachers, principal and county superintendent thought the epidemic would pass, but it continued day after day until 134 students in the twelve grades were absent. That was more than a third of the total enrollment. The officials met, considered the options, and decided to close the school for thirty days.

Nobody was happier about that than Billy. He was one of Miss Hunter's third-graders who had escaped the measles. At least he thought he had.

Miss Hunter suggested he and the other students spend at least part of the time off reading and doing multiplication tables. They all nodded like they would, even though Miss Hunter knew better.

Billy figured he'd spend the thirty days running traps he'd set out along the creek, sledding down the hills and building snow forts, doing chores only when he couldn't get out of them.

The school had been closed just a couple of days when Billy noticed his mother eyeing him one evening before supper. Since she had no thermometer, she held her hand to his forehead. Billy nodded when she asked if he was catching a cold.

The next morning he had red splotches over much of his skin. Doc Cain showed up later that morning, tossing away the cigar he always smoked before coming into the house. He asked Billy to stick out his tongue and say "ah." Doc listened to the heartbeat and made the usual "hmmmm" comment which sounded more ominous than it was.

As soon as he left, Billy was ordered to his upstairs bedroom. The blinds were drawn. "Doc's orders," his mother said. "You'll have to stay in bed three, four, five days." Billy thought he could fool his mom by protesting that he couldn't read his lessons or do arithmetic in the dark.

"By the end of the day you're not going to feel like doing either," she said.

She was right. The next day Billy was so sick he wished he was well enough to study. A few days later, when he was on his way to recuperation, he would deny ever making such a wish.

When he was better, he was given the run of the farmhouse, but still was not allowed to go outdoors. He read everything he could comprehend, including the *Bedford Daily Mail*, the *Grit* and an assortment of farm magazines. When he complained about having nothing to read, his mom mentioned the school books he had brought home.

"I was just about well. Now I think I'm going to get sick again," he told her.

He eventually was allowed to go outside, but the thirty days off school seemed more like a year than a month.

When school resumed, Billy and the other third graders decided there were a lot worse ways to spend a winter month than being confined to a classroom. They actually paid attention to what Miss Hunter was trying to teach . . . at least for a few days.

Walking in Dad's Footsteps Was a Big Job

Tad was ten when he decided he was man enough to do about anything his dad could. And like most farm boys that age, he soon learned what was meant by being too big for his breeches.

Tad wasn't one to stay around the house on Saturdays when his dad was working in the fields. That's why he went along with his father that February morning after the milking and feeding were done.

His dad explained it was an ideal day to sow Big Red clover seed in the forty acres of winter wheat out west of the house. The temperature was about twenty-five, the ground frozen, the skies overcast. There was no wind. That meant, his dad explained, he could walk through the field without the top of the soil turning to slippery mud and that the seed would fall where he intended it to go without being carried away in a wind. Then when the ground thawed the seeds would seep into the soil to germinate

when the weather warmed.

Tad listened, helping throw two big sacks filled with clover seed on the wagon, which was already hooked to the tractor. Clover seed was small and compact and heavy, the bags weighing about 180 pounds each. Tad had trouble holding up his end.

His dad sat on one of the sacks adjusting the straps on the seeder while Tad drove the tractor to the field.

The seeder looked simple enough. It had a bag for the seed, and an adjustable gap that dropped seed onto a fan that was turned by a crank.

Tad dipped the seed from the clover sack with a small scoop, letting it slide into the seeder bag held open by his dad. After about three scoops, his dad said, "That's about right."

He slipped each arm into the straps on the seeder so the crank would be on the right side. That's when Tad asked, "How can you tell where you're goin' and where you've been, pa?"

"I'm gonna step off five paces from the side, then set my eyes dead ahead to the opposite end of the field.

"The idea, Son, is to adjust your

pace and the rotation of the crank so you're getting the right amount of seed on the ground. Each pass through the field I'll be coverin' about thirty feet."

Tad nodded, and his dad went on: "At the far end I'll have to take about ten paces—or thirty feet—before starting back again. Same each time from then on."

Tad's dad was a big man, who walked fast, turning the crank on the seeder to match his stride. It was a pace he'd developed through experience.

Tad made a couple of trips from one end to the other and back, walking far enough behind his dad so the seed wouldn't hit him.

Bored with that, he spent some time across the road examining a ground hog burrow and watching a couple of squirrels play high in a tree. When he moseyed back to the field his dad was refilling the bag on the seeder.

"Think I've got the hang of it, Pa. Let me make a trip while you rest."

"Don't know, Son. Ain't as easy as it looks."

Tad persisted. His dad relented, helping Tad put the seeder over his shoulders, then pulling the straps to make them tighter.

Tad hadn't gone far until his dad noticed he was having trouble keeping a good rhythm. When Tad walked slow, he turned the seeder too fast, when he walked fast, he rotated it too slow.

A couple of times, Tad stopped, flexed his right elbow a couple of times, indicating his arm was tired. At the opposite end of the field he took ten steps, all right, but they were about equal to seven his dad took.

Coming back toward the tractor, he meandered more than he walked a true course. But he made it, ending up fairly close to his destination.

He didn't wait for his dad to ask if he'd had enough. He ripped the straps from his shoulders, handed the seeder to his dad and said, "How'd I do, Pa?"

His dad said, "Well, son, there ain't no way to tell until we cut the wheat in June and see what kind of clover crop we got underneath."

That June it was easy to see where Tad had been. Where he had walked too slow and turned the crank too fast, the clover was too thick. Where he had walked too fast and turned the crank too slow, there was no clover at all.

As he and his dad walked through the stubble after the combine had harvested the wheat, Tad asked: "This what Pastor Cox means when he preaches about everybody reaping what we sow?"

"Something like that, son," his dad said, grinning, not minding the weeds that were beginning to grow where the clover should have been.

How Warm Is the Barn, Billy Joe?

It was a simple statement, followed by a casual question not meant to elicit an answer, but Miss B., the substitute teacher, didn't know Billy Joe very well.

She was substituting for Miss Hunter, the regular third-grade teacher, on a cold January day in 1939. The students had just returned from recess, and as usual, Billy Joe was the last one to come through the door. He didn't bother to close it.

Which is why Miss B. said to Billy Joe, without raising her voice: "Close the door, Billy Bob. Were you born in a barn?"

Anyone but Billy Joe would have said, "No, Ma'am," and closed the door. But Billy Joe was different. He was smarter than the normal third grader at Heltonville and he didn't hesitate to try to show how much he knew. That made him argumentative at times, an evaluation with which Miss B. would soon agree.

He said, "Name's not Billy Bob. It's Billy Joe." He walked to the door and closed it. Then he returned to his desk, stood beside it and began talking about barns.

Billy Joe lived on a farm not too far from town and it was soon obvious he had paid a lot of attention to the barn there. "Everybody says the same thing about barns. They think barns are cold. Not all of them are," he said.

He continued, once he saw Miss B. was too confused by his speech to interrupt: "Well, our barn is about as warm as our house. We put strips over the cracks in the sides above the concrete blocks. The doors shut tight and the hay in the loft keeps out the cold."

When he paused for breath, Miss B. opened up the arithmetic text and said, "It sounds like you have a nice, warm barn."

If she thought that would stop Billy Joe, she was wrong. Instead, he resumed his unrehearsed and unsolicited dissertation. "Oh, we've got a good barn. But most barns are warm. You get all the stalls filled with horses and cows and let them start eating hay and heatin' up the place and pretty soon it's as warm as this classroom is right now."

Froggie, who was seated across the room, let out a bellow, like an old Jersey cow waiting to be milked. The laughter stopped Billy Joe's speech, but he still managed a few more sentences about how warm the barn was in the morning after the animals had spent the night in it.

Miss B. finally said, "Thanks, Billy Joe," accentuating the "Joe." "I'm sure we'll think twice before we ask anyone again if he was born in a barn."

Billy Joe smiled and said, "Come out to our farm and I'll show you how warm the barn is."

Miss B. said, "I'll take your word for it," then added quickly, "Okay, class, let's turn to page 93 of our arithmetic books."

The Fifth Season

Someone famous once claimed you couldn't throw a stone in Indiana without hitting a member of the literary establishment. But long before the rock could reach its target, it would be stolen, dribbled, and slam-dunked by a Hoosier high school basketball team.

Indiana didn't invent basketball, but its great players like Oscar Robertson and Larry Bird have helped perfect it from a clumsy backyard game into an exciting sport now characterized by angular grace and terrific bursts of speed.

Not too many years ago, when basketball scores were often so low they looked like baseball scores, in Indiana the game was played everywhere, by almost everyone, outdoors, on packed-dirt farmyard courts, and indoors, sometimes on nonregulation floors where driving toward the basket with the ball was taking your young life into your hands, inviting a collision with a nearby wall or a precipitous stumble on a squeaking floor board.

In Indiana, it was, and still is, the fifth season, separate in a way from the others and also helping mark the transition from cold weather into spring. In Southern Indiana it's said "it always snows during high school sectionals," and that's almost always true; it's also usually the last snowfall of the year.

At a time when winning was very important, but not the most important thing, character grew even when crops could not. High school basketball helped shape, in a mostly beneficial way, generations of Indiana youngsters, including the author of this book. It still does, in high schools blessed by special coaches and supported by strong communities with good, balanced values. —*MN*

Enemies . . . Just for an Afternoon

The magic is gone from Saturday afternoons on basketball sectional weekends. Gone with the small schools, gone with the camaraderie, gone with the five-cent Coke and the twenty-five cent hamburger. Gone, taking with it drama and excitement not found on any other weekend.

And the fans and the players and the merchants on courthouse squares are the losers.

For proof, turn back the calendar. It is 1946, the last Saturday afternoon in February. The place is Bedford, county seat, Lawrence County, home of the powerful Stonecutters.

It will be a day when country meets city, a day when rivals become friends, when old foes unite to support an underdog against a favorite.

It is like that, also, in Seymour, Washington, Bloomington, Vincennes, Madison—wherever cities are ringed by hamlets each with basketball teams.

By noon the Square around the Lawrence County Courthouse is filled with shoppers and fans. Conversations center on the semifinals of the sectional later that afternoon at the gymnasium five blocks to the west.

Among the final four are the Stonecutters, who have won five straight sectionals, five straight regionals. They are the big favorite again. They face Oolitic, believed their strongest threat, in the first afternoon game. Heltonville will meet Shawswick in the second game.

Coach Wilbert Gilstrap has let his Heltonville team come into town in private cars, knowing the players will want to stay in Bedford after the night game, regardless who wins. They arrive before noon, long before the first game at 1:30 p.m.

The players—as they always do—head for the north side of the Square. As usual, they make the John Katis poolroom the first stop. It's in the basement of the Masonic Temple and it's a favorite gathering place for the players from the rural schools. The pool and snooker tables are level and the balls carom true, the place is clean and Katis makes the best malts in Southern Indiana.

"Strawberry?" Katis asks Bogey, one of the Heltonville players who always gets a malt.

"Not today, John. Gotta be in shape when we meet them Farmers this afternoon."

The Farmers are from Shawswick. Dave Elliott, one of the Shawswick players, walks up and says, "Go ahead and have the malt, Bogey. You guys got no chance against us, anyhow."

Players from both sides begin to debate the merits of the two teams and the talent—or lack of it—acting as though they hated each other. Some of them are better actors than basketball players. A visitor would tell Katis later he thought the players meant every word they exchanged. Katis would just smile, knowing they were foes for the day only.

The players leave the pool hall for "The Quarry," which is what the Stonecutters call the gym, at about 1:00 p.m. That gives them plenty of time to find parking places, drop their satchels in the dressing room and find a spot to watch the Bedford-Oolitic game.

Bogey leads the team's cheers for Oolitic. The Bearcats play well through three quarters. The game is in doubt when Bogey and his teammates head for the dressing room. They learn later Bedford pulled away to win, 36-23.

When they come up to the floor to play, the gym is packed, mostly with fans who wanted to see the first game. Shawswick has a few hundred fans, Heltonville fewer.

Bogey has never played in the gym during the day. Somehow it looks different with the light coming through the windows. But the baskets are still as hard as ever to hit.

The warm-up period ends, Coach Gilstrap takes his team into the dressing room, reminds them they almost ended a long Shawswick winning streak a few games ago, losing only 31-30.

Wayne, the captain, says, as he always does, regardless of the opponent: "We can beat these guys, just like we did the Beavers," referring to a 30-18 victory the previous night over Huron. He sounds as though he means it.

It is wishful thinking. He and his teammates are outclassed, in size and talent, by Shawswick players like Elliott, Bob Jackson, Jim Graves and John Hodges.

The game is close for thirty seconds. Then the Farmers pull away. Far away, 33 points away, winning 51-18.

Nobody says much in the Heltonville dressing room. When someone

does say something, it's about the game. Gilstrap just seems glad the season is over.

Some of the players wait for the Shawswick team to leave the gym, and wish them good luck that night. They leave their cars near the gym, walk slowly uptown, stopping at the pool parlor. The first thing Bogey does is ask Katis for a malt, "Strawberry."

Players from other teams rib Bogey and his friends about the margin of their loss, but good-humoredly. Most of them have known defeat, many by 51-18 margins. The players shoot a few games of pool, then walk down by the railroad tracks for a sandwich. Seems like they face half the county on the way.

They return to the gym a half-hour before the game and watch Shawswick and Bedford in their warm-up drills. They join players from the other county schools in their support of Shawswick. Some of the Farmers give them the high sign, acknowledging the support.

It does no good. Bedford rolls to a 56-23 victory, moving into its sixth straight regional.

They talk later that night with some of the Bedford players, who want to know why everybody was against them. Bogey and the others explain it's nothing personal, that smaller schools just feel closer to each other.

Then, Bogey said, "We'll all be for you next week."

They were. That time they were on the winning side.

A Referee's Vision Went beyond the Game at Hand

B.B. was a Robin Hood in a striped shirt. B.B. had a name his parents gave him . . . but hardly anyone ever called him that. Sometimes they called him a lot of other names, though, names that in later years would become known as expletives-deleted.

B.B., you see, was a basketball referee back in the days when rivalries were keen and communities weighed their reputation on the high school team's won-lost scales.

B.B. was too old for World War II, too young to sit by the fire on Friday and Saturday nights. He had kept in shape over the years and knew all the rules set out in the Indiana High School Athletic Association's guide-

book for referees. That meant he was in demand when coaches and principals at Heltonville, Tunnelton, Needmore, Fayetteville and Shawswick were lining up officials for basketball games.

B.B. was paid $10 a night . . . and no expense money . . . for officiating in the 1940s. And that was for both the reserve and varsity games.

Some fans said he was overpaid, but that was usually because they were backing the team that lost the game he worked.

These fans didn't have the pleasure of his company out on the playing floor. B.B. thought basketball was a game to be enjoyed and he tried to make it so for himself and for the players.

He'd just smile at any player who looked displeased at his call, walk over and say, "Caught you that time, didn't I?" He seldom, if ever, had to call a technical foul.

By the time a game was into the second quarter he was in complete control, a benevolent dictator with a whistle dangling from his neck.

One of B.B.'s most trying nights came when the other referee didn't show up for a game between a couple of Lawrence County rivals. B.B. huddled with the two coaches, blew his whistle and waited for the teams to line up at center court.

He refereed both games by himself that night. Even the fans applauded him for his courage . . . if not his vision.

It was in the 1945–46 season when B.B. became a Robin Hood, at least for some of the Heltonville players. The team was ranked somewhere between bad to mediocre and played all its games on the road because the war kept a gym that had burned from being rebuilt.

B.B. knew Heltonville probably couldn't win the games he worked, no matter how much he helped. That may be why he seemed to give them any break he could, without being too obvious.

The players thought they were getting a lot of good calls, but B.B. never did anything to let them know for sure. Not until one night when the team was playing at Smithville.

Smithville took a big lead and B.B. became upset when the coach let his starters, who were big enough to hunt bear and old enough to shave, continue to widen the margin.

He blew his whistle, signaled a foul on a Smithville player and walked to the free throw line with Tyke, a Heltonville player. Before he handed the ball to Tyke, he winked and said: "That guy wasn't within three feet of you, but you guys need all the help you can get. Now see if you can make this free one."

Tyke sank the free throw.

B.B. gave the team a few other breaks before the game was over. It was a good thing, too. Otherwise the final score might have been worse than 56-26.

Don't Panic, but It's Live Radio!

Coach Wilbert Gilstrap was calm as usual when he broke the news to his Heltonville basketball team. "You're going to be on the radio," he said.

Gilstrap had been informed a radio station had opened for the first time in Bedford and would broadcast the sectional there. It was 1947, and radio seemed like a big deal to the players who were lucky to get their names mentioned in the *Times-Mail*.

Billy, one of the reserves, put his hand up like he was talking into a mike and said, "Starting for Heltonville against the Shawswick Farmers," then raised his voice and gave the starting lineup. When he finished, Bob, another reserve, began a verbal description of the way he thought the game might go.

When the excitement ebbed, Gilstrap showed some of the players the letter he had received from the station, asking for information about the team. The announcers wanted to know the season record and the scores of each

game played in the 1946–47 season, the name of each player, his class, height, weight and scoring average, and assorted other information.

Pokey, the team jokester, suggested the coach add a few points to each player's scoring average "to make us look good, and scare the opposition." He knew Gilstrap wouldn't give out any information that was wrong. And besides, the opposition had already beaten Heltonville twice during the season and knew what to expect from each player.

The anticipation of radio coverage made the days before the sectional drag on and on. The players told everyone they knew to listen if they didn't plan to be at the games.

"Never heard of the station," Fritz said to one of the players. "Where do we find it on the radio?"

Pokey didn't know, either. He just said, "Keep turning the dial until you find it."

What neither Pokey nor anyone else knew was that the station couldn't be heard more than ten or eleven miles outside Bedford. Or that because of the way the broadcast was beamed, the signal couldn't be received on battery radios.

That meant part of the rural area around Heltonville couldn't get the game, because it still hadn't been wired for electricity.

It was hard to tell whether the Heltonville players were more interested in the game or the radio station when they came out of the locker room just after one o'clock for their 1:30 game. They shot a few baskets before Bogey spotted the broadcast team in the southeast corner of the balcony.

"They aren't talking yet," he told Pokey, "so quit showin' off."

By the time the game started, most of the players had their minds on the game. They listened as Gilstrap told them how he wanted them to play defense, run the offense and concentrate on the game.

Billy, who knew he wouldn't see any action for a while, sneaked a look up at the broadcast booth and saw the two men talking like they were auctioning off a prize bull at a farm auction. But even Billy got caught up in the action—for a time—once the game started.

The game, though, wasn't all that exciting, especially for Heltonville fans. The Farmers had too much scoring punch from standouts like Jim Graves, Dave Elliott and Bob Jackson. By the time the game ended, neither Bogey, Pokey nor anyone else was too concerned about whether their names were on the radio. They watched the second afternoon game, then the two night contests before riding the bus back to Heltonville.

The next morning, some of the players decided to stop to visit Chuck, a friend who was sick at his home about a mile outside Heltonville.

"Caught part of the game last night," Chuck told Bogey, "but the station faded in and out so much I wasn't lucky enough not to hear the final score."

"You're lucky, too," Chuck smiled. "The announcers must have been butchers before they got their jobs. They used a meat cleaver on your name, so nobody will know you were even in the game."

The little radio station went off the air in a short time. A professional station, WBIW, eventually replaced it. But it was too late for Bogey, Pokey, Billy and the others.

The Losing Margin Gets Smaller as the Years Go By

It was impossible to grow up around Heltonville without hearing about the time the high school team played Bedford in the final game of the sectional.

The game was played March 3, 1928.

Fans were still talking about it March 3, 1945.

And as was often the case, the stories the fans recited about the game became more fiction than fact as their memories dimmed.

Bob, Jake, Tad and Tyke, who played on the Heltonville team in the mid-'40s, knew what to expect when an adult fan walked over to where they were sitting in Lute Thompson's restaurant one night after practice and said: "Ever tell you about the time we played Bedford in the finals of the sectional?"

"We" was the team. The man who asked hadn't been a player but he thought the team belonged to him as much as anyone else.

Bob and Jake knew it would do no good to tell the fan they had heard about the game a hundred times before. They just stared at the man, who said, "Yep. We had a good team then."

He was too wrapped up in himself to know that what he was saying was an insult to the players he was talking to. "Well, we had some players then, stars, in fact. Stars like Cladie Bailey, Ed Cain, Fred Maher and others. Best team we ever had."

Bob and Jake nodded, knowingly. The man continued: "When we played the Stonecutters in the final game there were seven thousand fans crowded into the four-year-old Bedford gym. There were less than five thousand seats. The other two thousand just stood tighter than a bunch of sardines in a can.

He went on for a while longer, before Tyke asked, "Who won the game?" But he already knew the answer.

The man said, "They did, but we gave them all they could handle."

Tad, who had more mischief than kindness, hadn't said much. He waited until a lull in the conversation, then pulled out a few paragraphs he had scribbed on yellow-lined paper. "This is from the *Bedford Daily Mail*, March 5, 1928," he said. He started reading: "By taking a 20 to 0 lead at the start, the Ivymen won the closing game of the sectional 49–11, from the net five of Heltonville."

The Ivymen were the Stonecutters. The Julianmen were from Heltonville.

Tad resumed reading: "The Julianmen made a gallant fight, but because of close battles in the second round and in the semifinals, they were somewhat weary and off form.

"Bailey, Heltonville's star floor guard, took numerous long shots but was unable to connect except in one case."

Tad read the scoring summary, then looked up at the man, somewhat embarrassed for setting the record straight so emphatically.

The facts didn't faze the man. He said, "I'd have sworn the game was closer than that. We would have done a lot better, except like the story said,

we had a rough draw. And then, too, Cladie and the boys weren't used to the glass backboards.

"And besides, we only had one hundred-twenty or so in high school. 'Spect Bedford had at least eight hundred."

Tad smiled and said, "Well, anyone can have an off-night."

The man said, "Yep. And besides, Bedford had the home-floor advantage."

The others nodded. They had heard enough about the 1927–28 Heltonville team to know it had been a good one.

"How about the seven thousand fans you mentioned?" Tyke asked the man.

Tad said, quickly, "The seven thousand figure was accurate."

It was the biggest crowd ever to watch a sectional at Bedford. At least it was according to historians.

The Big Winner Was Bill

He was a big kid, about six feet three with rugged features and an abundance of baby fat. At sixteen, he weighed maybe 235 pounds. He wasn't graceful or smooth, and he moved more like a tank than a tiger. But his size made up for that when it came to basketball.

He played ball for one of the high schools in Southern Indiana in the mid-1940s. The previous season players on other teams called him "Pig" because of his size and awkwardness.

That is, they called him "Pig" until a domestic argument took place at "Pig's" home.

Late in October, a few days before basketball season was to start, "Pig" was home primping a bit before going into the little village nearby for a soft drink and some conversation.

He came out of his room with his long hair plastered down with grease as heavy as his dad used on wagon axles. His dad made a few sarcastic remarks in jest, which "Pig," being a teenager and emotional, didn't appreciate.

Those words led to a few others. Finally "Pig" took a whack with his right hand, which was ham-size, and grazed the left side of his dad's head. His dad fell back against the pot-bellied stove and burned his back.

"Pig's" dad allowed as that would be enough of that. "Pig" allowed as how he was fed up with things at home and said he was leaving, never to return.

He started out the front door, his dad yelling for him to stop. "Pig" kept walking and his dad grabbed a loaded shotgun from a rack near the door, asked him once more to halt and then fired a blast of buckshot. The pellets hit "Pig" from behind.

During recuperation, when "Pig" found it difficult to sit down, he and his father settled their differences and decided to live in harmony ever after.

"Pig" didn't miss many basketball practices and was ready to play the third game of the season against Heltonville. By that time players throughout the county had renamed "Pig," "Buckshot."

Early in the game, the visitors from Heltonville razzed "Buckshot," nee "Pig," unmercifully because the blue dots where the buckshot hit were still visible on his legs. The big guy would just smile, muscle his way for a rebound, tip-in or hook shot.

"Pig's" team won going away. As usual, the Heltonville players reviewed the scorebook and one said, "Two, four, five, seven, nine, eleven, twelve, fourteen, sixteen, eighteen. That damned 'Buckshot' got eighteen points."

As they walked out of the gym, "Buckshot" was standing, holding his grip, talking to a fan. The Heltonville player who had counted up his points stopped, looked up at the big guy and said, "Bill, I ain't never gonna call you 'Pig' or 'Buckshot' again."

"I never took it personally," Bill smiled.

He jabbed Bill in the ribs and said, "You're a big, big man."

"You can call me 'Pig' or 'Buckshot' any time you want," Bill said.

Illustration by
Gary Varvel

Basketball Was a Labor of Love

His name was Lobie, but almost everyone called him Shorty. He was about five feet six, but that wasn't the true measure of the man. He stood a lot taller than that in the eyes of those who knew him well.

The fellow reading the news over WBIW radio in Bedford didn't know Shorty, or he wouldn't have seemed so detached when he reported Lobie White had died. It was an impersonal thing to him.

It wasn't that way for Shorty's friends, friends he had made at the limestone mill where he worked, friends he made driving a school bus, friends he made at his home in Heltonville.

Chances are none of them were more touched by his death than the thirteen to fifteen youngsters who played basketball at Heltonville in the difficult war years when the school had no gymnasium. Chances are they might have had no team at all had it not been for Shorty.

He wasn't a teacher or a coach. He wasn't an elected official. He had no sons in school. He was under no obligation to help.

It would have been easier for him to do what most other adults did and let somebody else worry about whether the team had a way to get to practice and to games. But that wasn't Shorty's way.

He helped talk principal Loren Raines and trustee Thornt Clampitt into renewing basketball at the school after the 1942–43 season was canceled when the gym and most of the school burned.

That took some serious talking. World War II was under way, gasoline was being rationed and the principal and trustee had serious doubts whether basketball was important enough to balance out the problems it presented.

But Shorty and colleagues like Marshall Axsom thought it was. And they prevailed.

The trustee and principal agreed, saying fans who wanted a basketball team would have to find transportation. Gasoline was too valuable to be used in school buses at night, they said.

Axsom, a sixth-grade teacher, agreed to coach the team and drive his car to practice at Shawswick, five miles away, and to the games, which were all on the road. Shorty said he'd drive, too, keep score and help out however else he could.

The war had depleted the male enrollment in the upper two classes and most of the thirteen players on the varsity and reserve were underclassmen. The few who were old enough to drive convinced their parents to let them use the family cars from time to time.

The team practiced a few times before the 1943–44 season was to open November 1 against Needmore. After the last practice before the game, Marshall Axsom said, "Fred, we'll need you to drive. You can take Junior, Bob, Wayne and Donald and Robert," pointing to Bob Hunter who was the student manager. "Shorty and I will take the others. We'll meet at the school at 5:45."

At 5:45 that night it was hard to tell who was the most excited, Shorty, the coach or the younger players. The players threw their grips in the trunks of cars, tossed the basketballs on top and found seats in the cars. Axsom told Shorty to take the lead.

Tad, Bunky, Bogey, Pokey and Jackie were seated in Shorty's car when he got in. Bunky asked, "Know where the school is in Needmore?" Shorty nodded. Bunky learned later Shorty knew how to find every high school gym from Owensburg to Hayden.

On the way he told them, "You'll be at a disadvantage. You didn't get a chance to play at all last year, you haven't practiced nearly as much as Needmore has, you'll be playing in front of strangers and you'll be playing against a good team. Just do your best. If you don't win, there's always next week."

He was right on all counts. The team lost, but Shorty had only kind things to say on the way home. "Surprised me how well you played," he said.

Heltonville won only one game the entire season, but Shorty never asked Axsom to relieve him from his voluntary obligation. And he never sounded discouraged, not even after games at places like Huron and Fayetteville where he and a couple of cheerleaders were the only fans the team had.

"Things will get better," he always said. "Someday the war will be over, we'll get our own gym and we'll beat the teams that are beating us now."

Bunky said, "By that time, we'll be out of school, married and working for a living."

Shorty said, "In that case, the hardships you've played under will just make life seem that much easier."

Shorty was right, as he almost always was. The team gradually got better, the war ended, school buses were used to transport the team, the gym was built and nobody was happier than he was the night the 1953–54 team won the Lawrence County tournament.

Chances are none of the players who rode with Shorty through the long winters of 1943 and 1944 ever thanked him for what he did. He probably didn't mind. He did it because he wanted to. Not for the thanks he'd get.

His Top Tip

When Al Brewster received a news tip, he didn't have to be asked to protect his sources. The sources knew he'd do that.

Al was sports editor years ago at the *Bedford Times-Mail*. He was consistently good at reporting what took place in the sports arenas around Lawrence County.

Each Friday night, like most sports editors on county-seat dailies, he'd cover a high school game, then go to the office and write about it while receiving calls from a half-dozen other coaches about their contests.

It was on a night like this, the last night of the regular basketball season in 1946, when three Heltonville players went to Al's office and gave him a report of a game that put him right in the middle of verbal warfare.

Al was told the truth that night by the three youths, and he never doubted it despite the outcries of scores of fans. Heltonville and Tunnelton, archrivals coached by brothers, had met that night at Tunnelton before a

packed gymnasium. Often the roar of the crowd was louder than the referee's whistle.

As the half ended, a Tunnelton player hit a basket and the referees and timekeepers argued for five minutes whether the shot was in the air before time ran out. They decided the shot was good. Score: Tunnelton 16, Heltonville 14.

The game stayed close the rest of the way. Tunnelton led, 34-32, when a Heltonville player hit a basket, again as time ran out. Another argument ensued over whether that basket should count, even though one referee signaled the game would end, 34-32, Tunnelton.

The brother coaches told their players to get dressed while they and the officials continued a conference. An hour later, Wilbert Gilstrap of Heltonville and Lester Gilstrap of Tunnelton came out of the conference. The Heltonville players were told it was decided the game would be recorded as a tie; that neither basket made at the end of each half would count. The final score, they said, would be 32-32.

As the team bus headed back toward Bedford for sandwiches before returning to Heltonville, a couple of underclass players discussed the fact that tie basketball games were unusual

and that it'd make a good spread in the paper the next day.

At Bedford, the two players, joined by an ally, took the scorebook from the student manager and headed up "J" Street to the *Times-Mail* office while the other players entered a restaurant. They handed Al the scorebook and explained that a basket made by Hayden Crane of Tunnelton at the end of the first half had been removed, making the final score 32-32.

Al agreed it was a good story, so good, in fact, it was picked up from the *Times-Mail* newspapers from Washington to San Francisco. As soon as the report appeared in the *Times-Mail*, however, Al was bombarded with irate calls from Tunnelton fans who said the final score was 34-32.

The brotherly-love decision by the coaches to call the game a tie never was explained by them to Al or to the fans. Had the game not been reported to Al, it would have forever been a victory for Tunnelton fans, a tie for Heltonville fans.

Despite the furor, Al maintained the scorebook he saw read 32-32. He never revealed who brought him that book.

Al's retired now. It's about time he knew just how much his sources appreciated his trust.

The Green Season

Don't believe all that in-like-a-lamb, out-like-a-lion (or vice versa) or groundhog-and-shadow stuff. Spring always comes to Southern Indiana dramatically. Whatever manages to slip in quietly beforehand doesn't really count.

Spring may come as a wet, unseasonable snowfall, so out of character it makes people notice, or, in years blessed by no late frosts, as a dramatic burst of redbuds, snow-white dogwood petals, and fruit-tree blossoms. Or, spring may be heralded by sudden warmth and heavy rains that send the last of winter's snow down hillsides, heaving up the ice on creeks and sending them out of their banks. And, of course, there are the dread tornadoes.

It is a tumultuous season when rural people launch themselves into a furious ritual of tasks, beginning with spring-cleaning (which young boys desperately, but usually unsuccessfully, try to avoid), brush-clearing, and burning. Pigs, calves, and lambs are born. Fields are plowed, disked, and planted, farmers racing against the weather with one eye on the soil and the other on the sky.

It is when gardening begins, and it is a time for lively rituals like the first trips to the swimming hole (which can be memorably interrupted by the untimely arrival of girls) and snaring the big suckers as they swim upstream to spawn.

There is no rest, because everyone knows there will be time to rest in summer, in the spaces between cultivating, haying, and hand-hauling water to parched home gardens. Meanwhile, everyone scrambles to wrest from Mother Nature a small measure of control over forces that are uncontrollable.   —*MN*

Broom and Dust, 'Twas Ever Thus

Spring housecleaning was more than a spring ritual. It was an event, an occasion, a production in the 1930s and '40s.

Spring was a time for a new beginning, Tad's mother always said. But as far as Tad was concerned, housecleaning could begin . . . and end . . . without him.

His mother and the other housewives around Heltonville set aside a week for the great cleanup. Usually it was the week after the school year ended in late April.

Tad compared it to getting out of jail, then being sentenced to a prison work detail. Tad didn't mind hard work. He just didn't like for his activities to be restricted to the house.

The cleanup was done a room at a time. That meant each piece of furniture was carried out into the yard. The floors were cleaned, the walls painted, covered with new wallpaper, or washed down. The woodwork cleaned or painted. The windows were washed inside and out, the curtains washed.

Tad helped each morning . . . for a little while. As soon as he could escape, he skedaddled.

By the time he was eight, he had learned to head to the fields where his dad was working. His dad always found something for him to do just so

Tad wouldn't have to lie when he told his mother he'd been working.

The fact was, Tad's father didn't like all the commotion that went with housecleaning, either, and he didn't want his son to grow up to be a house boy.

That alliance still didn't keep Tad, or his dad, from doing some housework each night after they finished the chores. They had to carry back in the furniture and set it down in a dozen different spots before the women decided where it would look best.

Midway through the housecleaning that year, Tad made a mistake of flexing his arm to show a bump he called a muscle and bragging to one of his sisters, "Got that from field work."

His mother smiled, then handed him the rugbeater, a device that looked something like a tennis racket.

"With muscles like that, you can save your sisters and me a heap of hard work. As soon as you finish eating, you take it and beat the dust out of the carpet hanging on the clothesline."

Tad said he didn't know how. One of the girls said, "Make like you're returning the whacks Mrs. Faubion gave you a couple of weeks ago." Mrs. Faubion was a music teacher who had paddled Tad at school for some mischief.

Tad took the wire beater, walked to the clothesline and whacked the carpet, jumped back and watched the dust fog. He kept at it, hitting the rug harder and harder, going from one side to the other like he was seeking vengence. Finally no more dust came from the carpeting, and he dropped the beater.

Then he stepped back, folded his

*Illustration by
Gary Varvel*

arms at the elbows, did a shuffle and hit the rug with his fists, first a left jab, then a right hook.

His mother finally said, "That'll be enough, son. Don't beat the carpet to a pulp."

Tad smiled, plopped down on the grass and said, "Mrs. Faubion won't be able to sit down for a week. And I just knocked Joe Louis out for the count."

His mom said, "See, rug-beating isn't such bad work."

Tad sighed and said, "Work? That was fun."

Rites of Spring
Crank to a Start

B.K. usually waited until late March to roll his Model T out of the shed at the side of his barn. It had been there since the first cold snap the previous fall.

B.K. was getting old when the 1930s came to a close, and he didn't like to drive much in warm weather, let alone when it was cold. The side curtains that snapped onto the top and the doors didn't provide much warmth. And besides, B.K. wasn't all that eager to crank the car to get it started when the temperature was below freezing.

If he needed a ride into town from his place east of Heltonville, he'd just ride along with a neighbor who was going anyway. It wasn't B.K.'s style to bother anyone, but he never saw anything wrong with taking advantage of any assistance when it was offered.

And B.K. knew when he could expect the youngsters from nearby farms to drop by on warm Sunday afternoons in the spring to help him bring the 1922 Model T back to life for another year.

There weren't many Model Ts around. The few there were caught the fancy of youngsters like Billy, Tad, Tyke and Larry, who were ten to twelve years old at the time.

B.K. expected the boys would be around that Sunday, when the temperatures warmed up enough to bring the snakes slithering out of their holes down along the creek. That afternoon, he had tugged open the big hinged doors to the shed, cleaned off the windshield and waited.

The youngsters showed up about two o'clock.

"Looks like you're fixin' to get the Model T runnin'," Tyke said.

B.K. nodded, then said, "Don't suppose you boys would like to help me, huh?"

It was like asking them if they'd like some of his wife's chocolate cake. They all said they would.

B.K. said he'd get in the car and steer while they pushed the Model T, which was parked on two-by-eights, out of the shed onto the grass. That job was easy.

B.K. told them to look the car over while he checked the gas and filled the radiator. Billy grabbed a rag and knocked off some of the dust.

Once B.K. had the car ready, he said, "I'll sit up here and adjust the gas and the spark and let you boys do the crankin'."

The boys had been around machines enough to know that a crank

was the handle at the front of the car that turned the crankshaft and started the engine. They also knew that a crank would kick, which meant if the engine recoiled, the crank would be flipped in the opposite direction.

Tad hadn't tried to start enough tractors and cars with a crank to know how to keep from getting hurt if the crank did kick. That didn't stop him, though. He grabbed the crank and gave it a turn with his right arm, letting his thumb reach around the handle toward his fingers for a good grip.

The engine didn't fire, but Tyke yelled out, "That's not the way to do it."

He said he'd been told to use his left arm so the fingers could unroll away from the crank in case it kicked.

B.K. had forgotten how youngsters could argue. He got down from the car and said, "Fact is neither one of you are doing it right. Let me show you how."

He held up his right hand, extended his thumb along the index finger and said, "You're supposed to keep your thumb on the same side of the handle. That way if the crank kicks back it won't fly back and break your thumb."

He checked the spark to make sure it was set right, then walked up to the crank and asked all four of the boys to step up close.

He made a jerking motion with his right arm. Nothing happened. He tried a few more times.

Panting, he got back into the front seat, readjusted the spark and told Tyke to try his luck. Tyke made two attempts, the cylinders took hold and the engine coughed to life.

B.K. let the engine warm up for a while, then took the boys on a ride down the dusty gravel road.

But Only a Mudder Could Ever Love It

When the frost left the ground, the mud arrived. Only the knowledge that spring was approaching made it bearable. MUD! A dirty, three-letter word. MUD! Wet, sticky, soft earth. MUD!

Your name is mud ... mud in your eye ... drag through the mud ... muddy the issue.

Throughout its long history, few kind words have been said about mud. None will be written here.

Somehow farmers around Heltonville learned to survive in the seas of mud in the '30s and '40s. Those were the years before the asphalt lobby convinced the world it should be paved with macadam to permit epidemics of chuckholes every spring.

But the mud was far worse than chuckholes. It is possible to go around or through chuckholes. It is impossible to move in mud. Mud could make entire rural areas almost immobile.

The late-winter thaws could creep down to the depth of the frost line, eighteen, twenty-four, thirty inches, sometimes deeper. Driveways to houses and barns, which usually had no more than four or five inches of creek gravel on them, became quagmires. Cars and trucks sank to their axles and the only way they could be pulled out would be with a big farm tractor with lug wheels or a strong team of horses. Even if the vehicle could be towed to the country roads, those roads wouldn't be much better. Chances are the roads would have "gone through," which meant they were mush down to solid earth.

It was a rare year when school buses didn't get hung up in the middle of Powerline Road, Hunter's Creek Hill, Gilgal Drive or almost any other route leading into Heltonville. Mud on roads got so bad on a few occasions students wished it didn't take so long to get to school.

Except for a few kids who lived in town, no one arrived at school without mud on his or her shoes. Some of the wiser treachers, like Irvine East, could tell where kids were from by the color of the mud. He said bright red clay meant they lived up around Dutch Ridge, which is near where the causeway across Monroe Reservoir now is. Mud that was kinda yellowish clay meant the youngsters who tracked it in lived out around Coveyville. Goat Run ran through Coveyville. They

called it that because a goat was the only thing that could run on the road during the thaws. The darker the mud, the better chances the kids had of being from some of the better farm areas south and east of town.

Some of the girls wore rubber boots to school, but the boys, unless they were kinda sissified, wore hightop boots with big treads on the soles. This meant the mud would cake in the treads and when the boys would shuffle their feet under the desks the dirt would dry and drop off. The boy who could leave the most dirt each day was considered somewhat of a folk hero.

Bob was the janitor at the school back then, and he had to clean up the mess. He'd ask some of the bigger students to stay after school and they'd lift the rows of desks, mounted on runner-like boards, so he could sweep up the red, yellow and loamy soil.

It took hours, but somehow Bob would have the school clean again in time for classes the next day.

The Garden Was a Family Affair

When it came to making a garden, no one was exempt. It was a family affair. And anyone who happened to be around was expected to help, too.

Folks didn't plant a garden, they made one. At least that's the way it was around Heltonville in the 1930s and '40s. They made a garden with the care that came from the love of the land and the things that grew from it.

Jeb and his wife, Maudie, made their garden that way. And they made

certain their four youngsters did, too.

Jeb was a big, rawboned man whose weather-worn face had more lines than a road map. His rough exterior betrayed the gentleness that swelled inside.

Jeb and Maudie made a garden like they did everything else . . . the very best way they knew how.

Jeb waited until the moisture was just right so the rich sod would turn mellow as he "broke" it with a walking plow pulled by his horses, Barney and Charlie. Jeb used the horses rather than his F-20 Farmall. "Tractor

packs the ground too much," he told anyone who asked why.

After that, he waited until the dark of the moon to disc and harrow the soil until it was pulverized into fine granules, none bigger than a peewee marble. Jeb said, "Anyone knows you don't plant taters 'cept in the dark of the moon."

No one who saw his potato crop ever argued about that.

When the ground was worked, it was time for Maudie and the kids to help. Maudie had already cut the seed potatoes into small pieces, each with an eye.

Jeb laid off the rows, pushing the garden plow, cutting the "V" for the potatoes deep into the soil. The rows for beans, peas, lettuce, onions and radishes were more shallow.

While he was still doing that job, Maudie directed the start of the potato-planting. She was a wisp of a woman who had made a garden for so many years she sometimes forgot youngsters like Bunky needed some direction from time to time.

Bunky was a nine-year-old from town who was visiting Pokey and had stripped off his shoes and rolled up his pants and followed all the others into the garden.

Maudie ordered Pokey, "Spread the fertilizer along the bottom of the row . . . about a handful every three feet or so." Then she told Bugsy, another son, "Take a hoe and cover the fertilizer with about an inch of dirt."

Bunky was looking on, wondering what he was to do. He didn't have to wait long. She said, "Bunky, you can plant the potatoes. Just drop the pieces about twelve to fifteen inches apart. I'll come along behind and cover them up after I put the girls to work with the onion sets."

Being boys, Pokey, Bugsy and Bunky tried to see how fast they could get the job done. Bunky had dropped about a row of potatoes the length of the 150 foot garden when Maudie stopped him. "You got to be more careful," said Maudie. "Drop the pieces so the eyes are facing up." Then she showed him exactly how she wanted each piece.

Pokey came to Bunky's defense. "It's some potato that can't find its way to daylight no matter where it starts," Pokey said.

His mom looked him in the eye and said, "Nobody likes a smart-aleck, son. When you plant potatoes, the eyes have it."

Both Pokey and Bunky were too young at the time to catch the humor.

Bunky redid that row, then was more careful.

When the boys were finished, they each grabbed a hoe. Maudie let them finish covering the twelve rows of potatoes and went across the garden to check on how the girls were doing.

They went from there to other rows, where Bunky learned to plant and set other vegetables. The more he worked, the sorer he got and he wondered how "old folks" like Jeb and Maudie could work so long without stopping.

He finally got so tired he plopped down at the end of the garden. When Jeb asked if he was all right, he said, "Just tired. Don't you ever wear out?"

"Nope. I just think of the rewards this work will all bring."

Pokey said, "Yeh, but Bunky won't get no reward from our garden."

Jeb said, "He can if he wants. All he has to do is come around when we're eating what we grow."

That pepped Bunky up enough so that he worked until all the rows had been planted.

He accepted an invitation to supper, satisfied his folks knew where he was.

After supper, Maudie told Jeb, "This has been such a good day we ought to go out to a barn dance tonight."

Jeb said, "No thanks. I've had enough hoedown for one day."

Bunky laughed with the others, happy to know that Jeb was probably as tired as he was.

A Bridge over Troubled Water

If you've ever been on rural roads around Heltonville, chances are you've driven over humpback bridges. A half-dozen of them are still in use, but the worst one has been abandoned. And that's a blessing.

The bridge that is now closed was at the south edge of town. A score of school bus drivers who used it out of necessity over the years will testify that it should never have been opened in the first place.

Drivers coming into town on Todd Road and Groundhog Road preferred to ford Leatherwood Creek rather than negotiate the bridge that was halfway between the two routes.

Back in the '40s Shorty drove the Groundhog Road bus, Everett the Todd Road bus. Shorty never did figure out what he did to deserve his route.

In dry weather, he eased his bus over giant geodes and other types of rocks in the creek bed, turned left at the Baptist Church and made another right turn on Ind. 58 to reach the school.

The only times he had trouble after crossing the creek was when a small geode got stuck between the dual wheels on the back of the bus. As soon as he heard a "thud, thud, thud," he'd stop the bus, comment on the "dadblasted rocks," grab the emergency ax in place beside his left arm and walk to the back of the bus. He'd knock the rock loose and resume his driving.

But Shorty's usual pleasant mood turned a bit sour when the spring rains came and the creek rose. He knew as soon as he started the route he'd have to cross the humpback bridge.

Sometimes he'd head into the ford, just to take a look. If it was too deep to be safe, he'd back up and ease the bus along the connector lane toward Todd Hill. Just west of the humpback bridge he'd cross a wooden bridge that seemed like it'd collapse every time. It never did.

Anyhow, the length of the bus made it impossible to turn left onto the humpback, so Shorty would have to drive up to Todd Road, back up and head back on the connector road in order to cross the bridge.

Before he started across, he'd have to blow his horn to make sure someone hadn't started up the other side. The one-lane bridge was humped so much it was impossible to see a vehicle on the opposite side.

Shorty never had an accident, but it wasn't because some engineer decades earlier hadn't made one possible.

Mom Insists: Ring Those Pigs

As far as Butch's mother was concerned, hogs were the root of a lot of evil. If not evil, a lot of upheaval.

It didn't bother Butch or his dad too much if the pigs on their farm near Heltonville ran hog-wild, as long as they stayed in the lot that was fenced off for them.

But Butch's mother wanted the farm, including the hog lot, to look neat and orderly, something like the pictures of places she saw in the *Farm Journal* and *Country Gentleman* magazine.

Butch's father wasn't impressed. "Show me places like that and I'll show you places owned by rich city slickers, who don't know a barrow from a sparrow. They keep the farms for show, not places to make money."

He was wasting his breath, though, and he knew it. It made him feel better to lose a spat when he put up a good argument.

Butch knew what to expect by the time he was ten. As soon as a spring litter of pigs was about big enough to start rooting, his mother would say: "A couple more days and the pig lot will look like it has been plowed."

She'd repeat herself morning, noon and night, knowing sooner or later the menfolks, as she called Butch and his dad, would tire of the refrain.

His dad always said about the same thing: "I'd sooner hear a pig squeal than her growl. As soon as we get the

Illustration by Gary Varvel

corn planted, we'll fix the pigs so they won't dare root."

Butch didn't take either his mom or dad too seriously when they talked like that about each other. He knew most of what they said was in jest.

What his mother didn't know, though, was that the pigs would be ringed before they were old enough to root, anyhow. If they weren't, they'd soon burrow a place under the woven wire to flee to unfenced freedom.

Ringing pigs was like a lot of other things. The hardest part was getting around to it. It was like that in the spring of 1940.

Butch's dad reached overhead on a two-by-six in the garage and found the hog rings and the ring clamps. The hog rings were copper wires about two inches long. The ring clamps looked something like wire pliers and had little slots where the rings fitted. Once the handles of the clamps were brought together, the rings closed to form a triangle.

They penned the pigs, which had been weaned for a couple of weeks, into a corner. Then it was up to Butch to show his athletic ability. He had to catch each pig, straddle its back and hold its front legs while his dad clamped a ring through its nose. It took maybe four or five minutes to ring each animal, longer if Butch had trouble holding on.

When the pigs were released, they ran along the fencerow nudging their noses toward the ground, then squealing once they felt the pain again.

His dad would watch them for a while, then say, "Hogs are a lot smarter than some people. They don't have to be taught something twice."

Back at the house, Butch went through the cabinet and cupboard looking for cookies to snack on before supper.

He stopped and laughed when his mom yelled: "Bring me the hog ringer, dad. I got a boy here who keeps sticking his nose where it don't belong."

This Tale's "Morel" Is That Riches Are Often Close By

Spring had arrived in Southern Indiana. One warm April day had followed another, turning the grass in the pastures deep green, bringing forth the wildflowers and sending the dogwood into bloom. Mayapple plants had worked their way through the ground, then released their leaves to open like wings that waved gently in the warm breeze.

A light rain had fallen overnight and the fresh smell of a new season had replaced the mustiness of winter.

It was a good time to be alive. Tad finished his chores early, dressed quickly and walked to the roadside to await the bus that would take him to school in Heltonville.

He set his lunch on a fence post and walked across the gravel road to look at the vegetation that was awakening after a long winter sleep. It was then that he spotted a mushroom, a yellowish morel that rose four to five inches high. He scanned the wooded area and saw more, lots more.

He ran to the springhouse, grabbed a ten-quart bucket and returned. He

gently lifted each mushroom from the earth, placing each in the pail as softly as he would have eggs from the nests in the henhouse. He counted to 5, 10, 15, 20, 21, 22, 23, 24 as he searched out the mushrooms that hadn't exposed themselves in open view. When he reached 30, he saw the bus coming. He sped across the road, up to the house, shouting to his mother about his find.

Shorty White, the bus driver, waited patiently for him to run back to the bus. Tad told him his story in the same manner Christopher Columbus must have informed Queen Isabella about discovering America. Shorty just smiled as he usually did.

Tad seldom fibbed, but that didn't stop the other ten-year-old boys on the bus from razzing him.

Billy said, "If you picked that many mushrooms, there must have been leprechauns jumping around between the mayapple plants to show you where they were."

Ray said, "You acted like you were daydreaming when you went mushroom-hunting with me. Maybe you dreamed you saw all them mushrooms."

Tad didn't let the teasing bother him. He just shrugged and said, "I'll be thinking of you guys tonight when I rake them morels through the butter on my plate and let them slowly dissolve before disappearing delightfully in my mouth."

At school, Tad's teacher heard about his find and said, "Forget about bringing me an apple. A pound of mushrooms will be just fine and do wonders for your grades."

Tad knew the teacher didn't take bribes, but he did promise to bring him some, just in the spirit of goodwill.

No one was more surprised than Tad's father when he returned home from his job at the stonemill and heard about the great mushroom find.

"Been checking that spot every spring for twenty years and never saw a single mushroom there," he said, adding, "Just proves that good things in life sometimes are right in front of you, if you just open your eyes and see them."

Tad's mother winked at their son and said, "Thanks for finally noticing."

It was still daylight. Tad asked, "Wanta go out and look for some more mushrooms, Pa?"

His dad nodded and said, "You got mushroom fever, son."

Tad said, "I reckon them big morels are something like gold nuggets. The more you find, the harder you look for more."

Taking No Chances

B.K. wore both belt and suspenders and didn't take any other chances, either. He didn't gamble with life . . . or with money.

B.K. lived on a small farm on Powerline Road in eastern Lawrence County and didn't leave except when he had to go into town to pay his taxes or buy something his wife, Lil, wanted. He still owned a Model T when his neighbors were driving 1935 Chevies, Fords and Terraplanes. He didn't plant hybrid seed until other farmers showed him how much more corn it would produce per acre.

B.K. was conservative, but he wasn't backward. His neighbors said he had a sharp mind which was a lot more active than other folks thought. While his neighbors were thinking of ways to add to their income, B.K. was figuring out how to eliminate the chances of something going wrong.

His farm was almost free of hazards, especially for B.K. and Lil, who were in their late sixties. He kept things orderly and neat and in good repair.

That's how he happened to have a new galvanized roof put on his barn one spring in the late 1930s. The old one didn't leak, but B.K. didn't wait for trouble. He anticipated it.

And he anticipated the thunderstorms that swept across the horizon each April, too. As soon as the last sheet of roofing was nailed into place, he asked the carpenters if they could come back the next day.

"What for?" asked one of the carpenters. "We're done, like in finished."

"Need you to come back tomorrow to put on the lightning rods. Have to go into town this afternoon and pick them up," he explained.

The lightning rods and other supplies were waiting for them when they returned the next morning.

There were four rods, each three feet or so long with points at the top. The carpenters spaced them at the apex of the roof, anchoring each firmly. They then connected them by a cable that ran down each end of the barn. The cable then was attached to rods that had been driven ten to twelve feet into the ground about two feet out from the barn.

B.K. explained to Tad, a neighbor youngster who often came to visit, "Ol' Ben Franklin had the idea first. He figured rods driven into the soil would cut down on the chance of electrical charges in the ground attracting bolts of lightning from above.

"But if lightning does strike, the cable will conduct the stroke safely to the ground without causing damage to the barn."

Tad nodded like he understood.

A few nights later a severe electrical storm moved through the farm country. Tad and his dad saw no damage at their place the next morning, then decided to walk over to B.K.'s place to see if he and Lil were okay.

When they spotted B.K. out by the barn, Tad's father said, "Don't know about you, but I didn't sleep much. Kept thinking one of them lightning bolts might hit the house or the barn."

B.K. looked up at the lightning rods, then at Tad and winked.

"What storm? Me and Lil slept like logs. When you anticipate problems, you don't have to worry about them when they come."

This Ride Home Didn't Come without a Hitch

He had red hair, but he didn't have a temper. At least he never showed it in public.

The color of his hair wasn't the first thing most people noticed about him. His smile was more obvious. That's why he was called Ed instead of Red most of the time. The only time he was "Edmond" was when he painted his mailbox or signed official papers.

Before he sold his truck and moved to Bedford, Ed lived on a small place east of Heltonville about a half-mile south of Ind. 58.

Ed died in 1985. His death caused the people who knew him to recall their favorite stories about the man who enjoyed life and the people around him. One of the stories was told by a man who was known as Tad when he was a boy and lived near Ed.

Tad was hitchhiking home from college one afternoon in late spring in the 1940s. He was thumbing a ride at the west edge of Seymour on U.S. 50 when he noticed Ed's truck approach. Ed saw Tad about the same time, stopped his truck, threw open the right door and said, "Hop in."

Tad stuck his laundry bag on the floor board and said, "Thanks for stopping."

Ed laughed. "I should be thanking you."

Tad asked why.

Ed replied, "You'll see, you'll see."

Illustration by Gary Varvel

Tad asked, "What are you hauling?"

Ed laughed, a suspicious kind of laugh, and told Tad he'd find out soon enough, giving a clue, commenting, "Sure glad you don't dress up when you hitchhike."

He didn't say any more about his cargo until he turned south off U.S. 50 at Medora Junction and drove a couple of miles before turning in to a farm lane. He backed up to a shed, using his rearview mirrors to guide him.

"Here's where you find out what I'm hauling," he grinned, turning off the ignition.

The cargo was six tons of fertilizer, neatly stacked on the truck in eighty-pound bags.

"One hundred and fifty eight-pound bags," Tad thought to himself, knowing he'd been had. He laughed, appreciating the humor.

He and Ed took their time, taking turns, one on the truck, one on the ground carrying the bags into the shed. It was a warm day and by the time they had finished, Tad had taken on·an odor not unlike that of the 2-12-6 fertilizer.

Ed left a bill for the farmer, brushed off his pants with his hands and started the truck. Ed bought soft drinks on the way home. Tad held up his Coke and said, "This, and a ride home, too? I must be living right."

Ed shook the little store with laughter. When he stopped in front of Tad's house, he asked: "You going to be at the same spot next Friday afternoon in case I come by with a load of fertilizer?"

Tad said, "Not if I can save enough money to buy a bus ticket."

Ed drove off, a smile on his face, as usual.

Geodes Were Hard on the Guy behind the Plow

NEWS ITEM: A geode, believed the largest ever found in Lawrence County, was discovered recently in a small creek just north of Heltonville.

Geode is the official name for rust-looking round rocks found around Heltonville, but most folks call them "confounded nuisances." Especially farmers, who also used an ethnic term to describe the rough exterior of the round rocks with insides of "crystal."

Sid, who has farmed the rolling ridges east of town for seven decades now, said he has no doubt that the geode Joe Green and Ronnie Prince found washed out of a creek bank weighed 247 pounds.

"But, shucks, man," Sid said, "I don't think that's a record. Seems to me like some of them I rolled out of the fields every spring weighed a quarter of a ton. They got bigger every year. Only thing that grew faster was the national debt."

Sid asked his visitor, "You 'member when you were back on the farm in the '40s and your dad spent a few days every spring clearing rocks from that west field before it was dry enough to plow?"

The visitor said he remembered. "Extremely well. That's when I learned a rolling stone gathers no sympathy, especially from the people

doing the rolling," he said.

Geodes are endemic to only a few Indiana counties and then only in a narrow belt through Monroe, Lawrence, Orange and Washington counties. In Lawrence County, that band reached from Heltonville east to Zelma. Geodes were easily spotted in the beds of Back, Henderson, Hunter's, Little Salt, Leatherwood and other small creeks.

They weren't bad in the creeks, though, except the problems caused by trespassers from the cities who came to haul them away for flower-bed edging, decorative walks and other purposes. But in fields, they were irritants to be cussed, kicked, stomped on and occasionally shattered with a sledgehammer.

Sid said, "There was nothin' worse than to be breaking ground with a walkin' plow and hit a buried geode. The plow would jump outta your hand and scoot along the ground until you got the team stopped.

"Wasn't much better, either, with a tractor. The impact of the plowshare on the rock would cause the plow to trip. You'd have to back up, drop the plow and ease the point back into the ground."

The younger visitor agreed. "I had the same experience dozens of times. That's probably one reason I left the farm. I remember one time my dad made me break one of the fields with a walking plow. Thought at the end of the day my arms would fall off. Even thought it would be a blessing if they had."

He added: "Never realized until then why dad wanted the rocks cleared out of the fields as soon as they appeared."

Sid struck a match on the seat of his overalls, lighted his pipe and asked, "Ever figure out whether them geodes actually grow or not?"

His visitor said, "Never conducted an official experiment. Imagine it just seemed that way."

When it was time to leave, the visitor asked: "By the way, Sid, would you mind if I drive down the creek and pick up a load of those rocks? Need a few more to finish that flower border out in back of my house."

"Take 'em all, son, take 'em all," Sid said, waving goodbye.

A Swimmin' Hole Prank Backfires

It was a perfect place to swim, that deep pool of water in Back Creek on Wes Wray's place. It was east of Heltonville between Ind. 58 and U.S. 50 in an isolated valley where the nearest house was out of sight a half-mile away. That allowed Pokey, Bogey, Bill, Tad, Tyke and the others to drape their clothes over their bicycles and leap off the root of a big sycamore into the cool water. Nude.

Most of them had never seen swim trunks, let alone own any. They didn't need any . . . until one warm May day in about 1942 when Froggie joined them.

Froggie was maybe fourteen or fifteen, a couple years older than they were. He wasn't a bad sort. He had a big heart, but a mean streak that sometimes was even bigger.

The boys didn't notice him until he jumped into the water. They hadn't seen him take their clothes off their bikes and sneak about one hundred-fifty feet up the wooded bank, where he dropped them in a heap.

Froggie was a big storyteller. He held the boys in awe with some of his tales for several minutes before Bogey decided he'd better start home. He climbed up on the sycamore root and looked toward his bicycle.

"Somebody's stole our clothes," he shouted. "Only thing out here is Froggie's overalls."

Froggie couldn't keep from laughing at his own prank. Bogey said, "Better tell me where they are."

About that time Pokey, who wasn't more than five-foot-three, tackled Froggie in the water and said, "Okay, smartie, where are they?"

Pokey was joined in the playful attack by the others, including Bogey, who had jumped back in. Outnumbered, Froggie finally told them.

Pokey bolted out of the water, then jumped back in, the tan on his body suddenly red.

"Whatsamatter?" Billy asked.

Some girls drove to within thirty to forty feet of the creek bank and stopped, the dust churned up by the car settling in behind them. They pranced out of the 1938 Ford V-8, wearing homemade bathing suits.

Except maybe for Froggie, the boys were still more interested in Bob Feller's earned run average than they were in the vital statistics of teen-age girls. Froggie was sort of casual around girls, but he suspected he ought to do something nice to repay the boys for being mean. He raised up in the water as far as he dared and said, "For God's sake don't jump in the water. We've been fightin' off water moccasins for the last hour.

"Besides, the water's colder than a well driller's backside."

"You're spoofing us, Froggie," one of the girls cooed, sticking a toe into the water, which was just murky enough to keep her from seeing too far into it.

Froggie let out a blood-curdling yell, then bobbled around in the water, waving his arms. "Damned ol' turtle's got me by the big toe of my left foot," he screamed.

The boys were sure Froggie was acting. The girls weren't so certain. The performance was enough to make them wonder whether they really should get in the water. It wasn't good enough to make them want to leave. "Why don't you come out and we'll wrap your poor toe?" one of the girls asked.

Froggie was a quick thinker. "Best thing for a turtle bite is to let it wash out," he said.

He eased across the soapstone bottom of the pool and whispered to the other boys, "We'll be here for hours if we don't figure out something."

By that time they all were beginning to shrivel from the water.

"We need some divine intervention," Froggie said, pulling out a phrase he'd heard on "Backsliders Brought Back," a radio program out of Del Rio, Tex.

He'd no more than said that when a black snake slithered out of the grass on the creek bank. The girls darted for the car, slamming the doors behind, quickly rolling up the windows. The boys couldn't tell whether they looked back or not. The dust was too thick to see.

Froggie pulled on his clothes, then retrieved the duds for the others. "First time a snake in the grass ever done anything for me," he said.

It Was Always Mother's Day on the Farm

Farm boys who grew up around Heltonville after the Great Depression had a special bond with their fathers.

They turned to their mothers when things didn't go right.

The boys grew up alongside their fathers.

Fathers taught them how to mend fence, plow, plant, harvest, cut wood, and care for the land and the things that lived on it.

Mothers showed them how to pick berries, make a garden, separate cream from milk, dress neatly, be humble, and care about people as well as things.

Boys sought approval from their fathers, love from their mothers.

Fathers were their friends, advisers, confidants.

Mothers were their disciplinarians, making them walk the line when their fathers were too permissive.

Fathers taught sons the work ethic, the belief that success belonged to those who earned it.

Mothers taught them that work was important and success admirable, but that there also was more to life.

Fathers gave them farm machinery instructions to read.

Mothers handed them good magazines and great books.

Fathers bought them bib overalls, high-top boots, and pocket knives.

Mothers saw to it they had dress pants, Sunday shoes, and pocket combs.

Fathers made sure they were up at dawn to help with the chores.

Mothers made certain they were ready when the school bus came.

Fathers looked upset when their report cards were bad.

Mothers appeared disappointed.

Fathers said, "Boys will be boys," when they got into trouble.

Mothers cried.

Fathers accepted the fact they sometimes wanted to skip church on Sunday mornings.

Mothers fretted about salvation.

Fathers would rant and rage when they did a job poorly or carelessly.

Mothers reminded them gently, "Anything worth doing is worth doing well."

Fathers had the answers to their questions.

Mothers posed questions and let them search for the answers.

Fathers were sometimes caustic, sometimes scathing.

Mothers were, it seemed, always even-tempered.

Fathers rebuked them at times, making them angry enough to want to leave home.

Mothers told them, "Dads have bad days like everyone else. By tomorrow everything will be all right."

Mothers were more often right than wrong.

Fathers wanted sons to make things easier for their mothers.

Mothers wanted the boys to help ease their fathers' burdens.

Boys bragged to other boys about their fathers.

Mothers were taken for granted.

But they never complained.

The Night of the Weasel

Luke was an honest, hard-working farmer who never could quite make ends meet. He and his wife lived alone on eighty acres that ranged from "hollers" to hills.

About the middle of March each year his wife would order baby chicks from the hatchery at Brownstown. It was about April 1 one year when the post card came telling her the chicks could be picked up that day.

As soon as Luke came in from the field, Lucille told him: "The baby chicks are ready. I've got the brooder house all ready so let's go get them."

Luke knew that meant, "like, right now." He looked at his checkbook and said: "Now Lucy, them 300 baby chicks is gonna cost me $50. I only got $27.43 in the bank. Just how you plannin' on me payin' for 'em if I don't go to the bank first?"

Lucy kinda snorted and said, "Luke, you oughta done that Saturday when you was in town, settin' on the Courthouse Square and yakkin' with all them other fellers."

"Okay, okay," Luke replied, "let's go."

At the hatchery, he helped put the chicks in the back seat of his 1931 Chevrolet. He then wrote the check for $50 and told the hatcheryman, "I'd appreciate it if you'd not cash this for a couple of days. Need time to borrow some money from the bank."

"Sure," said the man, who had done business with Luke and knew his word was good.

Luke and Lucy took the chicks home, built a fire in the stove in the brooder house, put chemicals in the water and put out feed for the little cheepers.

Next day, Luke went into the Stone City National Bank at Bedford and told the president he needed $50 for sixty days. The banker said, "Sure, just sign this note at six percent interest."

All went well. For two days.

On the third morning, Lucy ran out to the barn to tell Luke the bad news. A weasel had gotten into the brooder during the night and killed all but about a hundred of the chicks. Luke had some choice words for "those stinkin' sneaky varmints. Ain't no good for nothin'," he said. He sat down on a milk can while Lucy sobbed.

"Ain't nothing to do but buy me some more chickens," he said. A few days later he was back at the bank for another small loan.

"Better luck next time," said the kindly banker.

Luke and Lucy bought 200 more chickens and took turns staying up to watch for the weasel. It never returned.

About two-thirds of the chickens turned out to be roosters and they were sold for fryers when they weighed three pounds. The other 100 were pullets that later became good laying hens.

Luke paid the banker from the sale of the fryers. As he handed over the money he told the banker, "It's a hard way to make a livin'."

"But you'd never be satisfied doing anything else," said the banker.

"I know, I know," said Luke, waving his big hand as he walked toward the door.

He Was Unrefined but He Wasn't Unappreciated

His speech was unrefined, punctuated with cain't, hain't and ain't.

His manner wasn't smooth and polished.

His hair wasn't well trimmed or neatly combed.

His shoes carried a film of dust from the farm.

His bib overalls looked out of place on visits to town.

His felt hat had lost its shape from years of wear.

His son, Chig, began to notice those things when he started to compare his father to other men.

He was ten, maybe eleven, at the time, old enough to be embarrassed for his dad and himself in the company of well-dressed strangers.

He needn't have been. His dad made no pretense of being something he was not, a trait other people respected. Chig learned that one Saturday in June about 1940 when he went into town with his father.

"We'll stop at the Stone City Bank to pay off the loan I got to put out the crops," his dad said, picking up a check he had received from his job at the Heltonville Limestone Co. He worked nights at the stone mill to supplement what little income he had from the farm during the lean years of the Depression.

Chig was apprehensive about walking into the bank with his dad. The bankers wore white shirts with ties drawn snug against their necks and shoes that reflected images off the toes. Chig thought he and his dad would be out of place in the bank.

He was surprised when they walked into the building on the northeast corner of the Courthouse Square in Bedford. Some of the tellers nodded, called his dad by his first name, and waved at Chig.

His dad deposited the check, then asked, "Is Mr. Jourdan in?"

The teller motioned toward an office in the rear. Jourdan arose when he saw them, came out through the swinging door, shook hands with Chig's dad, then with Chig, and asked about the rest of the family.

They followed him into his office. "Came to pay off the note I got a couple of months ago," his dad said, appearing as if he felt at ease in the setting.

The banker reached into a file, looked at some papers and said, "It isn't due for another week. If you need the money, you don't have to pay the loan until then. Or, I can even extend the time at the same interest rate."

Chig's father said he'd prefer to pay off the note then. "Don't like to owe anyone," he said, tugging a worn checkbook from the bib pocket of his overalls.

Jourdan looked at the check quickly, then at Chig. "When you grow up', be like your dad. He pays off his debts when they're due. Too bad all our customers aren't like him."

He then looked at Chig's dad. "Anytime you need a loan, just drop in. All we need is your name on a note. That's better than collateral any-time."

When his father stopped to talk to a friend outside the bank, Chig said, "I'll be back in about five minutes."

As he ran to the J.C. Penney store, he made a vow never again to worry about his father's appearance. He pulled from his front pocket the money he'd saved for July 4th fire-crackers, then picked out a blue-pat-terned handkerchief, big enough for a bandana.

He gave the handkerchief to his dad the next day for Father's Day. His dad liked the gift, but not as much as Chig liked having him for a father.

No Memories Here on Memorial Day

The cemetery was a lonely, desolate place, far from any church or town, or anyone who really had rea-son to care. It was abandoned except for the elements and the animals. The descendants had moved on to places like Missouri, Iowa, Nebraska—some to Oregon and California—as the country shifted westward. Few would ever return. They left behind the cemetery where their ancestors were buried.

The cemetery was—still is—on a little knoll about an eighth of a mile from where Powerline Road connects with Possum Hollow Road a mile south of Ind. 58 east of Heltonville and south of Zelma. It was isolated, off the road. There were no paths to it except across the end of one farm field and down a fence row. That may be why few people took time to visit it or fret because it was overgrown with briars and bushes.

"Out of sight, out of mind," said Tad's father, who owned the farm where the cemetery was located.

It was about 1938, and Tad was about eight years old when he first be-came interested in exploring the cemetery. Interested enough, that is, to overcome his fear of the place. Then he had to have the company and the assurance of his friend.

The two toted a wooden keg of cool water to the field where Tad's pa was cultivating corn when they decided it was time to look the place over.

"Ain't nothing there that will hurt you, boys, except the stickers on the blackberry bushes," Tad's dad said.

They climbed through a barbed wire fence and walked about thirty yards to the cemetery. The first thing they noticed was an old wrought-iron fence that had rusted and collapsed with time, replaced with woven wire to keep out the livestock that occasion-ally were pastured nearby.

They stepped over the farm fence—into the past. It was a lesson in his-tory. Births on the tombstones dated back to the early 1800s, most of the deaths from mid-1800 into the early 1900s. Only a few were after 1920, the most recent loss in the mid-1930s.

Tad told his friend he remembered that last burial. "Some farmers dug the grave by hand. Ambulance drove down to that ditch and the pallbearers carried the casket the rest of the way."

Some of the graves were marked with large monuments. A few of these were elaborate. Some graves were

noted only by a metal holder that held a printed message, faded almost to obscurity.

Once in a while the boys took a stick and scraped off the grimy coating of decades to check the dates. They were too young to relate time to history. That would come on later visits.

That night Tad asked his Dad who owned the cemetery and why no one seemed to care for it.

"Reckon I own the land, Tad. The deed for that place calls for eighty acres and it don't say nothing about an acre being set aside for a graveyard. It was there when I bought it.

"I've offered several times to give the township trustee, whoever he has been, a right-of-way down the end of the field and down the fence row for a road. They all wanted one straight from the county road to the cemetery, right through the middle of the field. That'd ruin the place."

"Can't somebody cut the brush off the graves so the grass can be mowed, Pa, like it is down at Mundell?" Tad asked.

"The trustee has a fund for that, but there aren't enough relatives of the dead to make him do it," his dad explained patiently.

As the years passed Tad helped his dad and others clean the cemetery. But only a few people ever noticed. Like maybe a distant relative who brought flowers on Memorial Day, or a descendant checking out dates for a family tree.

But it was something those who helped felt good about. It was the least that could be done for those who stopped and stayed and died, leaving only their graves as reminders. Graves for which Memorial Day had no meaning.

Illustration by Gary Varvel

Time To Catch Girls, not Frogs

It was a warm day and Tad had stopped by to see if Pokey wanted to catch some frogs down along Leatherwood Creek. It was spring 1941, a time for twelve-year-olds to search out the mysteries of the world that was reawakening around them.

In springs past, Pokey's older brother, Butch, had led them on trips along creeks, through woods and up hills and down hollows around Heltonville, passing on what he had learned about nature from someone older than he. But Butch had turned sixteen a few weeks earlier. He just laughed when Tad asked him if he wanted to go along that day.

Butch was in his room, running a black comb with sharp, narrow teeth through his hair with one hand, watching the dandruff fall into the other. He did that for several minutes, seeing no decrease in the flakes, before he yelled, "Hey, Mom, we got anything to get rid of dandruff?"

Tad looked at Pokey and said, "Since when did he start worrying about dandruff?"

Pokey said, "Since he found out he had a date tonight. Thinks he's in love. Ma says that happens to teenagers in the spring."

Butch's face turned red. "You guys get outta here."

About that time, his mom walked in and said, "We don't have anything unless you want me to try to find some stuff I used one time on your big sis."

Butch looked desperate. "Go ahead. I gotta get rid of this dandruff," he said to his mother, rubbing his right hand through his hair.

Pokey and Tad followed her into the kitchen. They watched as she found the solution.

"What is it, anyhow?" Pokey asked.

She explained. "It's made out of some grains of resorcin, which we use sometimes to treat skin irritations, a little glycerol and some diluted alcohol. I'll add a few drops of perfume to kill the odor."

She took the solution back to Butch and said, "Part your hair in two or three places and I'll rub this stuff in. Supposed to use a medicine dropper, but we don't have one."

Pokey and Tad stood by sniffing the perfumy smell of Butch's hair and laughing about it. Butch finally combed his hair in place and looked pleased at himself in the mirror.

His mom said, "You'll have to use the stuff several times before the dandruff's all gone. But your hair's oily enough now so she won't notice any dandruff."

"She" was the girl Butch was taking to the show in Bedford that night.

Butch nodded to his mom, the closest he ever came to a "thank you," and said, "My dress shoes squeak. Everybody will notice me when I walk down the aisle at the Von Ritz theater."

His mom smiled and said, "Do what your pa does. Put a few tacks in the center of the sole. That usually stops the squeak. Just make sure the tacks don't come through the inside."

Butch had put his shoes on the last on the porch, and was driving in the

tacks when Tad and Pokey finally decided to leave.

"What show you taking your girl to?" Tad asked.

"She wants to see Cary Grant in 'Penny Serenade.'"

Pokey held his stomach and acted like he was about to throw up and mumbled he'd rather see a cowboy show than a love story.

"Come on," he told Tad. "Let's go catch frogs. I'd rather fall in the creek than fall in love."

The Biggest Catch Is Just Being There

Chig must have been about seven years old when he told Tyke he'd like to go fishing. It was a warm spring day in the late 1930s and they were sitting next to each other on the school bus en route home from school at Heltonville.

"Let's go, then," Tyke said. He was a couple of years older than Chig, with whom he shared most of the wisdom he had learned.

Chig said, "Ain't got no hooks, no lines and no poles. So how can we go fishin'?"

Tyke said, "We'll just improvise." Improvise was a word he had picked up listening to Miss Hunter and Miss Mark talk at school. "I'll go home, tell my ma I'm going fishing, and be back."

"What's improvise mean?" Chig asked.

Tyke explained, "It means that we'll bend straight pins from your mom's sewing basket into hooks, find some string, grab a beanpole from the pile leanin' against the garden fence, and dig up some fishin' worms.

Chig was waiting when Tyke arrived. He had stuck some pins in the striped railroader hat he was wearing, and had picked out two beanpoles and was untangling some string.

The boys walked together to a small stream that eased through the farm and spotted some sun fish in a pool that was about three feet deep.

The fish nibbled two or three worms off Chig's pin-hook before Tyke said, "If you see one eating the worm, jerk the pole real quick and snag him, like this."

He flipped a three-inch fish onto the bank, looking pleased at himself. He eased the catch off the pin and dropped it back into the water.

"What did you do that for?" Chig asked.

"Didn't intend to keep any fish. The fun comes in just bein' here."

They stayed on the bank until Chig hooked a couple of fish, which he, too, tossed back into the water.

As they walked up the hill from the bank, Tyke said, "That was lesson Number One. This weekend we'll try something else."

He was true to his word. He arrived at Chig's house at midmorning Saturday and said, "Let's meander down to Back Creek and do some real fishing."

Chig said he'd have to get his hook, string and pole.

"Don't need none of them things," Tyke said. Chig found out later what he meant.

They moseyed across the bottom field on Wes Wray's farm toward a big sycamore next to the creek. The boys looked into the clear water and saw some suckers, fifteen to twenty inches long, darting about in the six-foot-deep pool.

"We're going to snare a couple of them," Tyke announced confidently.

He found a pole that had been cast aside, then pulled a roll of fine wire from his pocket. He tied one end of the wire to the pole, then unrolled about eight feet or so of it, bent it back and forth until it broke, and fashioned a noose on the loose-end.

He plopped down on sycamore roots, cleaned of earth by high water a few weeks before, tossed the wire into the water, and whispered to Chig, "As soon as one of them suckers gets in the right place, I'll snap the pole and have me a fish."

The fish swam through the trap time after time, always more quickly than Tyke could react. Chig tried also without success.

Tyke said, "Fish lesson Number Three. Don't give up."

He finally caught one that looked to be about fifteen inches long and weigh three or four pounds. He looked pleased. So did Chig.

"Know how to clean it?" Chig asked.

"Nope." said Tyke, tossing the wriggling catch back into the water. "Guess cleaning is lesson Number Four, which you'll have to have someone else teach you."

That didn't bother Chig. He looked at the fish resume its swim and said, "Like you said the other day, the fun comes in just being here."

Learning about Life among the Dead at the Cemetery

A cemetery was as much for the living as for the dead. At least, it seemed that way at Mundell Cemetery as Decoration Day neared. It became even more obvious if a grave had to be dug.

The graveyard was next to the church in a farm community a few miles southeast of Heltonville. It was a place where neighbors looked after one another, a place where visitors went from strangers to friends in the time it took to say "howdy."

No one ever had to hire a grave dug in the 1930s and early 1940s. The work was done by the farmers, who thought nothing of taking time off from work in the fields to show up at the cemetery, mattocks and shovels in hand.

They worked for nothing, but they were paid for their effort in something worth more than money. The pay came in the form of an inner richness that made them feel good about themselves and the other men around them.

It was a ritual to honor a departed friend. Or a tribute to a former neighbor who had moved away, but who had asked to be buried in the cemetery.

Tad tagged along to the graveyard whenever he could. He knew some other eight-year-olds would be there, and his dad told him he could learn

about life as well as death at the cemetery.

Tad soon learned who were the workers and who were the talkers at the gravesite. Some of the men said little while they waited to jump down into the grave, nothing once they started to work. Others talked a lot while they waited, then complained about how hard the ground was once they started to shovel. Men who scarcely knew the person who was to be buried talked a lot about him, exalting him, making him seem more of a friend than he had been. Others who knew the deceased much better, said little. Their loss was written among the wrinkles on their weathered faces.

Tad and the other youngsters enjoyed listening when the men relived the life of their departed friend. They told stories about him, good-natured stories that caused them to reflect on the man and his life.

The grave-digging took a half-day, sometimes longer, giving Tad time to walk through the cemetery, reading gravestones bleached by the sun and worn by the rain. The tombstones were lessons in history, a march of time, a record of the men and women who had come and gone, leaving their mark on the place they lived.

Tad noticed few strangers ever stopped at the graveyard except for Decoration Day. He watched them one day in May when they did. Some went quickly to a gravestone, left a bouquet of flowers, looked solemn and returned to their cars. Others sat down at the grave, and a few cried.

Once Tad strolled back to the grave after the grave-digging work was finished. One of the men looked down and said, "We preached his funeral several times while we dug his grave. If he doesn't get to heaven, it won't be our fault." The men stepped away from the grave, putting their hands to their backs, trying to straighten up.

On the way home, Tad's pa asked, "Learn anything today son?"

Tad said, "Yep. I learned a graveyard is a harder place to be for the living than it is for the dead."

The Ties That Bind for Boys

The first night Billy, Bob, Gordy and Frog came home draggin' to the tune "I've Been Working On The Railroad."

The second night, they just came home draggin'.

The four were each fourteen in late April of 1944. School was out at Heltonville for the summer and they decided they could make more money working on the Chicago, Milwaukee & St. Paul Railroad than they could helping their fathers on the farms and picking up a few odd jobs now and then.

"I can make five dollars a day puttin' down new ties and rails up between Kurtz and Freetown," Frog told his Dad.

"Hey, you ain't but fourteen," his Dad said. Frog had a ready explanation: "Everybody who is eighteen or older is either farmin' or in the Army, Navy or Marine Corps. All I gotta do is tell 'em I'm eighteen. They don't even ask for proof."

Frog's Dad wasn't any dummy, so he just said, "It's your conscience. And your back."

Frog said, "Ain't nothing harder on my back than settin' out tomater plants. Besides, I can have some spending money without askin' you all the time."

Billy, Bob and Gordy told Frog later that they had almost identical conversations with their fathers.

After that second day, they began to wonder if the job was really any easier than setting out tomatoes.

Tad and Tyke didn't go to work for the railroad. Their father was a bit firmer. He told them, "First of all, you ain't gonna lie. Second, you know I've contracted with Morgan Packin' Co. to put out fifteen acres of tomatoes. Ain't no way I kin do that without you boys."

When their dad said, "You ain't gonna do that," Tad and Tyke knew they weren't gonna do that.

Their dad waited until the boys got over their mad spell, then explained to them that they'd be better off at summer's end than Frog, Billy, Bob and Gordy would be. "We'll divvy up the profits. Then you'll know whether you'll have more money left to start school than they do."

Tad and Tyke just kinda pawed at the gravel in the driveway at their home the first couple of nights that the four railroaders stopped by to tell of their experience "on the C.M. and St. P," as they called it.

The railroaders even figured up how much they might have by the time the July 4th celebration rolled around.

Bob, kinda holding the small part of his back like it was sore, said, "That's about ten weeks away. Reckon we ought to have about three hundred bucks apiece by then."

Neither Tad nor Tyke had much appetite when their ma called them in for supper. They sulked for about a week. The sulking stopped, though, one day right after dinner when Bob, Billy, Frog and Gordy came walking across the tomato field where Tad and Tyke and their pa were setting out Pritchard plants.

"Railroad shut down?" their pa asked.

Bob fixed his chin against his chest and said a bit more softly than he usually spoke, "Nope. We were fired. They found out our ages. Besides that, they said, 'Somebody done hired some boys to do some men's work.'"

Nobody said anything else for a while. Then Bob looked over at the farmer and said, "Reckon you could use some help setting out these 'maters?"

"Yep, we sure can. But the pay is still $1.50 a day."

"We'll take it," the four said almost in unison.

About an hour later, Frog said, "Heck, this isn't nearly as hard work as I remembered it being last summer."

Tad and Tyke grinned for the first time in days.

Lazy, Hazy, Crazy Days

Scientists assert that summer commences with the June solstice and ends with the September equinox, but every Hoosier schoolchild has always known to a certainty that it begins with the Indianapolis 500 and ends when some well-intentioned teacher asks you to write about what you did during your summer vacation. Then it's all over for sure.

Teachers have always chalked up their students' hesitation in answering this question to their resistance to putting words on paper in general. But maybe there's another explanation. I remember (it was in *The National Geographic*, I believe) that the people of some third-world tribe object to having photographs taken because they fear thus preserving an image will kill the subject.

Maybe that's the way youngsters have always felt about describing summer. In their clumsy efforts to describe it, maybe they're afraid they'll kill it. And who are we to force them to commit it to paper before they can get it down true, preserve it instead of kill it? They'll find out soon enough that the magic of summer comes and passes quickly.

I suspect that Wendell Trogdon's strategy was to write about something the teacher would approve, and not, for example, about riding to Indianapolis with thirty other teenagers in an International truck equipped with a noisy airhorn and shelled corn, or about sipping beer, roasting delicious chickens, and telling tales in a Southern Indiana cavern.

So, take heart from these stories, children. The next time your teachers ask you what *you* did, you don't have to tell them the good stuff, either. Like the author, you can save it till later, when you can tell it true and share it with family and friends. —MN

Grain, Pain, Rain

It hadn't rained for several days and the farmers were becoming more and more concerned about their corn crops. That was the main topic of conversation that Sunday in July about 1940 while the men waited for services to start at Mundell Church near Heltonville.

The corn was shooting, which meant ears were forming under the silken husks and tassels were appearing. It was a crucial time for the crop and the amount of moisture in the ground could make the difference between profit and loss.

It was Sherm who came up with a suggestion on what could be done to preserve what little moisture remained in the fields.

"Best way to retain the moisture is to run a heavy object between the rows. That packs down the soil and keeps what dampness there is from coming to the top of the ground and evaporatin'," he said.

Some of the farmers looked kinda quizzically at Sherm, the way they did at people who talked like they might be a little touched in the head.

"Where'd ya hear that?" Zed asked.

"From some fellers who farm down

around Springville. They know how to farm and they said it worked for them. That's good enough for me."

"How'd they go about doing it?" Zeke asked.

"They used wheels off mowing machines, which you know are heavy as . . . well, I'd better not say what right here and now," Sherm said, looking up toward the church door.

"Corn's too tall to drive a team through a field," Alex said.

Sherm said, "What they do is hitch one horse to one wheel and let it go between the rows. The wheel not only packs down the soil, it throws up a ridge of loose dirt against the roots of the corn."

Some of the farmers agreed the idea might have some merit. Others weren't sure.

Clem was one who couldn't make up his mind, but he never hesitated to try something new as long as it didn't cost him anything.

There still was no rain in the forecast a couple of days later when he blocked up the horse-drawn mowing machine and removed one of the wheels. He lifted it onto the wagon, harnessed the horses and drove to the nearest field.

He tied one of the horses to a fence post, removed the single-tree from one side of the wagon tongue and used a short chain to fasten it to the mowing machine wheel. He hooked that single-tree to the other horse. Then he tied the two reins together and tossed them around his neck, tugged on the lines and guided the horse in between the first two rows.

He had gone no more that a couple

of hundred yards when he stopped the horse, rolled down the sleeves on his shirt and tied a big red-patterned handkerchief around his neck to keep the dry corn blades from cutting his face.

He worked throughout the morning, changing horses from time to time, worrying more about the animals than himself. He stopped only a couple of other times that morning for a drink. By noon he was covered with a quarter-inch of dust. His wife made him wait outside at dinner time until she swept off the dirt with a broom.

He returned to the field that afternoon and worked until it was time to milk. His wife met him at the barn where he was unharnessing the horses.

"I brought you clean shorts, shirt and overalls. You ain't comin' near the house until you jump in the creek."

After the chores were done Clem cleaned up as he was ordered and still managed to get to church in time for the revival meeting. He told Sherm about running the mowing machine wheel up and down the rows all day.

"Man you did it the hard way. I just hitched up each wheel and put my two boys up on each horse and said, "Go to it." They sat up high enough not to get cut by the blades on the stalks. I just sat back in the shade and watched."

Clem said, "Ain't no wonder you were so all fired excited about promotin' that idea."

He waited for Sherm to quit laughing, then said, "I sure hope all that work did some good."

He never did find out. It rained that night.

After-Work Hours

Each small town in Indiana had a place where the men gathered at the end of the workday to drink a bottle of pop, buy a loaf of bread and spin a few yarns before going home.

At Heltonville, the spot was Roberts & Sons general store at one of the turns where Ind. 58 crossed the Chicago, Milwaukee & St. Paul Railroad tracks.

Most of the men stopped there after eight hours of work running diamond saws, planers, travelers or other machinery at the Heltonville Limestone Co. mill one and a half miles east of town.

One would pull up to the gasoline pumps out front, pump the handle back and forth until six gallons showed in the glass at the top and let it flow out into the car. Then the man would go inside and tell Bob, one of the sons in Roberts & Sons, "I put in six gallons."

"That's a buck," Bob would reply.

The man would brush the limestone dust off his overalls, pull out a battered wallet and ease out a dollar. Then he'd turn to one of the men in the car pool and say, "I'll match you for the orange pop tonight."

The loser would have to hand Bob a dime for two bottles. He'd then go to the double-door cooler where the pop was chilling, take out two bottles in one hand and open them, shake off the water and bring one back.

"Get you tomorrow night," he'd tell the winner.

They'd saunter over to a group of other men already sipping everything from grape to Dr. Pepper and describe what chores awaited them on their small farms. The worst thing they dreaded was milking on hot August evenings. "Those cow tails can kill you," one would say.

"Best flyswatter ever made," replied another.

It was during the lean years of the late 1930s, and no one ever complained about how hard he worked. Most were happy to get their checks, which averaged about $25 to $30 a week.

After a half-hour or so, they'd begin to leave. Someone would pull out "orders from the old lady" from the bib pocket of his overalls and yell for Molly, one of the employees.

"Slice me off a pound of that cheese there, Molly. Keep the knife handy and rip off another pound or so of that balogna and then reach in the cooler there and get a handful of them wieners."

Molly would oblige and weigh the meat on the new set of white scales, pull the roll of brown paper out just far enough to provide enough wrapping for the meat and cheese, state the price and hand the package to the buyer.

"Molly, you'd better come home with me," the man would say.

She'd look startled and ask, "What for?"

"Cause I've bought that right hand of yours you weighed with the meat a hundred times," the man would reply. Then he'd roar with laughter.

Molly would smile as usual and say, "Get outta here."

If anyone ever left mad, nobody knew about it. Someone might get miffed and stay away a day or two, but he'd always be back.

After all, it beat facing a cow's tail.

This Poison Ivy Remedy Required Some Nerve

Farm boys didn't have to look for work. Their fathers pointed it out to them.

Like when the corn had been laid by, the wheat harvested and the hay put up.

Chig learned that when he suggested maybe he'd just loaf one July day. His dad had other plans.

"It's time to mow the fence rows," he announced. Mowing the fence rows meant more hard work, but Chig, who was eleven, knew better than to offer anything more than a token argument. His dad would have been disappointed if he hadn't offered at least some protest.

The mower on the tractor could get within a few inches of the fences on level ground. But not many fences on the farm east of Heltonville were built on level land. That meant the weeds and briars had to be cut with a scythe, a device with a sharp blade and a long handle that could only be swung with effort.

The job looked harder than it was before Chig's dad showed him how to swing the scythe with the least possible effort, even on steep banks. The least possible effort still required hard work.

"We'll work about twenty-five minutes and rest five minutes," his dad said.

It was during one of the five-minute breaks when his dad walked up to a post covered with ivy and jerked away the green vine.

Chig said, "That stuff's got three leaves, which means it's poison ivy, which means you've just caught a case of the itch."

His dad laughed. "I got sense enough, Son, not to attack something I'm afraid of. I learned when I was no older than you that it's possible to become immune to poison ivy. It's like a lot of other things. You've got to show you're not scared of it."

"If you learn to conquer it now, you may build up an immunity that will last a lifetime," he said, adding, "if you've got the nerve to try it."

Chig wasn't about to say he didn't have that much nerve.

"Okay," his dad said, "walk over to that post, grab the leaves and pull off the vines."

Chig did as he was told, then asked, "You sure this will make me immune?"

His dad said, "Wouldn't advise it for everyone. But you're a chip off this old block. Just get back to work and don't think any more about it."

Chig never mentioned to his mother his self-induced poison ivy immunity. He just waited to see whether he would wake up itching one night. He never did.

A week or so later, his mom mentioned that the weeds along the garden fence were unsightly.

"Why don't you take the sickle and cut them?" she asked Chig.

Chig feigned a worried look and said, "I'd be happy to whack 'em down, but I might get poison ivy."

His dad gave him a wink and said, "I'll take care of them right after supper."

July: Fishing and a Country Baptism

A caravan of cars, moving slowly, churned the red clay dust on the gravel road into blankets of fog. The cars stopped and a man got out, swung open the big farm gate and got back in. The caravan passed through. A passenger in the last car closed the gate.

In the cars that golden summer day were members of a rural church en route to a baptizing. The cars proceeded down a lane before turning at the banks of Back Creek, a stream that meandered across Pleasant Run Township east of Heltonville. The drivers parked the cars as best they could under the shade of the trees that lined the creek.

Faubie, who was about eight, noticed the horses swish the flies from their backs with their long tails. Cows munched on the few blades of grass that were still green. The dried vegetation crackled under the feet of the congregation as it walked slowly to the creek. The members edged to the west bank, where they could view the minister, who waited on a sand bar. A group of youngsters in their teens stood near the preacher.

The water was clear, the sandstone bottom visible a half-fathom deep in a pool twenty-five feet wide and seventy-five feet long. To Faubie, it looked as big as an ocean. He noticed the fish in the creek. Beams from the sun found their way through the overhanging leaves, turning the iridescent scales on the goldfish into a bright glow.

Faubie's mind was more on fishing than on the baptism, but he tried not to let it show. His commitment to the Lord would come later.

Illustration by Gary Varvel

The congregation broke into song, "Shall We Gather at the River." The only accompaniment was the distant mating call of a bobwhite.

The minister used a stick to steady himself and waded out into the water. The young women who were to be baptized followed slowly, fearfully. The boys came more quickly, yet more reluctantly, they would confess later.

Faubie made a mental note of what followed. He was to recall four decades later, "Individually, sacredly, solemnly, the minister immersed each of the new members. Some of the faces came up from the water with an ecstatic shine. One or two gave a shout of joy."

More hymns followed the final immersion. It was a time of joy and celebration, Faubie thought "an unbounded, uninhibited praise to the Creator and His Son," he recalled later.

A final prayer was said. The congregation and the newly baptized, still in wet clothes, returned to their cars and the caravan departed as it had come.

Faubie followed reluctantly, casting one last glance at the few fish he could see in the water, which had been stirred a light-brown from the baptism. He made a mental note to return, someday, to fish and to recapture the meaning of that July day.

A Bountiful Feast Was His Reward

Being a country boy had its own rewards. And many of those rewards came each time he sat down at the table, especially in mid-August.

The meals were fit for a king and his court, which is how most farm wives considered their husbands and children. Those meals were even better on Sundays when company came, especially the preacher. Farm wives in the 1930s and '40s counted no calories and spared no effort to make every dish a delight to themselves as well as to their guests.

Tad's mother, Millie, was no exception. She tried as hard as the other wives in the Flatwoods community southeast of Heltonville to outdo each other to please the minister and win his praise as he left the table.

Tad was ten before he learned just

how good a cook his mother was.

He'd often heard the youngsters in Heltonville talk about eating dinners at restaurants in Bedford and thought how rich their parents must have been to afford such a luxury. About the only time he ever went into a restaurant in the county seat was on a Saturday when his dad bought him a ten-cent fish sandwich at one of the spots on the west side of the Square.

Bugsy was a friend of Tad's who lived in town and sometimes got to eat at plush restaurants. It was Bugsy who made Tad realize just how good a cook his mother was.

Bugsy had come home with Tad after a Saturday matinee at the Lawrence Theater in Bedford, spent the night, gone to church and come back to have dinner before going home.

The boys and Tad's parents, brothers and sisters arrived home from

church before the minister, who had to wait until the last of the congregation left the church. Tad's mother put on an apron immediately and started assigning chores to the children.

Tyke: "Get two gallons of milk from the springhouse and bring up some butter in a one-pound mold." The milk was fresh from the morning. The butter had been churned two days earlier.

Neil: "Clean a dozen ears of corn and make sure you have all the silks off." The corn had been grown in the garden, picked with the dew of the morning.

Marty: "Check on the ice cream. Make sure there's enough ice left around the freezer." The boys had made the ice cream that morning and packed it with ice, throwing on burlap bags to slow the melting.

Tad: "You and Bugsy, bring up a watermelon and muskmelon from the springhouse." The melons had been bought earlier in the week from a grower in the White River bottoms between Medora and Vallonia.

In a couple of hours, the table had been set and the boys and men had washed in a dishpan, splashing water onto their faces and drying with a towel made from a mash sack. The minister had undone his tie and looked as if he were at home on the farm.

Once everyone was seated, the minister said grace and explained he would have prayed longer had not the smell of the food distracted him. Tad thought that was a blessing in itself.

The biggest problem diners had was finding a place on the big twelve-inch plates for all the food. There was chicken fried from broilers raised on the farm. There was roast beef, once

steer on the hoof. There were fried potatoes from a new crop freshly dug from the garden. There were corn on the cob, green beans, beets, peas.

And there were biscuits, homemade from wheat taken from the thresher to Heltonville, where Jerry Jones ground it into flour. For those biscuits there was a wide choice of spreads: fresh dairy butter, apple butter, maple syrup and an assortment of jellies.

About the only words spoken were, "Pass the . . ."

Tad thought it was the first time he'd ever spent any time with the minister when he wasn't trying to save souls.

Just when everyone began to ease their chairs back from the table, Millie mentioned the assortment of desserts. Desserts like fresh apple pie, fresh raspberry pie, chocolate cake. Desserts like homemade cookies. Desserts like the homemade ice cream. And banana pudding. And watermelon and muskmelon.

The minister said it was more difficult to make a choice than it was to pick a sinner to save in one of the taverns in Bedford.

He finally opted for a piece of apple pie covered with ice cream, followed by some banana pudding. Bugsy had chocolate cake, apple pie, pudding and ice cream, not necessarily in that order. Tad had a little of about everything.

The minister praised Millie until she was so flustered she wrung her hands in her apron. But Tad knew she was pleased.

Bugsy thanked her too, then said: "Tad don't know how lucky he is. Your dinner was better'n any I ever had at any fancy restaurant my dad and mom ever took me to."

Tad was prouder of his mom than he'd ever been.

About 4:00 p.m., the minister said he'd best be leaving for some solitude that would help him prepare his evening sermon. Bugsy said it was time he started home, too.

But neither one left until Tad's dad brought out the big butcher knife, brought the watermelon from the basement and cut them each a big slice. The preacher stayed to eat his.

Bugsy held his big slice with both hands and nibbled on it as he started the long walk back to town.

Rollin' On to Riverside

The summer of '47 had been memorable in Heltonville for its uneventfulness. Oh, there was a lot going on, but not enough to keep teenagers throbbing with excitement. That's why twenty or so high school youths signed up when Ope announced he would take a truckload of people to Riverside Park up in Indianapolis if he could make expenses.

Ope wasn't much more than a teenager himself. He'd saved enough money while in the Navy to buy the truck, figuring he'd work for himself and wouldn't have to take orders from any more bosses who acted like chief petty officers.

Ope kept the big International spotless, washing it from time to time in Leatherwood Creek behind his house. He was dependable and likable and farmers didn't hesitate to give him all the hauling jobs he could handle.

Ope didn't have any trouble getting thirty or so boys and men to pay a buck each for the trip to Indianapolis on an August Sunday. He even borrowed chairs from the Baptist church in town so they could sit down if they wanted on the ninety-mile trip.

At Needmore, Ope picked up a few

more riders, then drove off Ind. 37 into the town of Guthrie, where he woke up the sleepy little burg with a blast of his airhorn and three more teenagers rubbed their eyes and climbed aboard.

He'd driven no more than a few miles when the riders from Pleasant Run Township got into arguments with the passengers from Marshall Township about everything from apples to zebras. There were a few scuffling skirmishes, but no fisticuffs. By the time Ope had driven through Bloomington the arguments had ended and everyone decided to peacefully coexist.

About that time, some of the younger passengers decided it would be fun to throw some shelled corn that had been left on the bed of the truck at passing cars and hear the noise as it hit the roofs.

That proved not to be a good idea. Near Waverly, a southbound car wheeled around and began a chase with Ope, who was perplexed when the driver pulled alongside and motioned for him to pull over.

The driver, irate and swearing, informed Ope in no uncertain terms that he ought to call the state police.

"I'm takin' my boy home from the

hospital. He had an eye operation and those idiots back there on your truck threw corn into the car. You could have blinded him for life and caused me to have a wreck."

Ope had to agree with the man. He apologized, climbed up on the bed and berated the passengers for the benefit of the man, who seemed to be satisfied that Ope meant business.

In Indianapolis, the passengers had to put up with hoots and yells from the city slickers. They answered in kind, except at stoplights, where they didn't take any chances.

At Riverside, Ope parked and told everybody to be prepared to leave at 4:00 p.m.

Tad and Chig took off together. They managed to make it on a couple of rides before boarding the airplane glide, which went in a circle. Both of them got sick, which didn't set too well with some folks down below.

If they hadn't felt so queasy, they would have been embarrassed when the operator of the ride got the thing stopped and they tottered off. They stumbled back to the truck, where they collapsed.

It seemed at least forty-eight hours before 4:00 p.m. arrived and Ope and all the other riders returned. Ope noticed their condition and offered to get them some refreshments, but Chig said he preferred to die with his stomach empty.

They didn't feel too well until they saw the "Leave Monroe County, Enter Lawrence County" sign up the hill from Harrodsburg.

At home that night, Tad's mother took one look at him and said, "The only thing worse than your looks is your smell. Was the trip exciting?"

Tad didn't have the heart to tell her the truth.

"Yep," he said. "I'd like to go back sometime and take a good look at the place."

Ragweed Cream a Real Scream

It was a dry, hot August, the grass in the pasture had been gnawed down to the roots and the cows had turned to the weeds for forage.

Among the weeds they found—and digested—was *Ambrosia artemisia folia*, better known as ragweed. Some folks called it hogweed. It was probably all right for hogs.

The cattle didn't complain, either, but Tad and his folks did. Especially when the four milk cows on their farm near Heltonville chewed and re-chewed the ragweed. Ragweeds had a flavor that was so strong it could be tasted in the milk the cows gave . . . and in any byproduct made from the milk.

Tad was just old enough to help turn the cream separator in the dry years of late 1930s. He usually stuck a tin cup with a handle under the milk spout as it came from the separator, savoring the warm milk even on hot days.

The first time he tasted the ragweed, though, he ran to the door and spewed the milk against a big beech tree near the milkhouse. Then he ran to the spring, took a cool drink, rinsed out his mouth and gagged for a while.

His mother took a smaller sip of the milk, knew what was wrong and said, "We'll have to give this to the hogs. If they'll drink it. They can have the cream, too."

Tad said, "We're going to sell the cream, anyhow. Why do we have to throw it out? Won't nobody know what it tastes like but us."

His mother said that would be "selling a product under false pretense, and besides it might get Ern into trouble." Ern was the man who picked up the cream and took it to a dairy in Seymour.

That night Tad and his father closed off the pasture where the ragweeds were and turned the cows into a stubble field, where red clover had just been cut. Within two days, the milk tasted like it was supposed to and Tad went back to drinking it straight from the separator.

He'd almost forgotten about the ragweed a year later when he poured out a big bowl of corn flakes for breakfast, then covered them with cream. He took his first bite and knew the cows had been in the ragweeds again.

Tad mentioned the experience to his friend Chig a day or two later. "You think that's bad?" he asked, using the tone he saved to relate a personal experience. Tad knew he was about to hear something exciting.

Chig pulled up the overall gallus that had fallen over his left shoulder, and said, "When I was milking the other night I noticed the milk smelled different. Told my parents about it, but they said they couldn't smell anything."

Tad waited for Chig to go on. "Well," Chig said, "we saved some of the cream to make ice cream. Me and Pa cranked on that old three-gallon ice cream maker 'til we were blue in the face. We finally finished and could hardly wait to eat the ice cream. Ma dipped out about three big scoops for me and I sat down on the grass, leaned against the smokehouse and thought that was about the closest to heaven a boy could ever get."

Tad knew that wasn't the end of the story.

Chig said, "But that was before I tasted the ice cream. It was vanilla with ragweed extract. Man, I swallowed one bite and I knew I wasn't in heaven. It was more like hell."

Tad laughed, then said, "Hope you didn't say hell in front of your parents."

Chig said, "Nope, but my dad did. And he also said, "'This damned stuff would make a preacher cuss.'"

Tad was still laughing when Chig topped off his story: "But Mom wouldn't let him save some of the ragweed ice cream to take to the social to see if the preacher did cuss when he tasted it."

No Harvest This Time

Donny and Ward had talked for days about headin' west to join the wheat-harvesting crews as they worked their way north through the Great Plains from Texas into Canada in the summer of '47.

They were sixteen, adventuresome, or so they thought, eager for new experiences and anxious to throw off the traces of parental restraint and seek temporary independence.

Most of the field work was finished for the summer on the farms their parents operated in Lawrence and Jackson Counties, and there wasn't much to keep them occupied except for fence-building, barn-painting and weed-cutting, chores that were not only hard but unimaginative.

It took several days for Donny and Ward to work up enough courage to tell their parents of the plans. They were met with a reaction that fell far below the enthusiasm· mustered by each of the boys.

The fear of the unknown was used by the parents in an attempt to discourage them. Instead it only whetted their desire to prove fright would not be their master.

Ward finally convinced his parents he'd be back home in time for school in September and that he'd be careful, watch whom he associated with and keep his money in his sock.

He met Donny that night at Norman where high school players from Heltonville and Clearspring met regularly for a basketball game in the dust bowl just north of C.E. Cummings' store.

"I'm all set," he said.

Donny said, "Still got some convincin' to do with Ma. Dad says O.K., though, so I'm halfway there."

He assured Ward he'd be ready to start hitchhiking the next afternoon.

"Meet you down at Horace George's store," said Ward. "Hard tellin' how far we can get before dark."

"I'll be there," Donny said.

He was, too, when Ward came trundlin' in with a bunch of clothes in what looked like a knapsack.

"Where's your duds?" he asked Donny.

"Can't go," Donny said. "Ma won't let me."

Ward frowned, dug a Dr. Pepper out of Horace's pop cooler, shook off the water and said, "Guess I'll be headin' off alone.

"See you this fall, Donny."

Ward walked a block over to Ind. 58 and lost himself in thought until Roy came along and picked· him up.

"Looks like you're headin' for someplace besides home," Roy said.

"I was, but my plans were changed. Just drop me off at home," he said, forlorn.

Neither his mom nor dad were too surprised when Ward shuffled up the driveway, chin tucked into his chest.

"Just remember, things always work out for the best," his dad said.

Ward had to endure a lot of jokes the rest of the summer from friends who talked a lot about the wheat being separated from the chaff. Ward got used to it, though.

"Root Hawg" Was a Winner

Come August, Depression or no Depression, almost everybody who wanted a job had one in an area from Heltonville to Brownstown in the '30s and '40s.

Credit for the positions, if you could call them that, was due Morgan Packing and a few other canning companies. They bought tomatoes, corn, beans and pumpkins. That meant jobs for pickers in the field, truck drivers and loaders and workers in the canning factories.

The work was hard, the hours were long and the pay wasn't much to brag about. But it beat nothing, which is what a lot of people had back in those days.

Jimmy was ten in the summer of 1940. The most money he ever had before was the dime his dad would give him once in a while to have a triple-dip ice cream cone at C.E. Cummings' general store in Norman. But he made what he thought was a fortune that summer, helping set out plants, hoeing weeds and then picking the tomatoes when they got ripe.

He earned a nickel a crate for picking the tomatoes, and through hard work and short breaks he could make $1.50 or so a day.

He didn't fool around like a lot of the pickers. That caused Clarence, a farmer for whom he picked, to mention one day, "That boy's goin' at it root hog or die." That caused the other pickers who weren't as conscientious to call him "Root Hog," which didn't bother Jimmy. At the end of picking one week, Clarence paid off the pick-ers, and Jimmy had more money than any of them.

He let out a big "Rooooot Haaawwwgg" that echoed off the tin roof of a barn in the distance.

Jimmy's brother, Elrod, worked for a trucker who hauled the tomatoes to Brownstown. Elrod was muscular for a thirteen-year-old, and by the time he loaded dozens of truck loads that summer he was strong and mean enough to play with the Washington Redskins. More than one person who razzed Jimmy ended up getting a rotten tomato rubbed in his nose. Compliments of Elrod.

The parents of Jimmy and Elrod worked at the canning factory for a couple of months in the harvest. They'd leave home early and get home late, often working fourteen or so hours a day seven days a week. Like the boys, the parents were too tired to spend any money at night, except for food and a few soft drinks and maybe a little candy now and then.

By the time the canning factory shut down the family had amassed a fair amount of money. When they showed up in Norman one Saturday night in a shiny used 1937 Chevy, the townspeople started saying things like, "You folks must of had a rich uncle who died."

"Ax," the father who got his name from a sharp tongue, just grinned and said: "It was easy. Me and Ma and the boys just worked like hell for the last two months. You might try it next summer."

One of the fellows who wasn't known for his interest in work, said, "I think I prefer to stay poor forever." He did, too.

From the Mouths of Caves, Legends Gathered

Spring Mill was the place to go for guided tours of caves.

But youngsters around Heltonville in the 1930s and 1940s didn't have to make the 23-mile trip to the state park to explore caverns. Caves, deepened and mystified by local legend, were just over the ridge above Leatherwood Creek.

They were uncharted. Some old-timers claimed one cave wound its way from its opening on the Ramsey Place through the subterranean limestone to an exit near Leesville. That would have been a seven-mile venture, even without the turns and twists.

The intelligent young accepted the legend, some as fact, some as fiction. It was something they'd prefer neither to prove nor disprove.

They did make some cursory attempt at exploration, but seldom dared creep more than a hundred yards from the opening of the cave. Lanterns could burn out of coal oil, flashlights could be dropped, never to be found again, matches could turn moist and unusable.

The cave, though, was an ideal spot for picnics and fun, for times best enjoyed in isolation away from the watchful eyes of adults.

Chig, Pokey, Bogey, Tad and their teen-age friends met occasionally at the cave to roast chickens over an open fire, to sip a few beers obtained from older youths and to loll away warm Sunday afternoons. They soon learned the water inside the cave was a good

spot to keep the beer cold and to relax from the summer sun.

They'd exchange stories they had heard about the cave. None could top the tale Chig claimed he had been told by his dad. His dad, he said, had made the underground journey to Leesville so often he had the route etched in memory.

Pokey wanted to know why he had made the trip that often, adding, "Once would have been enough for me."

Chig said, "For very good reasons, or at least Pa said they were good reasons."

He explained that Leesville was a place where men sometimes gathered to play poker, safe in the knowledge that the sheriff was twelve miles away in Bedford.

Chig said, "Pa claims he could leave the car at home, tell Ma he was going to walk into Heltonville to a meeting at the Oddfellows Lodge, then take the cave route to Leesville where he'd say, 'deal me in.'"

The others knew the story was more fiction than fact. But they didn't interrupt.

Chig said, "Pa even played upstairs one night at the Granny White House."

The Granny White House was a cabin made of logs from an old fort near Leesville.

That's when Tad finally broke in: "The Granny White House is at Spring Mill State Park." It had been moved there from Leesville.

That didn't bother Chig. He said, "It is now. Has been ever since Ma kicked it there after she learned Dad had been playing poker upstairs."

The laughter was broken only by the opening of the beer bottles.

What the boys didn't know was that Chig's dad had made the entire trip through the cave to Leesville once. Or at least he claimed he had.

Just Plain Folk

Hoosiers were and are individualistic, hospitable, honest, unassuming, thoughtful folk. Kin Hubbard's popular cartoon character of the 1920s and '30s, Abe Martin, sitting and reflecting on a barbed-wire fence, didn't quite have the image right: no real Hoosier would sit there very long without inventing a more practical perch.

Rural-Indiana patience is sometimes taken for laziness. An example that comes to mind is some young cabin-builders who were hired not so long ago to do the difficult job of raising the log walls of a Southern Indiana resort. The general contractor got very nervous when, two and a half weeks into a three-week deadline, the young men still hadn't shown up. He was ready to believe the worst rumors about local shiftlessness when the builders appeared with an ingenious device they had invented and built to make their work easier. They raised the log walls in three days.

Hoosiers are often underestimated. There's the possibly apocryphal story about the man from Southern Indiana who, seeking higher education, figured the best way to get it was to travel to Harvard. Arriving by bus on campus, he immediately asked a nattily-dressed Easterner, "Where is the library at?" "Sir," the other answered haughtily, "this is Harvard University, and we do not end our sentences with prepositions." "Excuse me," apologized the Hoosier, thoughtfully. "I'll rephrase the question: Can you tell me where the library is at, you pompous son of a bitch?"

The nicest thing you can say about people from Indiana is that they are "just plain folks." That means they are extraordinary in every important way. —*MN*

Town Just Wasn't the Same after W.C.'s Departure

Bogey was loafing after school at the general store in Heltonville when he heard the men talking about the death of W.C. Roberts.

"This town will never be the same," someone said. The other men nodded solemnly in agreement.

One of them looked at Bogey and said, "You knew Mr. Roberts, didn't you, son?"

Bogey was only nine at the time, which was in 1939. "He lived in the big white house on the hill at the end of town," Bogey replied, pointing eastward.

The house had high pillars in the front and appeared as big as a plantation home to Bogey. Cedar trees stood tall in the manicured yard, which extended down to Ind. 58.

"And he used to be principal at the school here before he left to go to Tunnelton," Bogey added.

The man replied, "That's right. But it only tells part of the story. W.C. was a lot more than an educator. He was a man of character, a friend, a person who did a lot of things for a lot of different people. Every town has someone it can look up to, and W.C. was that man in Heltonville."

W.C. had died earlier that day, a victim of food poisoning.

The men took turns recalling the things W.C. had accomplished.

A farmer mentioned that W.C. and his wife, Gussie, were recognized as experts in poultry-raising. And that W.C. helped plan the first county farm products show, thirty years earlier.

Someone else mentioned that W.C. was Lawrence County school superintendent from 1918 to 1925 and helped establish the county's first consolidated school near Mitchell.

Another man said, "What none of you know is that he and Gussie used some of their own money to help schools stay open in the Depression. W.C. was too modest to let many people know about that."

One of the younger men said, "W.C. was principal here when I was in high school. The school's first yearbook in 1933 was dedicated to him by the junior and senior classes.

"You know any other principal students would have that much respect for?" he asked.

No one did.

Another former student called W.C. a "patient, understanding teacher, who once said he'd like to shield us all from the evils and troubles of the world."

When the tributes ceased, one of the men looked at Bogey and said, "If you ever climb the ladder of success, son, remember it was men like W.C. who held the ladder for you."

Bogey told them he'd remember.

A couple of years later, the big house where W.C. had lived burned. It was never rebuilt. The man who had set an example for the residents was gone. So was his home.

The town seemed to lose some its enthusiasm, some of its zeal to become a better place to live.

And Bogey remembered that afternoon in 1939. The men had been right when they said the town would never be the same without W.C.

No Job Was Too Small for Mayor Emmet

The signs on Ind. 58 east and west said:

HELTONVILLE
Unincorporated

That meant the community had neither a city nor a town charter. There was no local government except for that dictated from the Lawrence County offices in the Courthouse at Bedford.

But, like every other hamlet, Heltonville had a "mayor" without portfolio. In some places he got that title by virtue of his wealth, in others for his community spirit, in others by just being around.

Emmet got his title as mayor of Heltonville by just being around. And he kept it, without having to stand election, by staying around and doing good in his own way.

Emmet wasn't his real name. Some of the people who remember him fondly might be offended if his right name were used, even though this is

intended as a tribute and not a put-down.

Emmet owned no land and seemed to have few worries. The times he worked to earn money were rare.

Emmet was like some real mayors. He didn't accomplish much and didn't exert himself doing that. And he agreed that qualified him for a political job like mayor, even though such an official position didn't exist.

Emmet liked the honorary title. He'd spend his days walking up and down the railroad tracks, checking to see if the crossties were in place. Sometimes he'd watch the water run down Leatherwood Creek, maybe dreaming of a dam for a reservoir. He'd stop at the barber shop, feed mill, restaurant, post office, general store and anywhere else he thought his advice might be needed.

If he ran out of people to talk to, Emmet would just sit on the steps at the Methodist Church or the Odd-fellows Building waiting for one of the young people in town to stop for conversation and consultation. Those were occasions both Emmet and the young people enjoyed. Most of the young people, at least those who had been brought up to respect their elders, called him "sir."

None of their parents objected to them talking with Emmet, that being an era before suspicion and doubt clouded innocence with fear.

Oh, once in a while one of the women would caution her son about a rumor Emmet had spent time in an "institution," an "institution" being a mental hospital. A lot of the boys in town already had heard about that rumor, having been at the barber shop one Saturday morning when an indiscreet boor happened to comment, teasingly he thought: "Emmet, you're as crazy as a bedbug."

The shop got deadly quiet and most of the customers cleared their throats and looked down at the tongue-and-groove floor like they were counting the hairs that rested in clumps.

Emmet didn't say anything, either, for a while. Then he reached into his pants pocket, pulled out a worn wallet and gently removed a tattered piece of yellow paper. Then he walked over to his accuser and said softly, "I ain't crazy and I got papers right here to prove it." What he purportedly was holding was his release from the State Hospital at Madison.

Nobody bothered to check the "papers." So Emmet put them back in his billfold and walked out. If the encounter bothered him, he didn't let it show.

Emmet died a few years later and a lot of people mourned his death. A newcomer to town wondered why, saying insensitively, "He was just a make-believe mayor who didn't really do anything."

A friend of Emmet's responded: "Yes, but he did it better than anyone ever did before."

Or after.

He Healed the Sick in Body and Mind

Jasper Cain was a family doctor by profession. He was a friend, adviser, confidant, farmer, hunter, humanitarian by choice.

He often said, usually to young people: "The best thing you can say about a person is that he cared about the people around him."

"Doc" cared. He cared so much he forgot at times his own welfare and comfort. He kept going even when it would have been easier to stop.

Doc had a little office in Heltonville, but he didn't confine his practice there. He'd range for miles through the hills and hollows in the 1920s and 1930s, sometimes in the 1940s, to do what he could to make someone feel better.

He often had to wait to be paid, but he didn't fret about it. He knew most people would pay him whenever they could. Sometimes he'd accept eggs, butter, apples or whatever a poor farmer offered him in lieu of money.

Doc didn't get much satisfaction from making money. There were a lot of other things that thrilled him more than visiting the bank. He didn't make much money for serving two terms as Pleasant Run Township trustee, but he thought he was doing something worthwhile by seeing the school was run properly.

Doc seemed happiest when he was on the land, farming, hunting, walking, watching the wildlife.

Some of his best times came on hot summer days when he'd go to a farm where his son was harvesting wheat for a friend with their Allis Chalmers tractor and combine. He'd perch on a sack of new wheat, light up a cigar, make sure the match was snuffed out and just relax with the farm owner and his son, occasionally blowing smoke rings.

Whatever Doc said was worthwhile. There were no "X-rated" remarks. He talked about the war in the Pacific and in Europe, about rationing, about his life as a country doctor, about the people of the community.

When Ed stopped to unload the hopper, Doc would help hold the sacks as the grain augered into them. Then he'd teach the farm boy, slowly, clearly, patiently, how to tie a miller's knot.

He'd laugh as he watched the boy chase a rabbit that had leaped from the wheat as the combine neared. Once in a while, a rabbit might get caught in the cutting blade of the combine and lose a leg. Doc would take it gently from the boy and tie a tourniquet, then ease it to the ground, watch it hover in fright, then flee.

Doc liked to joke, but never maliciously. And he'd never leave a person with a false impression.

On one of his last hunting trips, he was duck-hunting when some birds flew over. He aimed his shotgun and a bird fell. His companion said, "Good shot, Doc."

Doc just smiled.

That night as he left his friend, he confessed, "There's something you ought to know. I wasn't shooting at the bird I hit. I was shooting at one off to the left."

The friend said, "You didn't have to tell me that, Doc.

Doc grinned and said, "I feel better for doing it, though."

Boss' Son Was 'OK'

This is a second-generation story, one that isn't easy to relate to readers who have never been inside a stone mill.

Reliance on other building materials has reduced the need for such mills, but in the '20s and '30s there were many in the Stone Belt that circled the Bedford-Bloomington area. The mills were super-long structures, usually covered with galvanized metal, often with railroad spurs running through them. It was in the mills where quarried rock was cut to size, planed and sometimes sculptured.

Near the top of the mills were what the stone workers called travelers, machines that hoisted huge pieces of limestone and moved them about the mill. Strong cable placed around the stone by "hookers" extended up to the traveler operator, who could place the pieces at a diamond saw, plane or wherever they needed to go.

Onto this scene in the '30s came the son of the owner of one mill. Young, inexperienced, he was a man whose reputation for fun exceeded his reputation for work.

He spent a few weeks learning the basics of the business before his father made him the night superintendent. That meant he was responsible for a crew of about one hundred men, a tough, hard-working lot of part-time farmers and Italian immigrants. They expected no favors and gave none, especially to newcomers. Bill didn't let that bother him. It didn't hurt any that he was a free spirit who wasn't overly impressed with his dad being owner of the place.

One night, while Wes was away from his saw, Bill removed the sandwiches, apple and hard-boiled egg from his lunch box and drove three No. 10 nails through the bottom and into a crosstie. He then replaced the items.

When the whistle blew for supper, Wes as usual jerked his lunch box to head outside. But this time the bottom came out. He spent most of the thirty-minute break picking up crumbs that once had been his supper.

An hour or so later, Bill was aboard the traveler when he dropped a small chip of stone on Wes, yelled down and asked, "Hey, fella, how'd you enjoy your lunch?"

That's when Wes playfully grabbed a water hose and directed it up at Bill.

Electricity and water don't mix, of course, so when the spray hit the electrical wiring, sparks flew across the traveler's track, knocking out power over much of the mill.

Wes figured he'd either be fired or spend the next ten years paying for the damage. Instead, Bill climbed down from the stalled traveler, smiled at Wes and said, "We gotta get this damned mess fixed before Dad gets here tomorrow morning."

He called in some electrician friends from Bedford, who spent the night rewiring, splicing and patching. Before the other workers left, Bill told them, "I don't want any of you to ever mention this. What Dad don't know won't hurt him."

All Bill said to Wes was, "Hell, a man's gotta have some fun once in a while."

In the years to come Bill looked on Wes as a friend and confidant. And the millworkers looked on Bill as an all-right guy.

This Poor Man Was Always Rich in Friendliness

Dan wore bib overalls and a big smile. The overalls came from J.C. Penney's. The smile came naturally.

A few folks around Heltonville didn't think Dan had much to smile about, but that was because they associated happiness with wealth.

Wealth was just a six-letter word that had no real meaning to Dan. It wasn't relevant to the world in which he lived. He lived in a world populated by poor men like himself, men who worked hard to support big families that gave them more enjoyment than they would have received from all the money in the Stone City Bank at Bedford.

Dan carried no trace of fat on his big-framed body. His weather-worn face only accentuated his grin.

Almost everyone in Pleasant Run Township knew Dan. Adults knew him because he drove a truck for Fred Dulin. Youngsters knew him because of his sons, Marvin, Bob, Edwin, Myron and Gerry. Dan had infected them with his contagious good nature.

Dan usually started work before dawn, especially on days he had to haul livestock to market in Indianapolis. He'd drive out to a farm, greet the farmer warmly regardless of how cold the temperature might be, back up the truck to a barn door, pull the chute from under the truck bed and put the side-racks in place.

He seldom stopped talking, no matter how hard it was to drive the animals up the chute onto the track. If he ever got disturbed, he didn't show it.

Dan showed a lot of youngsters how to stack ninety or a hundred bales of hay on the truck and tie them down and be confident none of the load would be lost, no matter how rough the roads. Some men would have lost their patience, and their tempers, teaching some of the boys Dan had to work with when hauling hay, moving furniture and unloading fertilizer. But Dan just accepted their ineptness as inexperience, saying, "Everybody's got a right to learn before being criticized."

But Tyke thought even Dan would lose his temper after a traffic incident one night in the mid-1940s. Tyke was playing cat-and-mouse with one of Dan's boys. The mouse was the car Tyke drove, the cat was a car driven by Dan's son.

Tyke stopped his car in the center of a bridge over Leatherwood Creek, planning to accelerate as soon as he saw Dan's son drive up behind. His plan went awry. Dan's son came up too quickly. His car smacked the rear end of Tyke's.

Back in town, Tyke expected the worst. "It was my fault," he admitted, kicking a stone to avoid looking at Dan.

Dan didn't blink an eye. He just raised his right hand, which was big enough to hide a ham, laid it on Tyke's shoulder, gave a gentle squeeze and said: "Wasn't any more your fault than it was my boy's. The cars can be fixed. And both of you have learned that cars aren't playthings."

He never mentioned the incident again.

Dan grew older and the boys became men. He never failed to wave at them if he was in the swing on the front porch of his home on Ind. 58 as they drove by.

Somehow, they always seemed to be in too big a hurry to stop and talk.

Dan would have been happy had they done so. He was never too busy to be friendly.

The house where Dan lived burned later. But the fire didn't destroy anyone's memory of him.

Going All Out To Enrich the Lives of Youngsters

Dutch didn't have to work day and night at his government job, but a lot of teenagers around Heltonville became better people because he did.

The social engineers who formulated policy for President Franklin D. Roosevelt thought rural youngsters had a right to enjoy competitive sports as much as those in cities. That's where Dutch came in. He was hired to direct youth recreation in Pleasant Run Township in the later years of the Depression. It was a job he turned into a personal challenge.

Most of the young people he worked with came from poor homes, homes where disappointments outnumbered joys. Defeat, they thought, was more likely than victory, immediate survival more important than long-term ambition.

Dutch gradually turned their feelings of inferiority into confidence and gave them enough self-assurance to dream of accomplishment. Dutch used some adults to show the way. He organized a semi-pro independent baseball team, called it the Heltonville 400s and coached them to a winning season in which they didn't lose in tournament competition until the

finals of the state championship.

The success of that team was an elixir for the teenagers in the community. It gave them an incentive to work harder at the games they played.

In the summer, Dutch's youth baseball teams became winners on diamonds he had shaped from flat brown spots in broomsage fields. The self-worth of the players grew with each victory.

Dutch turned the boys of summer over to the high school coach when classes resumed in the fall, but he didn't stop coaching for the winter. Girls, he decided, should have an equal opportunity at competitive sports. He organized a basketball team, scheduled games with other high schools and began using his coaching talents to teach the sport to girls who had never before played in spirited competition.

By the first game, Dutch knew he had a good team. Elsie, Nellie, Geneva and the other players had gained the self-confidence Dutch had taught his baseball players earlier. They practiced hard, played harder.

Some of their parents didn't believe in girls playing sports, but they allowed their daughters to play as long as Dutch would provide transportation and be responsible for their welfare.

The girls went through the season

losing but one game, that one to Bedford, 9-7. They won the first three rounds of the county tournament and beat Springville for the championship February 26, 1940.

Nellie and Geneva read the results of that game in the *Bedford Daily Times* the next night: "Coach Walter Holt's Heltonville girls annexed the county basketball championship by defeating Springville in a listless game, 7-2."

Geneva kind of frowned and screamed, "Listless, spiffless, we won and that's what counts."

She sounded like a winner. "Too bad there isn't a state championship tournament," she said, confidently.

Dutch was given a trophy symbolic of the league championship. He turned it over to the school principal. It was the first county championship trophy won by any team from the school.

Putting Religion to the Test

Abner was a soft touch for hell-fire and damnation preachers. He got religion almost as often as most men around Norman and Heltonville got haircuts. And it lasted about as long.

Actually, Abner was religious, but not always in the way some of the preachers demanded in their fist-clenching sermons. He was a good sort, a hard worker who minded his own business and took care of his family on a limited income.

Most of the time that income came from working in the Lawrence County stone quarries. But, sometimes, when orders for cut stone declined, he got laid off from that job and had to seek work elsewhere, which he did instead of going to the unemployment compensation office in Bedford.

That's why he happened to be on a three-man Lawrence County highway crew on a scorching, humidity-soaked August in the late 1940s, clearing brush from roads out by Mount Pleasant Church in Shawswick Township.

Being the oldest, he was more or less the straw boss, a title bestowed on him by Jimmy and Freddie, the other two members of the crew. Jimmy was about thirty, a janitor when school was in session. He worked mainly to have something to do in the summer months. Freddie was nineteen, a college student who worked because he needed the money.

Abner picked them up at the general store in Heltonville each morning and headed to wherever the highway superintendent told the crew to work.

Brought up by God-fearing parents, Jimmy and Freddie had been exposed to religion ever since they were born, but that didn't stop them from being a bit irreverent from time to time.

Abner had been exposed to religion, too, a lot of it in a lot of different forms, from moderate reasoning to the fanatical. Jimmy and Freddie listened to him expound on whatever philosophy he had absorbed at prayer meetings. Some was valid, worth accepting, worth storing in the recesses of the mind. The rest was subject to debate. It gave them something to test Abner's commitment, to challenge him, to make him question what he

might otherwise accept as fact.

They did so more out of curiosity than meanness, searching themselves for whatever Abner hoped to find in his nomadic search for salvation.

The three never lost their tempers, despite discussions that were as hot as the sun that beamed down on the crushed limestone roads, bounced back up against the bills of their caps and reflected into their eyes.

The sweat ran down their bronzed faces and soaked their denim shirts. The heat parched their throats. They all believed in giving an honest hour's work for their $1.75-an-hour pay, but they rested ten minutes or so each hour to preserve their energy.

It was a day like that when Jimmy yelled to Freddie: "Sure would like a good cold beer, how about you?"

Freddie said, "Is the Pope Catholic?"

"Not me," said Abner. "That's the devil's brew."

Jimmy and Freddie didn't give up. They kept talking about the beer until Abner said, "Okay, Freddie, take my car and go get whatever you want. I'll keep track of how long you're gone and we'll work that much longer before quittin'."

Freddie was back in a few minutes, carrying a ten-quart bucket filled with ice and six Oertel's 92 bottles. He opened one, handed it to Jimmy. He opened another, and took a long drink, sighing at the taste.

The sigh didn't escape Abner. He said, "You know, boys, maybe the Good Man wouldn't care if I had one beer."

Freddie ripped open the cap, and handed a bottle to Abner. Abner took a long swig, then turned his head skyward, squinting into the sun, like maybe he was asking the Lord to forgive him.

Freddie had one more beer, but Jimmy said he thought he'd quit after the first one. Abner said there was no point in the beer going to waste. He had the other two, each time looking up to get permission.

The three talked for maybe forty-five minutes or so before returning to work. The respite actually was beneficial to the county, because the three worked harder and faster than before the break. And they stayed an hour later on the job, just like Abner said they would, despite a few complaints from Jimmy and Freddie.

They loaded their tools in the car about 5:30 and started to head back to Heltonville, when Abner stopped and said, "Pick them bottles up, Freddie. We better destroy the evidence."

He stopped at a roadside dump and pitched out the bottles, saying if his wife found them she'd kill him and the preacher would be the first to forgive her.

When Abner dropped the boys off at the store he said, "Just because I had some beer is no reason to think I've lost my religion, boys."

"We know. You were just a victim of your environment," Jimmy said.

"You're a credit to your religion," Freddie said.

Abner changed churches a few more times before finding one he stayed with. And, as Freddie said, he was a credit to all of them.

A Big Man Shows a Big Cave

Web was about seventy-five years old when a young whipper-snapper reporter from the *Bedford Times-Mail* came out to his place near Heltonville one warm day in late winter.

"Name's Duane," the newsman said.

"Name's Duane," Web repeated, before smiling and asking: "Are you sure you are a reporter? 'Name's Duane' sounds like you might be a poet."

"Reporter," Duane said, "at least I'm trying to be."

"Must not be trying too hard, or you wouldn't waste your time stoppin' here talkin' to an old man like me," Web said, teasingly. Then he asked more seriously, "What can I do for you?"

Duane said he'd been told by people in Bedford that a network of caves extended amid the limestone in eastern Lawrence County and that Web knew more about them than anyone else this side of a spelunkers' convention.

"You got some good information, son," Web admitted. "When I was a boy, me and my buddies used to almost live in them underground formations."

Duane pulled out his notebook, then had a better idea, asking Web if he'd like to show him some of the caves.

"Don't think I can today. I'm getting up in years and besides I'm feeling kinda puny. Been under the weather lately."

He saw the reporter looked disappointed, then said: "Well, I suppose I could go along if you don't walk too fast. But you can't wear them good clothes you got on. You'll ruin them where we're going."

Web took the newsman into the basement and handed him a pair of bib overalls and a pair of boots. "These will save your clothes." Duane wasn't used to such hospitality.

Web said he'd drive. "Easier than directing you," he said. He stopped the car about a mile east of Heltonville on Ind. 58, grabbed the lantern he'd brought along and told Duane where they were headed: "We're gonna cross the railroad, wade through the crick and walk up and down two hills to that high ridge you see over yonder. Then we'll go down until we find the entrance to one of the caves. You'll have to go slow 'cause I told you I ain't been feelin' well."

Then Web took off at what Duane thought was a gallop. Once in a while the reporter had to yell up ahead, just to get Web to slow down.

It took about fifteen minutes to find the mouth of the cave. Web waited another five minutes for Duane to stop huffing and puffing, then lighted the lantern and said: "Follow me."

They walked, crawled and crept maybe three hundred feet or so into the cave before the newsman said he thought that'd be far enough. Web handed him the lantern so he could lead the way out, retracing the path they'd entered through.

Outside, Web blew out the lantern and walked back up to the top of the ridge where he waved his hand southeast. "This cave goes for about seven miles in that direction. People don't

believe me when I tell 'em I've gone in this entrance and come out way over by Leesville."

But Web had made a believer of the newsman. "I believe you," Duane said.

Web said he was sorry Duane hadn't had more time so they could have gone farther into the cave.

"So am I," Duane lied.

"At least you got the feel of what it was like," Web said.

Duane nodded, wiping the mud off his borrowed boots on a piece of limestone that jutted up out of the ground.

Web drove back to his house, where Duane took off the boots and overalls.

The young reporter shook Web's hand, thanked him with sincerity and told him how much he appreciated his help.

Duane arrived back at the newspaper office just as the editor was leaving.

"Find the caves?" the editor asked.

"Sure did. Found a big cave and a bigger man," Duane said, explaining how Web had been his guide and how he managed to walk the hills and hollers.

Then he added, "Man, if he was under the weather, I'd like to see him when he was feeling good."

Jasper Lives On in the Lives of Many

You could learn a lot just watching Jasper. If you were helping him, he expected you to pay attention and to catch on fast.

He didn't like to have to explain something twice, even to a twelve-year-old. Pokey learned that the first time he tried to help Jasper after school on a barn being built for Pokey's dad on a farm near Heltonville in the early 1940s.

It was a time before power tools and electric saws. To speed up his work, Jasper measured the lengths for several boards he had to saw, writing down the lengths.

He'd tell Pokey what sizes of lumber he needed and expected him to have the boards ready to slide onto the sawhorses when he was ready to cut them. "Need three one-by-sixes," he told Pokey. Pokey strolled over to the stack of lumber and brought back three boards. Jasper reached down, blocking Pokey as he started to scoot a board onto the horses. He looked the boy in the eye.

"This is a one-by-eight. That means it's eight inches wide. I asked for a one-by-six, which means it should be six inches wide."

He then reached into his carpenter's apron for his steel tape, pulled it out to four inches and said, "This is four inches. When I say I want a one-by-four, this is what I want." Then he did the same thing at six, eight and ten inches, pointing out the widths firmly but quietly.

Pokey nodded and Jasper said, "Just pay attention, use your eyes and your head and we'll get along just fine."

Except for some occasional lessons like that, Jasper and Pokey got along well until the barn was finished.

The next summer, Jasper returned to paint the galvanized sheets on the hip roof of the barn. When he asked Pokey if he'd help, the boy looked up to the peak of the roof thirty-five feet above the ground and said, "I will, but I'm not too excited about it."

"Don't intend for you to get up on the roof," Jasper said. "What I want you to do is keep the rope I tie to the ladder anchored on the opposite side of the barn. You can tie it to the steel-tired wagon, then roll the wagon along as I paint from one end to the other."

Jasper painted from the ladder on the roof, squatting down at the top of the barn when he wanted to move the ladder. He'd yell for Pokey to untie the rope. Then he'd move the ladder where he wanted it and tell Pokey to retie it to the wagon wheel.

All went well until Pokey got careless and didn't knot the rope like he was supposed to. It let Jasper and the ladder on the roof slip down maybe eighteen inches before it caught somehow, so Pokey could reknot it the way it was supposed to be.

Jasper stuck his head up over the peak of the roof and said, "You almost let me down, boy. Remember to pay attention. Carelessness is what gets people killed." He didn't look half as scared as Pokey.

It took two days to paint the roof. Jasper had painted for several hours on the siding, working from scaffolding that stretched from one ladder to another. Pokey was moving one of the wooden ladders when he somehow stubbed his toe, letting the ladder fall

shatteringly to the ground, breaking it in two. Fortunately, Jasper was standing on the other ladder.

Jasper didn't say much, except to remind Pokey to watch what he was doing. He wasn't the kind to get excited and cuss up a storm. Instead he said, "I've got another one at home, but it's too late to get it today. I'll just bring it with me tomorrow."

Jasper took money for a new ladder, reluctantly, when Pokey's dad settled up with him after the job was done. "Pokey didn't break it on purpose," he said.

A couple of years after that, Jasper came to the farm to lay some concrete blocks for a foundation for a corn crib. Pokey had the radio in the truck turned up as loud as he could get it, listening to the World Series while he mixed mortar.

When he paid more attention to the game than he did the thickness of the mortar, Jasper told him firmly: "It's okay to enjoy yourself while you work. Just don't let it interfere with what you're doing."

It was the last advice Jasper gave Pokey, who grew up and left the farm a short time later.

Jasper stayed in the community, continuing to be the best carpenter he knew how to be. He did what he was content to do. That was to live a quiet life with his wife, Doris, on his isolated little farm at the end of the gravel road about one and a half miles north of Ind. 58.

He liked being his own man, independent and free, living an uncomplicated life.

Jasper Bowman died in 1982. But a part of him lives in Pokey and the other boys who grew to manhood remembering the things he taught them.

They Deserved Oscars for Their Daily Dramas

Some people thought Sid and Jeb disliked one another. It was an erroneous supposition.

They were just good actors when it came to joshing each other. They had perfected the art through years of practice.

They were neighbors. On the surface, that was one of the few things they had in common.

Sid was six-feet-two, rawboned, wiry, with muscle growing on muscle. He was intense, a workaholic who seldom let his mind or body rest.

Jeb was five-feet-eight and thin and the muscle he had came more by nature than through hard work. He was low-key, easy-going, seemingly unconcerned about life beyond tomorrow.

The two men farmed east of Heltonville by day and worked at the stone mill in Heltonville by night. They shared rides to work with Fritz, another neighbor. Fritz was never sure when Jeb and Sid were serious and they never gave him any clues to help him figure it out.

Besides, Fritz was an agitator. He didn't hesitate to foment what he thought would be a dispute between Sid and Jeb.

The three were among a group of men who gathered on the slabs of stone at the mill one night at supper. Fritz looked at Jeb and said, "You really think Sid ought to plow under his corn and plant it again."

Jeb looked serious. "Sure, I do. It's the sickliest-looking field I've ever seen. Looks like it has yellow jaundice."

Sid acted like he was hurt. Jeb went on, "My fields are dark-green. The plants are healthy. Guess Sid won't have the best corn in the neighborhood this year."

Sid slammed the top of his lunch bucket shut. He avoided looking at Jeb, probably to keep from laughing. He turned to Fritz and said, "Jeb's corn may look good now, but you just wait. I got 220 pounds of fertilizer to an acre in my fields. As soon as the corn starts growing and the roots get into that nitrogen my corn will overtake Jeb's."

Jeb feigned a move toward Sid, but Fritz stepped between them. Sid pushed up his sleeves. "It ain't how fast your corn takes off, it's how well it finishes," he said.

Jeb said, "We're not talking about races. We're talkin' about corn."

Sid waved his right arm and said, "You could put everything you know about farmin' in a corn flakes box."

The two men were still on stage when it was time to return to work.

When they dropped Fritz off that night, he said. "If I quit agitating you two, will you settle your differences?"

Jeb nodded, "I will."

Sid shook his head, eyed Jeb and said, "No way I'm going to get along with him."

Fritz walked toward his house, shaking his head.

Jeb and Sid retained their scowls until they drove off. Then they broke into laughter, ending another nightly performance.

The Funeral Competition Died

Death was no stranger to Heltonville. It was not, however, a daily visitor.

In a bad week in the 1930s, when the population was listed as 602 by the census bureau, no more than two people died.

Leston Jones, the mortician, never had more funerals than he could handle with care and dignity. That's why a lot of people were surprised when Tom Thurman opened a new mortuary at the west edge of town in 1939. His funeral parlor was in a nice location in a home on the south side of Ind. 58 on a bank above Leatherwood Creek.

Tad, who was about ten at the time, had heard his dad mention Thurman's name in the past. He related the news about the new funeral home at supper that night.

"How well do you know him?" Tad asked.

His father said, "Well as I know anybody. Tom and I grew up together, explored the same caves, swam in the creeks, joined in the same pranks and became good friends back years ago when we were boys."

Tad wanted to know if the two men were still good friends.

His dad nodded yes, then explained, "We haven't seen each other too much. Tom hasn't been around Heltonville much. He worked as an undertaker in Bedford, but the only time I saw him was a chance meeting now and then on the Square."

He went on for a while, talking about the things he and Thurman had done together as boys. When he stopped, Tad asked if there had ever been two funeral homes in Heltonville before. His dad said he didn't think so, then listed the men who had run the one funeral home.

Tad learned that Leston Jones had bought an existing business about ten years earlier and had operated it for about five or six years on the ground floor of the Odd Fellows Building. Then he moved it to his home down by the Baptist Church. Before that, E.O. Winklepleck, D.F. Stafford and Jeptha Newkirk, who also built coffins, were funeral directors in town. It was the first time Tad knew Winklepleck, who taught the fifth grade at Heltonville, had been an undertaker. He mentioned that to his dad, who laughed and said, "I'll bet it was a lot more peaceful being a mortician than it is teaching some ten- and twelve-year-olds."

Tad laughed, too, then became serious. "Guess since you and Mr. Thurman are good friends you'll let him handle our funeral if any of us die."

His dad, said, "No. We'll have Leston do it."

Tad looked perplexed.

His dad explained, "Leston's a friend, too. Besides, he was in business first. I don't think a man should come into town and open up a place when there's just enough business for one person."

The Thurman Funeral Home handled a few funerals in the next few years, but not many. It never became a success, closing almost unnoticed. Not because Tom Thurman wasn't a good funeral director or a good friend. It was because too many people felt the same way Tad's father did.

No Purring About Help from the Shredders

Herman lived somewhere between the past and the present.

He wasn't too far behind other farmers around Heltonville. But he hadn't caught up with them, either.

He still cut and shucked his corn in the late 1930s after mechanical pickers had appeared on neighboring farms.

Herman had been a big man, independent and powerful, but age and hard work had stooped his shoulders and forced him to ask others for help.

That's why he called one of the area farmers who owned a corn shredder and a big tractor to run it. Herman haggled a bit over the cost, which he normally. did, before telling the owner-operator: "Bring out your rig whenever the ground is frozen down a few inches. Just give me a day or two warning so I can line up some help."

It was mid-January when the tractor lumbered into Herman's barnyard, towing the shredder, a machine that looked something like a grain thresher, except that it was smaller.

The owner pulled the machine up to the barn, secured it with chocks, unhooked the tractor, then lined it up with the shredder. He unrolled a big, heavy belt and draped it over the pulleys on the tractor and shredder. He then backed up the tractor until the belt was snug without being tight.

He cranked out the blower pipe into

Illustration by Gary Varvel

an opening to the barnloft toward an area that had been cleared of hay.

By that time, the neighbors helping Herman had loaded some of the shocks onto flatbed wagons and were waiting for the shredder owner to start the operation.

He engaged the pulley on the tractor and the shredder shuddered into a constant series of motions. He stepped onto a platform, explained how he wanted the shocks unloaded and waited for a wagon to be driven up next to where he was standing.

He fed the stalks into the shredder. It stripped the ears from the stalks, letting them drop onto a conveyer that dumped them into a wagon. The stalks were chopped up and blown into the barn.

The operation went well until mid-afternoon. By then, the crew was working in harmony, wasting little motion.

Fritz, who was one of the helpers, thought things were getting a bit monotonous. When a cat rubbed against his leg, Fritz picked up the animal and set it on the platform with some stalks. He thought the shredder operator would laugh, hand back the cat and make some joking comment.

He didn't. He pushed the cat into the shredder. Its remains ended up in the hayloft.

Herman loved animals almost as much as he loved his wife. The cat's demise didn't set well with him.

"You got a whole litter of cats around here," Fritz said. "It ain't like you lost your only child."

That comment only added to Herman's blustering fury. He didn't calm down until the last shock was hauled in from the field and shredded.

After that, he always carried a cane wherever he was. Some people said it was to make his cats scat when a neighbor came near. Others said it was to whack shredder operators to make sure they were paying atttention.

Nowhere To Hide

When Bob talked, Tad, Tyke and Pokey listened. Bob was three years older . . . and six years wiser . . . than they were and what he said usually was informative. His advice wasn't always useful, though, like that he gave them one April afternoon in 1940 when they were on the way home from school at Heltonville.

Tad, Tyke and Pokey were seated in the back of Shorty White's bus talking about what they might do the next day, a Saturday. Bob turned his attention from the girl he was sitting next to and said: "If any of you have a lick of sense you'll clear out of the house as soon as you have breakfast."

Pokey, who was nine, asked, "Why is that?"

Bob winked at the girl and said, "For your own protection. If your mom is like every other farm wife around here, she'll be cleaning house, since it's the first warm Saturday in April. And she'll expect you and your sisters to help."

Sure enough, Pokey's mother announced that night the annual ritual would begin the next morning and that all the kids would be expected to help, providing they weren't old enough to

work in the fields. Pokey's dad turned down his plea to help with the plowing, telling him, "Your ma needs all the help she can get."

Pokey had an alternate plan. He helped with the chores the next morning, then told his sister, "I'm going to mosey on down to Grandma's house for a while."

Pokey would have been better off if he'd stayed at home. It turned out his grandma was smart enough to know he was trying to avoid some kind of work at home. She greeted him friendly-like, as she always did, inviting him to sit a spell and have a piece of flat chocolate cake and a glass of whole milk.

Pokey was thinking that was a lot better than working at home when his grandma said, "Glad you came by. I've got plenty of things you can help me do today."

Pokey looked like he'd swallowed a fly. Before he could reply, she told him he could help move the furniture in the bedrooms, hang the carpets on the clothesline and beat the dust out of them with the rugbeater.

When that was finished, she said it was time to empty the ticks on the beds and fill them with new straw. "Straw's in the southwest corner of the barnloft. Dig out enough until you get some that's still bright and clean," she told him.

He did as he was told, knowing when his grandma talked, she meant business. She praised him for getting the right amount of straw in the ticks, then said, "While we're at it, we'd just as well untack the big carpet in the living room, take out the old straw under it and put in new."

Pokey knew there was no need to argue—even though there hadn't been

more than twenty people in the living room in the last year and the straw beneath the carpet was still soft and cushion-like. It was like changing oil in the 1935 Chevy after driving it twenty-five miles.

At dinner, when Pokey asked the blessing, he added an aside under his breath, "Don't you think you've punished me enough, oh God, for running off from home this morning?"

God didn't answer.

That afternoon Pokey had to move more furniture, wash windows and clean out the lint from the corners of the baseboards. Just when he thought there was nothing else to do, his grandma handed him a can of black polish and a brush and ordered him to give all the stove pipes a new coat.

It was five o'clock when he finished. His grandma let him have two pieces of cake and two glasses of milk before sending him off, telling him thanks and acting sympathetic when she said, "Hope you're not too tired to do your chores."

Pokey had a lot of explaining to do at supper. He told his folks about how hard he'd worked all day.

His mom said, "Served you right, Son. Now that you're experienced, you can help us house-clean next Saturday."

Pokey's sisters just sat and smiled like they knew something he didn't.

"Didn't you get finished today?" he asked.

"We didn't start," his mother said. "We knew you'd want to be here to help."

His dad added, "And to make sure you're here, we'll put a leash on you."

Pokey said, "No need of that. I done learned you can't run away from work."

Wardy's Wealth Was Between His Ears

Wardy wore a smile like a decal. It seldom left his face, even when things went wrong, which they seldom did.

Wardy wasn't like the hellions who grew up with him in a farm neighborhood near Heltonville in the 1940s. He always seemed older than his age. He was usually working on some hobby at home when his ragamuffin friends were perpetrating Halloween pranks or gallivanting in search of fun and mischief.

Wardy wasn't a vacant youth full of himself. He turned attention from himself to others, preferring to give praise rather than to accept it.

Everybody trusted Wardy, but no one more so than his dad. That trust was evident one rainy autumn Saturday when Tad and his father decided to spend the day looking for a used car. Wardy, who had been driving for about a year, asked to go along.

The harvest was still under way on the farms, but the season had been a good one for crops. Both yield and prices were up and the income was sure to exceed the cost of production.

Wardy hadn't yet made himself comfortable in the back seat when Tad, who was about four years younger, asked, "Think you'll buy a car today?"

Wardy said, "If I can find one worth the money."

That was another thing about Wardy. He didn't spend money foolishly.

Tad said, "How much you got to spend?"

Wardy said, "No set amount." Then, without bragging, he mentioned he had a blank check signed by his father.

Tad said, "I'd expect some cockamamia from other people, but not you. Don't tell me you got a signed check and that you can write in any amount you want?"

Wardy's dad wasn't exactly poor and no one who had heard his name would reject a check he had signed.

Wardy didn't say anything. He just looked embarrassed and handed the check to Tad. Tad whistled, looked at his dad and said, "Think you'll ever trust me to buy a car with a blank check?"

His dad, enjoying the exchange, kept his eye on the road and said, "Maybe." He thought for a while, then added, "Any boy who has spent seventeen years on a farm ought to have learned enough common sense to use good judgment. Wardy's dad knows what he's doing."

World War II was still under way and quality cars were hard to find. The three checked the lots in Bedford, then drove to Bloomington, where the supply wasn't much better.

Tad pointed out two or three he thought Wardy might be interested in. Wardy examined them closely, listened to the engines, but saw none he wanted to drive home.

Tad's father said, "Just as well keep the one we have as buy any of these. Ain't no point in trading one clunker for another."

Wardy still had the check in his wallet, and a smile on his face, when he

stepped out of the car that late afternoon.

"There goes a feller who knows the value of a dollar," Tad's father said as they watched him walk down the lane to his house. "He's a good example of an educated boy."

Tad wanted to know what he meant by that. His dad said, with a wisdom he often kept to himself, "Education is thinking, and thinking is looking for yourself and seeing what's there, not what you're told is there."

Tad said, "Maybe I'd better take him along if I ever decide to buy a car."

His dad nodded in agreement.

A Harrowing Trip Just for a Bargain

Hobe's frugality brought him a lot of flak from the other farmers in the Flatwoods community southeast of Heltonville.

They razzed him, not to be mean, but to hide their envy that came when he paid cash for farm equipment and supplies they could only buy after borrowing.

"You're such a tightwad you squeak when you walk," Sharm told him one Friday afternoon in the late 1930s when they were all picking up some items at Roberts' general store.

Hobe took the razzing in the spirit of friendship with which it was tendered, then said: "Well, if I can pry my billfold open and it don't snow or sleet tonight, me and the boys are gonna drive down to English tomorrow and buy a new farm wagon."

"How come you're gonna drive all the way to English?" Jim asked. "That's sixty miles and besides you can get the same wagon in Bedford."

"To save money. Ain't no point in goin' through a middle man when I can buy it outright from the factory down there," Hobe explained.

As usual, Hobe was up the next day before the sun, awakening his two boys, Fats, twelve, and Freddie, ten.

The sun was just beginning to rise over Ben Kindred's farm when they set out in Hobe's 1932 Buick sedan.

When they reached English about 9:00 a.m., the boys moseyed around the factory while Hobe negotiated the deal. They walked up beside their dad to hear him say: "If you want that much to deliver the wagon, I'll just take it home myself."

The wagonmaster asked, "How? Behind that Buick?"

"That's right," Hobe said.

The boys helped roll the orange running gears up behind the car. The wagon had big wheels with wooden spokes running to the hubs from the outer rims, which were covered with three-inch steel rings about a half-inch thick.

Hobe used a small logging chain he carried in the car to fasten the tongue to the back bumper. Hobe told Fats to ride up front with him and Freddie to ride in the back seat to make sure the wagon was following.

Then he pulled back onto Ind. 37 and headed north over the winding road that was one turn after another. There was little traffic. Freddie was glad for that.

Each time a car went by, the wagon seemed to weave to the left toward the center of the road, missing the cars that went past by inches. He warned his dad a few times, but Hobe had both wheels on the road and appeared to be praying nothing bad would happen.

Once in a while Freddie would yell "a car wants to pass" and Hobe would steer the car to the right, giving the motorist as much room as possible. It seemed to Freddie, though, the wagon always went out toward the center of the road instead of the side.

The worst part came on the down side of hills. The tongue would slip under the bumper and the wagon looked as if it was going to run right up against the spare tire on the back of the car.

Fats was no comfort to Freddie. The temperature had dropped since morning and it was his job to wipe the frost and steam off the inside of the windshield so his dad could see to drive.

The eighteen miles to Paoli took about forty-five minutes. Motorists in town gave Hobe a wide berth as they saw him round the Orange County Courthouse there. Some shoppers stared at them.

Freddie felt uncomfortable as he rested his knees in the seat and kept his eyes on the wagon.

The terrain flattened and the road became straighter toward Orleans, into Mitchell and north toward Bedford, and the miles seemed to pass more quickly. At the bridge over White River, a motorist on the other side waited for them before starting into the bridge. Hobe honked the horn on the Buick in gratitude.

Hobe took a route through the least-traveled streets of Bedford. Except for the wagon running over the curbs and corners, nothing went wrong. They reached Ind. 58 and headed east on a road that would make Ind. 37 north of English seem straight. Cars with shoppers heading home backed up behind the wagon, but Hobe didn't speed up.

"Tell 'em to keep their shirts on," he told Freddie. Freddie knew they couldn't hear him.

Hobe pulled off the highway a couple of times to let the cars pass. That kept the other drivers from fuming too much.

Once they reached Hirscher's crossroads, it was easy going. They kept going straight on Powerline Road, leaving Ind. 58 for its 90-degree left turn toward Heltonville. There was no more traffic, although the wagon ran into the side-ditch a few times.

Back at the farm, Fats jumped out of the car and opened the farm gate so Hobe could drive through. When he pulled the wagon up beside the barn, it was about 3:00 p.m.

As they unhooked the wagon, Hobe said, "Expect you boys are hungry as I am." Both nodded.

Freddie said, "But I won't be able to eat anything until I get my heart out of my mouth."

"I won't be able to until my hands thaw," Fats said, still holding the rag he'd used to keep the windshield clear.

"I won't, either, until I get my fingers straightened out," Hobe said, holding up both hands to show how they had cupped as he had gripped the steering wheel of the Buick.

Squaring Things to a T as Easy as A, B, C, or D

A boy could learn more than woodworking in the shop classes Loren Raines taught. Raines was the industrial arts teacher. He was the principal. And he taught a Bible literature class. If that wasn't enough, he was a preacher who ministered to a congregation in Bedford on Sundays.

Students in high school could elect whether to take the Bible literature class. But the seventh-grade boys had no choice about woodworking shop. It was required.

Their apprehension about taking a class taught by a preaching principal was understandable. Most of them had a special vocabulary to use when they hit their thumbs with a hammer. The words weren't the kind they'd want Raines to hear.

Most of them had little to be concerned about, it turned out. Bogey and a couple of other students were the exceptions.

Classes usually were easy for Bogey. When he didn't get an A he got a B and seldom if ever a C. He thought he was just about the smartest student in class. But he soon learned his ability to cope with reading, arithmetic, geography and history had little to do with what he was expected to accomplish in shop.

Raines spent the first few class sessions explaining the tools the students would be using. He showed them how to tighten the vices without harming the wood, adjust the planes, drill holes and use the saws. Then he handed each of them rough pieces of boards about three inches wide, six inches long and an inch thick.

"I want each of you to plane and square these pieces. Your first grade will depend on how well you do that," he said with all the seriousness he used in his sermons.

He showed them how to start on a flat surface, using it to square each of the sides and ends later, plus the bottom side.

Students like Hubert and Gordy, who seldom made good grades, quickly squared the top, then the side, then the end of the board. In the meantime, Bogey struggled.

He planed and sweated, sweated and planed, stewed and fretted. It took him three days to square a flat side for the top. Then he struggled even longer to get the side squared. He'd plane a few minutes, take the board and the square to Raines. Raines would hold the square against the top, then point out the gap on the edge of the board, saying, "You don't have it square yet."

Bogey placed the board back in the vice and planed some more. Meantime, Hubert and Gordy had finished their boards and gone on to another project.

Bogey began to lose sleep at night, realizing for the first time some students could do things better than he could. Days passed before he mentioned his problem in the class to his dad.

"You're trying too hard," his dad said. "All of us have things we can do better than others. And all of us have things we can't do as well as others. Just because you're having trouble doesn't mean you're a failure. Just relax. Someday you'll get the hang of it and you'll wonder why you were so concerned."

A couple of days later, Raines issued his first grades in the class. He gave Bogey a D. He gave Hubert and Gordy each an A. Bogey smiled when they showed him their grades. It would have been easier for him to cry.

A couple of days later, he finally finished the board. It was difficult to tell who was the most relieved, Bogey or the teacher. Raines handed him another board. "See how quickly you can square this one," he said.

Bogey squared the board in less than an hour. Raines looked pleased.

Bogey never did catch up with Hubert and Gordy, but by the end of the semester he had improved his grade to a B. And he had learned you don't have to always be better in everything than everyone else.

Soapsuds Signal of Week's Start

To Molly, cleanliness was next to Godliness, even if it caused her to work like the devil. Molly and the other farmwives who lived in the rural area around Heltonville in the 1930s and 1940s treated dirt as a sin to be washed away each Monday.

The odds were with the dirt, but it never won. The women could have looked at the handicap they faced each wash day and thrown the dirty towels back into the hamper and given up. But they never did. Especially Molly.

She didn't dwell on the fact there was no electricity in the house, no water heater, no running water, no pushbutton washer and no tumble-dryer.

She just did what she had to do, the way she had to do it even on cold winter days.

Molly was a wisp of a woman who converted every ounce of her 110 pounds into a bundle of perpetual motion that generated what energy she needed from 5:00 a.m. until 9:00 p.m. or later each day. She wouldn't have had it any other way, even though her husband, Fritz, and her five youngsters could have survived with less care and attention, and clothes that weren't quite so clean.

At least that's what they told her each Monday when they helped her prepare to do the laundry. The preparation started almost as soon as Molly and Fritz were awake. As soon as Fritz brought a few embers to life in the potbellied stove in the living room, he started a fire with kindling and corncobs in the kitchen range.

Then he rousted his two boys, Pokey and Joey, telling them: "You boys pump the wash water out of the cistern and fill the kettles while I start a fire under each one."

Molly always told them to wait until she wiped each of the black kettles free of dirt and dust. The kettles held about fifty gallons each, and the boys made endless trips, each carrying two three-gallon buckets.

By the time the kettles were filled and the fire blazing under them, Molly had breakfast ready. She always thanked them for their effort, never forgetting to mention to the boys it

was nice of them to have stacked enough scrap lumber and broken tree branches to keep the fire going most of the day.

Molly waited until Fritz left for his job at the stonemill and the kids for school before she started the washing. The water would be boiling by then, and that's how she liked it.

She restarted the gasoline engine on the Maytag, which Fritz had warmed up and filled with gasoline and oil before he left. Then she carried water from one kettle, dumping it into the big tub on the washer. When it was about two-thirds full, she measured out the right amount of soap powder, then dropped in the clothes that had been pre-sorted. She pulled the lever on the side of the washer, starting the agitator inside.

While that batch of clothes was washing, she refilled the big kettle, put overalls and other denims in the other kettle and stirred them around a few times with a big paddle to make sure they were properly soaked. She washed them last.

Once the clothes had washed in the washer, she ran them through the ringer and folded them into a big pan. She then drained the tub on the washer, letting the water run down a little trench beside the washhouse. She refilled it with hot water, started

another load of clothes and carried the first batch to the clothesline, which she cleaned by holding a cloth on it and walking from one end to the other.

If the wind and rain bothered her, she didn't let on. Sometimes the wind bounded over the hill to the north, dropping the temperature so quickly the clothes would freeze before they dried, leaving ice cracking as the overalls swayed back and forth.

Molly didn't stop until the clothes were washed and hung out to dry, and still her work wasn't finished. She had to remove the clothes from the line, fold them and dampen them down. Ironing would have to wait until tomorrow.

Molly always managed to finish in early afternoon, giving her time to have supper ready at 5:30. That was when Fritz would complain about how rough things were at work, Pokey and Joey gripe about how much work their teachers had given them and the three girls moan about how cold Shorty White's school bus was in the winter.

Sometimes one of them would remember to ask Molly how the washing went. She always smiled, like she had been sitting inside all day reading a love story, and said, "Fine."

But life was never much of a problem, for her.

By Their Sports, Ye Shall Know Them

Tad might never have become a baseball fan if the preacher hadn't come to dinner that October Sunday in 1938.

The preacher was a friendly man, but Tad, being eight years old, didn't feel comfortable around anyone with whom he had to watch his manners as well as his language.

And besides that, the preacher said long prayers and preached half-hour sermons full of hell-fire and damnation. That made Tad feel guilty, even though he'd never done anything worse than snitch an apple from a basket outside a grocery store in Bedford.

Tad's mom didn't spare any effort to provide a bountiful dinner for the preacher, trying her best to prove to him she was the best cook in the Mundell Church congregation southeast of Heltonville. It was the noon meal, but farm people called it dinner, mainly because it was the biggest meal of the day and much more than a lunch.

The pastor was impressed, saying it was the biggest dinner he'd ever sat down to, but he often used exaggeration to stress a point. The minister prayed a long time, explaining there was so much food it took a while to bless it all. Tad's mother just kind of laughed and acted a bit flustered at all the attention.

Tad noticed it took longer than usual to eat dinner. That was because all the kids were minding their manners, which they seldom otherwise did.

After dinner, Tad's mother sent the men into the sitting room, keeping Tad's sisters to help with the dishes.

Tad sat in on the conversation between his dad and the preacher for a half-hour or so, before figuring there were better ways to spend the afternoon.

That's when he sneaked through the door into the living room, turned on the big console radio powered by a dry cell battery, and twisted the dial until he found some excitement. The excitement was the play-by-play of the fourth game of the World Series between the Chicago Cubs and the New York Yankees.

The Yanks were leading when the announcers gave the score at the end of the third inning. They had scored three runs in the bottom of the second off Bill Lee, who won 22 games for the Cubs during the season.

In the top of the fourth inning, the Cubs scored one run off pitcher Red Ruffing, who had beaten Chicago 3-1 in the series opener. The Yanks scored again in the sixth.

Chicago came back with two more runs in the eighth to cut the margin to 4-3. But that ended the Cubs' hopes.

The Yanks, with hitters like Frank Crosetti, Tommy Heinrich, Joe DiMaggio, Lou Gehrig and Bill Dickey in the middle of the batting order, ripped into Cubs pitching in the eighth inning, scoring four runs before Dizzy Dean, a name Tad knew, came in to get the final out.

The Yankees won, 8-3, to sweep the series.

After Tad had turned off the radio and walked back into the sitting room, the minister looked up and asked: "Cubs lose again?" Tad nodded.

The minister said, "I'm a Cub fan, but you can't beat a powerhouse like New York with singles hitters like Stan

Hack, Billy Herman, Phil Cavaretta and Joe Marty. I thought Lee or Charlie Root would win at least one game, though.

"Too bad Diz is over the hill. He would have won two games if he was still as good as he was in 1934. If he had been, though, the Cardinals would never have traded him."

The minister talked more about baseball until he noticed how surprised Tad look. Tad hadn't expected a minister to know that much about baseball. The surprise showed.

"Just because I'm a minister doesn't mean I can't like sports," the preacher said. "You ought to see me at some basketball games. Then again, maybe you shouldn't."

From that point on, Tad was both a fan of baseball, and of the preacher.

A Brief Trip to Unconventionalism

Young people seemed to understand Hardy better than the older folks did. Maybe they were more tolerant when his behavior was unconventional, or at least unusual to the people who lived around Heltonville.

Hardy was in the Navy in World War II. He was discharged a few months after the war was over and joined the 52-20 Club. The 52-20 wasn't really a club. It was a title made up by veterans who were eligible to draw $20 a week for 52 weeks, money the government said would help them adjust to civilian life while finding jobs. Hardy drew the money for a time, then took a job as a school-bus driver early in 1946.

He was just a few years older than some of the high school students who boarded his bus each morning, but he was a lot more experienced in life than they were. The boys who knew Hardy were excited when they learned he would drive the bus on the junior-senior trip to Madison in late April. They knew he would make the trip eventful, if not unforgettable.

They weren't disappointed.

Hardy and the students were models of decorum en route to Madison that Saturday morning. Miss Clark, a teacher who was the junior class sponsor, couldn't have been happier with their behavior.

The thirty or so students in the two classes had lunch at Clifty Falls State Park, tramped along some of the trails and enjoyed the scenery until mid-afternoon. It was then Hardy suggested maybe they ought to drive into Madison for "some ice cream and other refreshments." Miss Clark thought that sounded like a good idea, but she didn't know what "refreshments" Hardy had in mind.

He parked the bus and suggested maybe some of the students might want to walk across the Ohio River bridge into Kentucky "just to say you've been there." Some of them headed for the ice cream parlor, others toward Kentucky. Hardy whispered to some of the boys that he'd catch up with them on the bridge.

No one noticed where he went, but in a few minutes he walked toward the center of the bridge, said, "huddle around me, boys," pulled a pint of whiskey from a sack and took a swig.

"Anybody want a snort?" he asked. Nobody refused, figuring the fire in the whiskey would be less painful than the verbal jabs if the offer was refused.

Not even Hardy had enough to drink, though, to feel much effect from the alcohol. But Hardy had a good imagination and his power of suggestion made the boys feel more under the influence than they really were.

When all the students were aboard the bus, Hardy drove west on Ind. 256. By the time he reached Austin, he was in good form, leading the boys who had sipped the liquor in rendition after rendition of "Sioux City Sue." The more he saw Miss Clark's frown in the mirror, the louder he sang. He threw in a few jokes, none too off-color, to break up the music, then bellered "San Antone" from time to time just to add to the torment.

Miss Clark didn't say anything until the bus slowed down as it went through Crothersville. She said plenty, then, reading the riot act to Hardy, who had once been one of her students.

Hardy listened, said, "Yes, ma'am," and drove on toward Uniontown and Brownstown. His conduct was exemplary the rest of the trip. And he carried on an intelligent conversation about his experiences in the South Pacific.

The boys forgot "Sioux City Sue" and started talking to the girls on the bus.

Miss Clark forgot about how Hardy had carried on and thanked him for a nice trip when she deboarded back at the school.

Any thought she may have had about reporting Hardy to the principal or the township trustee had disappeared from her mind.

Eddie Wins More than Blue Ribbon

Eddie was a good kid who turned out all right despite his environment. He had a good home, the undivided attention of his parents and many of the best things in life. But with the help of friends he managed to overcome those handicaps.

Eddie was an only child. That set him apart from most of the kids who grew up around the Flatwoods community southeast of Heltonville in the late 1930s. Most of them came from big families, some so big it was difficult to remember the names of all the brothers and sisters.

Eddie lived in a nice house with running water and an indoor toilet. Most of the other houses weren't too nice and very few had indoor plumbing.

Eddie didn't have to worry about farm chores. About the closest he came to a field was a little work in the garden now and then. All the other kids had regular farm duties they had to do before starting on their homework.

The only old clothes Eddie had to wear were his own. And they were store-bought. The other kids had to wear hand-me-downs, which usually had been homemade, from older brothers and sisters.

Eddie always had a nickel or dime

in his pocket. A lot of the other kids didn't know what a nickel or dime were.

Despite all these advantages, or disadvantages, Eddie got along well with the other youngsters in Miss Hunter's third grade class—except for one occasion late in the school year.

It was April and the thoughts of the pupils were more on the summer vacation that would start in a few weeks than on the assignments Miss Hunter gave them. Realizing this, she agreed to compromise. If they would keep their minds on their studies for four days, she would let them relax on the fifth. They could, she suggested, bring something they had built, or drawn, or designed, or sewn, or stitched or grown to class on Friday and tell the others about whatever it might be.

"I'll give a blue ribbon to the best presentation." Some of the kids had to ask what a presentation was.

It was an offer the pupils couldn't refuse. They behaved well. Miss Hunter did as she promised, telling the youngsters on Thursday afternoon to bring in their handiwork the next day.

Barbie brought in a doll made of corn husks, Billy a peashooter he had made from an elderberry branch, Joey a bow and arrow he had fashioned from a hickory bush, Margie a pot holder, Julie a molded handprint, Betty a quilt for a doll bed, and . . .

Nobody was impressed until Eddie walked in from the school bus carrying a bird house. It was about eighteen inches square and was made of little pieces of limbs, each uniform in size and each trimmed of bark. The pieces were attached to upright pieces, also trimmed. The pieces were joined with little finishing nails, driven straight, and the ends of each were beveled at the same angles. The bird house was divided into four sections, each section having a perfectly round hole for a bird to enter. Miss Hunter was impressed. So were Eddie's classmates. Jealously so. There was no doubt who would get the blue ribbon, and Eddie won it as expected.

He toted the bird house back on Lobie White's bus that afternoon, sat down as usual beside his friend Tyke and tied the ribbon around one of the miniature logs.

"You didn't deserve that," Tyke told him, pointing to the ribbon. "Your grandpa made that bird house, didn't he?"

Eddie didn't say yes or no. He just looked hurt like he sometimes did when he couldn't have his way. He didn't say anything all the way home.

The next Monday, Eddie had the blue ribbon in his hand when he got on the bus.

"Gonna give it back," he told Tyke.

As soon as the first bell rang, Eddie walked up to Miss Hunter's desk like a man and said loudly enough for the entire class to hear: "I didn't make the bird house, Miss Hunter. My grandfather did. It isn't fair for me to have this." He handed the ribbon to her and walked back to his desk.

Miss Hunter took the ribbon, followed Eddie, looked down at him and said: "You've just won something that will last longer than this ribbon. And that's your own self-respect."

Eddie had more fun the rest of the year than he'd ever had before. And more friends.

Entertaining— and True, Too

It was Pokey's own fault no one believed him that Monday when he told the class the tale of the whale.

Pokey normally handled the truth about like he did life. Recklessly.

He wasn't really bad for a ten-year-old. He was never malicious or mean. He just believed in carrying fun to its outer limits and sometimes beyond.

And he was a storyteller who never let reality get in the way of his imagination. That's why all the kids in E.O. Winklepleck's fifth grade class at Heltonville kind of snickered when he told them about the whale he'd seen at Seymour over the weekend that fall in about 1940.

Most of the class had seen Pokey excited, but never as excited as when he related that experience. The words jumped from his mouth and his eyes danced and his arms waved in a flow of emotion. Ordinarily, Mr. Winklepleck would have tried to calm down Pokey, but he too may have been caught up in the drama the youngster was describing.

Pokey went on, "Like I said, Dad took Mom, me and the rest of the kids to Seymour yesterday to see this whale and some other sea animals that were on exhibition.

"They were on railroad cars parked on a siding about two blocks from downtown. Man, was there ever a crowd there. We had to park 'bout three blocks away, then stand in line for twenty-five to thirty minutes."

Some of the girls in class were cupping their mouths with their hands to keep from laughing at what they thought was another big yarn.

"Cost fifteen cents a person to get on the railroad cars. Dad said that was a lot of money, but it probably would be the only chance landlubbers like us would ever have to see a whale."

He looked at Mr. Winklepleck, who nodded for him to go on.

"Well, we finally got to see the whale. It was dead, of course, and it didn't smell too good. But we sure got a good chance to look it over.

"Mom and· my sisters left in a hurry, holding their noses. But Pa, my brother and me just hung around and listened to the information about that big old fish.

"Man who was doing the talkin' said the whale was a black whale and was fifty-three feet long and weighed thirty-seven tons."

Gordon, who thought he knew about everything there was to know about the life that occupied the land and the sea, said, "Sounds like a big fish story to me. Did Jonah jump out of the whale's mouth while you were there?"

Pokey didn't let that bother him. He smiled and said, "He did that a long time ago. Shows how far you are behind the times."

Pokey took a lot of kidding the rest of the day.

The next morning when Mr. Winklepleck arrived at school, he posted some information about whales on the board. It said black whales grew up to sixty feet in length and could weigh fifty tons or so. And one of the girls who liked Pokey brought in a newspaper that had the story about the whale in Seymour. It turned

out everything Pokey had said was true.

When the other students told him they were sorry they doubted him, he just shrugged his shoulders and said, "Hope this doesn't ruin my reputation as a storyteller."

Horses Dressed to the Nines, Seth the Twos

Horses had been a part of Seth's life for more than four decades. That's why he kept a team into the 1940s, long after most other farmers around Heltonville had traded their draft horses for tractors.

Seth treated his horses as well as he did his sons, better at times, they complained, jokingly. He brushed and curried "Dolly" and "Molly" morning and night and made sure they had their quota of oats, corn and hay, adding a special treat of sugar if they'd been in harness for hours.

The harness was the horses' work clothes and Seth made sure it was always in good repair. Each March he would lift the harness from the pegs where it had been stretched, lay it on the gangway of the barn and examine each piece, marking where repairs were needed.

He took care to fix each worn section, using rivets to splice the leather. Once the repairs had been made, he oiled the harness with a compound that contained neat's foot oil, oil of turpentine, petrolatum and lampblack. He worked the oil into the leather, making it pliable and soft. Hard, rigid leather could rub a horse's hide raw, causing sores that wouldn't heal for days.

Seth waited until the oil had soaked into the leather to put the harness on the horses. Once the bridles were on each horse and the harness buckled in place, Seth shined the knobs on the hames until they gleamed. He checked out the traces, wiped off the oil from the chains, then hooked them in place.

Most farmers would have stopped there. But not Seth, not one March in the early 1940s. He pulled out two red tassels he had bought a few days before and tied them on the reins. He then added some glistening brass ornaments to the harness. He took out his red handkerchief and tied in on the lines that led from one horse to the other.

When he was finished with the decorating, he stepped back to admire his work.

Clem, a neighbor, stopped by about that time. He walked up to Seth's side, took a long look at the horses and said: "Reckon that's about the best lookin' team I've seen since the Jackson County Fair last August."

Seth smiled and said, "Thanks, Clem."

Clem said, "Just kinda curious, though. How come you spend so much time making Dolly and Molly look so good? They'll work just as well without all them decorations."

Seth had heard the same comments before. "Horses need someone to keep them well-groomed and looking clean and neat. They can't take care of themselves," he said.

Clem took a long look at Seth, put his hand to his mouth and smirked. Seth was wearing faded overalls. Patches had been sewed on patches to cover holes at the knees. He had stuck a No. 6 nail on the bib to hold a gallus in place. Each of his rubber boots had broken buckles. His felt hat showed the grime of winter.

Seth caught the humor Clem had seen. "Never said I could take care of myself. Soon as I unharness these horses, I'm going up to the house and tell the wife that she'd better start dressing me as well as I dress my horses."

Clem knew he was kidding. Seth would never be happy dressed up as well as his horses.

Seasons of Change

For a youngster growing up in Southern Indiana during the 1930s and '40s, change (often called progress) was a bittersweet fact of life—a template laid over the changing blueprint of the seasons. Change was not, for the most part, intimidating, maybe because it came in imperfect lurches, something like a square stone wheel that gradually had to have its corners knocked down. There was some time to get used to new notions before they were quite refined.

The miracle of air transportation first came as a barnstorming pilot with a small airplane whose rudimentary engine sounded like a lawn mower, then as World War II fighter planes from a nearby airfield, and then made an emergency landing as one of Lockheed's first jets. Sometimes change brought plain joy— as when a farmer snapped on the lights in his newly electrified home.

These were notions people had to come to grips with. Less apparent but perhaps more difficult to deal with in the long run were the changes that came in on quiet feet, like the erosion of the beauty of a favorite natural place, the abandonment of a home where ten children were reared, the passing of a one-room schoolhouse.

There were plenty of reminders that change was not a one-way street, but a "mixed bag" with a price. Sometimes these were small reminders, a cat accidentally digested by a powered corn-shredder. Occasionally there were tragedies, like the foreclosure of property of an old farm couple.

As a result, Hoosiers have come to an uneasy accommodation to change that exists to this day. Just because they like to tinker doesn't mean they buy into the notion that all change is progress.   —MN

Devil's Backbone: Nature's Stability

It's no sin to walk along Devil's Backbone and enjoy the view. Never has been. Never will be.

Devil's Backbone was created with the universe, left there eons ago for those who appreciate the marvels of nature.

Tad was maybe eight years old when he made his first trip to the "Bone," accompanying his dad on the ten-mile trip from their farm near Heltonville. His dad thought the spot was something special. Tad wasn't impressed.

He made other trips before gasoline-rationing and World War II brought an end to leisurely drives. He never fully appreciated its beauty, always wondering why his dad thought visitors who came to their house would be interested in seeing it. He was amazed when they were.

"Ain't nothing special," Tad said one Saturday in April as he and his dad and Jim, a visiting friend, looked south across the bottoms to the north and to the south.

"It's special, all right, son," his dad

said, eyes glinting˙ as he looked into the spring sun. "You can never appreciate the world until you can appreciate the things around you."

Jim nodded, then said: "This may not be as exciting as catching frogs or playing mumblety-peg to you now. Didn't mean much to me, either, when I was a boy."

Jim waited for Tad to say something, which he didn't, then went on: "Now it means a lot. I just like to come up here on the ridge and enjoy the view and the stillness." He waved his arms to the north, then to the south, to emphasize his point.

Devil's Backbone was really a narrow ridge crossed by a graveled Lawrence County road. There were bluffs on each side, dropping maybe three hundred feet almost straight down. To the north, in Guthrie Township, Guthrie Creek snaked through a valley of rich, flat farmland, turning west at the bluff, seeking an escape into White River. To the south, at the bottom of the bluff, was the river, forming a crescent at the base of Devil's Backbone. Across the river, in Bono Township, lay more farmland, rich with silt left when the river ebbed after its frequent floods.

Tad's father and Jim talked about the richness of the land and the hazards of the floods. Tad listened, still not convinced there was anything special about the view.

On the way home, Jim turned from his passenger seat in front of the car to Tad in the back and said, "People may change. The things they make may change. But the things nature makes don't change. Chances are Devil's Backbone will be the same forty or fifty years from now as it is now. Come back then and see for yourself."

"By then you may appreciate it more," his dad said.

Years later, Tad was enjoying the solitude of his own company one day when he turned off U.S. 50, went through Leesville, and checked a map to make sure he remembered the route before heading toward Devil's Backbone.

The winding route, now paved, had not changed. Neither had the view, either to the north or to the south. The bottomland looked cleaner, cleared of brush and fences to expand the fields. In the stillness, the soft-flowing sound of the river rose to the top of the bluff, giving no hint of a force that days earlier had flooded the bottoms. Along the river's bank, the sun glanced off the shiny rails of the old Baltimore & Ohio tracks that led to and from the tunnels downstream.

Tad figured he was fortunate to have come when he did. In a few weeks, the trees would be filled with leaves, obstructing the view until late fall.

He walked along the road, looking both north and south, realizing at last why his dad thought it was a good place to visit. The problems of the world seemed far away. His dad and Jim would have liked that.

They wouldn't have liked the debris dumped along Devil's Backbone by others who never realized its beauty. Tad noticed the roll of rusted wire, the broken screen door, the plastic bottles, the used bricks and the cardboard boxes left there as a monument to man's insensitivity to the wonders of nature.

He wished he could tell his dad and Jim they had been right about the place.

He was grateful he couldn't tell them about the litter.

Thirty Seconds over Heltonville

It was a day like no other day, that day when the jet age came to Heltonville. It came from out of the sky as a Shooting Star, a P-80 Lockheed jet, skidded to a stop on Floyd Johnson's place out where Groundhog Road joined Powerline Road.

It was big news that fall Sunday in 1946, especially to youngsters around town, who had watched propeller-driven PT-26's from Freeman Field at Seymour fly over during the last two years of World War II. Many of them had daydreamed about becoming pilots themselves, wondering what it would be like to soar above the clouds in pursuit of the enemy.

The war had ended a year before and the PT-26's all but disappeared from the skies over Jackson and Lawrence counties. But youngsters like Don, Pokey, Bogey, Bog and Chig still paid attention to the aviation news and knew that jets like the Lockheed P-80 had been forced to land. The boys were all in Heltonville that afternoon, figuring out whether to watch the paint peel on the post office or watch the water run under the humpback bridge over Leatherwood Creek. Someone stopped by, shouting that a plane was down.

They ran to the cars they drove even though they weren't old enough to have licenses. The wheels on the cars tossed gravel as they sped uphill, but the noise didn't hide the excitement in their voices.

They envied the Johnson boys, who went to Shawswick to school, and Cecil Miller, who lived on an adjoining farm but attended school in Heltonville. "Cecil must have had a front-row seat," Pokey said, "All the girls at school will be asking him about it tomorrow."

They saw the crowd before they reached the entrance to the quarter-mile drive up to the Johnson house. They had to get up closer to see the plane.

By the time they arrived, authorities had sealed off the area around the plane and they couldn't climb over and into it as they'd hoped they could.

A farmer who lived nearby said, "Never knew government workers could move so fast. Man, they roared in here in nothing flat."

The plane was a few hundred feet from the farm house and except for some damage to the bottom of the fuselage, it looked none the worse for the experience.

"What happened?" asked Pokey.

"Flameout," Cecil said, hands in his overall pockets.

Pokey looked unknowing.

Don said, "Means the flame went out and there was nothing to power the jet-propulsion engine, which happens to be an Allison J33-A-9. Made in Indianapolis." Don knew a lot about planes, even though he was just sixteen.

"What happened to the pilot?" one of the boys asked, and was told by a bystander who had become an instant expert: "He's okay, probably changin' his pants. But don't 'spect him to talk. These planes are so daggone new the govamint don't want infermation about them to get out."

The boys stayed around until they made sure the plane wouldn't be left unguarded, then headed back toward town.

The next day, "govamint" workers came to the farm, dismantled the plane and hauled it away.

None of the boys paid much attention after that when a prop plane went over. But they kept an eye in the sky for the new jet fighters.

Snaring Customers with Freebies

Jim never left for Bedford on a Saturday morning without Flossie reminding him: "Remember to pick up the glassware when you stop at the Spur station to get gasoline." Then she'd tell him what item she wanted him to select.

Jim knew exactly what Flossie was talking about. He had picked up enough saucers, plates, cups and glasses from filling stations in Bedford to fill a china closet.

Almost every station in Bedford gave the items as premiums for each five gallons of gasoline. Competition required them to do so. There were about forty places in town where a motorist could buy gasoline in 1940 and each tried to outdo the other.

The Spur station on North "I" Street up by the Chicago, Milwaukee & St. Paul Railroad tracks went even further. It would fill gasoline tanks for one dollar on Saturdays. And if the drivers had time, they could get tires inflated, the oil checked, the floor board vacuumed and the windows cleaned.

Jim was as eager as the next motorist to get the free service. He just didn't like to wait for it. That's why he sometimes showed displeasure when the service took longer than he thought it should.

The wait, though, did give him a chance to look over the display of tableware on display at the station and to select the piece Flossie had asked him to pick up.

He was pleased when he returned to his home near Heltonville one Saturday and Flossie announced, "This teacup will give us a complete set of six cups, saucers and dishes."

Jim muttered, softly to himself, "Thank goodness."

Flossie didn't hear him. "Bogey is spending the night with Alex so he'll be here for supper. I'll just use them then," she said. Alex, who was ten, was their son.

Flossie was proud of the table settings that night. Alex could see she was. He thought he would make her feel even better by asking Bogey, "What do you think about Mom's fancy new dishes?"

Bogey picked up his cup which hadn't been filled with cocoa yet, eyed it carefully, and said: "It looks like the same kind we got at the Spur station in Bedford."

Bogey didn't know why Alex was kicking him under the table, but he didn't say any more. Flossie's face turned redder than the beets on the table. Jim stifled a laugh.

Alex was embarrassed for his mother. But not as embarrassed as Bogey was when Alex explained why he had kicked him.

Big-Time Money

To a college freshman who wanted to make big money over summer vacation in 1948, the ad in the *Bedford Times-Mail* almost leaped off the page: "Detroit auto maker seeks workers. Good pay. Apply at state employment office."

"That'll beat hauling baled hay, cutting brush for the highway department or picking tomatoes," he told himself. Within an hour he had lined up two friends willing to leave Lawrence County for Motor City.

A man at the employment office asked a couple of questions to see if the youths had all their faculties, said, "You fellas will do just fine," and told them to report to Detroit Monday. "The Hudson Motor Car Co. will want you," he said.

That was Saturday morning. The three spent the rest of the day jawing the possibility of how much money they might make. Most of the night was spent telling anyone who'd listen that they were heading to Michigan, the Big D, auto capital of the world.

Next morning it took them thirty seconds each to round up what clothes they had and about three hours to convince their parents they were good credit risks for some "starter funds."

About 11:00 a.m. they figured it was time to start Donnie's '39 Ford and head north. The V-8 was perking well and the three were in good spirits as they neared Greenville, Ohio, on U.S. 127. That's when a big brown Lincoln came off a rural road without slowing to look at a big red stop sign. Tin, chrome and steel tangled in a wrestling match that left both cars in a ditch.

The three youths checked their conditions and found themselves dazed but almost unscarred. The same went for the driver of the other car and his wife.

That night the youths stayed in a Greenville hotel. They left the next morning for Detroit by Greyhound.

It was midafternoon when they arrived with their worn, brown suitcases at the Hudson plant. "Here come some more little ole Southern boys to help the big city," a big dude laughed as the youths reported to the personnel office.

"Report at Gate 7, 6:30 a.m. tomorrow. Ready to work. Don't be late," said a man in the office.

That night, they found rooms in a house that should have been condemned when Detroit was still a trading post. The rooms were cheap. And dirty, noisy and hot.

The work on a preassembly paint line was easy for the country boys. So easy, in fact, that they got all their work done in the first two hours. That caused the foreman to get a message from the union steward to tell "those young punks" to slow down.

It didn't take long for the three to decide the slow work pace they were ordered to follow, the smell of the city, and the confinement of their rooms were not worth the money.

Four weeks later, they were once again aboard a big Greyhound, this time heading south. They agreed hauling baled hay would seem a pleasure.

First Experience with Crime

G.E. liked his younger brothers almost as well as he did his car and his latest girlfriend. That's why he invited them to ride into Bedford one Saturday night in the summer of 1940.

It would be the first encounter with crime for Tad and Tyke, who were eleven and twelve at the time.

G.E. had a two-year-old 1937 V-8 Ford coupe which he kept immaculate. He had a cover on the steering wheel, which had a spinner knob. A squirrel's tail adorned the antenna.

The chrome shone in the street lights and the paint glistened from hours of polishing. Reflectors on the mudflaps glowed in the beams of headlights.

G.E. parked the V-8 on "J" Street, helped his date from the car and told Tad and Tyke, "We'll meet you after the picture show," pointing toward the Lawrence Theater, which always had a double-feature starring celluloid cowboys like Gene Autry and Roy Rogers.

"You can stop for a milk shake or Coke after the movie, if you don't spend all your money on popcorn at the show," he added.

Tad wanted to know what G.E. and his girlfriend would be doing in the meantime. G.E. ignored the question. The girl smiled, like she was expecting a good time.

The movies lasted about three hours and Tad and Tyke spent another twenty minutes at a malt shop, debating whether to have a chocolate or cherry Coke.

They spotted G.E. and his date at the corner of "J" and 15th Street and walked with them toward where they had parked the car.

G.E. was the first to notice the car was gone. "Somebody has stolen it," he said with the same manner he would have shown had Tad and Tyke been kidnapped.

They walked back to the corner, where the policeman was talking to a taxi driver. G.E. reported the theft. The policeman took all the information about the car and said, "Suspect somebody took it for a joy ride. We'll find it, but probably not tonight. Chances are it'll be damaged when we do."

That comment didn't add to G.E.'s happiness.

Tad looked at Tyke and asked, "Wonder how we're going to get home?" Their folks had no telephone and most of the other people who had come into Bedford from around Heltonville had already left for home.

G.E. walked to the cab stand, asked the price for a cab ride twelve miles east, and let out a loud whistle. He thought for a moment and said, "OK. We don't have any other choice."

The four climbed into the cab, Tyke nudging Tad into the front seat, then following him. He was smart enough to know that G.E.'s disposition would improve if he and his date had the back seat to themselves.

The boys gave the driver directions to their farm. When he pulled up to the gate he said, "Like I said, this'll be six dollars." The figure sounded like the national budget to the boys.

G.E. said, "I'll have to go in and borrow some money from my dad."

He looked embarrassed for having to admit that in front of his date.

The boys waited for him to return. He handed the driver the money, held the keys to his dad's car in his hand and told his date he'd drive her home.

The next morning at breakfast, their father said, "Never had a car stolen, myself."

G.E. said, smiling, "Who wants a car that's coated with an inch of dust and no chrome, no radio, no mudflaps?"

His dad said, "You did last night, remember?"

G.E. stammered and said, "I remember. And I remember I have a date tonight . . . if I can use your car again."

His dad agreed. G.E. spent that Sunday washing it.

His car was found a few days later in Bedford. It was undamaged, except for some wear and tear.

G.E. was happy to have his car back. And his dad was happy to have *his* car back.

"Forbidden Movie" Not That Thrilling

Young people from around Heltonville started going to the Von Ritz theater when they learned there was more to life than cowboys and horses. The Westerns were seen on the screen at the Lawrence Theater down on "J" Street.

The Von Ritz showed big-budget motion pictures that won Academy Awards and starred actors and actresses whose pictures crowded the pages of movie magazines.

It was a place where teenagers took girls on their first dates and where the midnight movie that started at 11:00 p.m. each Saturday was a social event.

Some of the older fellas who had been dating longer said the best seats were in the back row of the theater, but the youngsters didn't yet know why.

There was a touch of class to the theater. Ushers carried flashlights and they made it a point to show their authority, shushing people who talked and threatening to eject anyone suspected of throwing empty popcorn boxes from the balcony to the seats below.

It was a place where you were proud to be seen, even by adult neighbors who might pass along words about your behavior to your parents.

With one notable exception, that is. The exception came one night in February 1943, or maybe it was 1944. The time is unimportant. The event was. Or at least it seemed so at the time.

That event was a special midweek movie, a movie billed as adult, revealing and educational, a movie restricted to an audience sixteen and over.

Jake, Pokey, Bogey, Tad and Tyke were among the thirteen- and fourteen-year-olds from Heltonville who had seen the thinly-veiled previews of the movie called "Mom and Dad." The insistence that no one under sixteen would be admitted was enough to convince them they had to see the show even though they had to use the ingenuity of their youth.

It took all the wisdom they could muster to do so. They agreed to tell their parents they would be home from basketball practice later than usual because they were going to a belated Valentine party.

They found a ride into Bedford with Chunky, who was sixteen and a licensed driver and who said he felt like he was embarking on a career of contributing to the delinquency of minors.

Chunky parked on the Square and told Pokey and the others he had to meet a friend at the pool room. "You boys are on your own. If you make it into the movie, fine. If not, you can wait here 'til it's over. Either way, I'll see you here when it's over."

After he'd left, Pokey said, "Okay, let's turn up the collars of our coats, slicken our hair, have our money ready and walk up to the ticket window like we're eighteen-year-olds."

Pokey got his ticket, and so did Jake, Bogey and Tyke.

When Tad handed the cashier his wrinkled one-dollar bill, she looked at him and said, "Are you really sixteen?"

Tad nodded. The cashier said, "And I'm Betty Grable and here's your ticket and change."

Most of the seats were taken, so Jake led his associates down the north aisle of the main floor. They were all too embarrassed to look either to the right or left.

It was probably just as well. A couple of their teachers were there, so was a Sunday school teacher . . . and some of their brothers and sisters.

The movie about a teen-age pregnancy and the miracle of birth wasn't all that explicit. Not to Jake, Pokey, Bogey, Tad and Tyke. Like most farm boys, they'd never paid much attention to the birds and the bees, but they had to the livestock on the farm.

Sex and reproduction didn't make them snicker like it did some of the crowd watching the movie, which seemed to go on forever.

By the time Chunky had dropped his other nonpaying passengers and stopped at Tad's house it was past 11:00 p.m. The kerosene lamp was still on in the house. Chunky said "good luck" as Tad headed up the driveway.

His mother and older sister were still up. His mother said, "Sis says you didn't look like you were having too good a time at the Valentine party."

Tad's face turned red. It was the first time he knew his sister had been at the movie, too. He acted like he hadn't heard his mother, who said, "Reckon your pa will have to say something to you tomorrow."

He did. But all he said was, "I can understand your curiosity, Son, and why you wanted to see that movie.

"But was it worth lying to see?"

Tad said, "Not really."

"Not many things are worth lying for," his dad said.

An Airborne Doctor Ahead of the Times

Zeb figured the doctor would drive out from Bedford that warm summer day in 1945.

"Wife's sick," Zeb told the doctor. "She doesn't feel like makin' the trip to Bedford. Both of us would be right thankful if you'd come out to the farm."

Coming out to the farm meant a ten-mile drive each way.

Zeb's place was east of Heltonville. He had driven into Bedford to express his concern about his wife to the doctor.

"You go on home," the doctor said. "I've got a few more patients to see here in the office, then I'll be right out."

Zeb thanked him, made a couple of quick stops on the Square in Bedford and drove home as fast as he could in his 1934 Chevy.

"Doc will be comin' before long," he told Bugsy, one of his sons. "He may not know which house is ours. Wait for him down at the gate and bring him on up to the house."

Bugsy planned to flag down the first strange car he saw, especially one that didn't have dust like most in the community did. "That'll be the 'doc,'" he told himself.

He waited for an hour or so, whiling away the time by picking up handfuls of gravel, then tossing one pebble at a time across the dusty road. If his mom hadn't been sick, he'd have complained about the uneventful wait.

Illustration by Gary Varvel

It didn't stay uneventful much longer. Within minutes he heard the drone of an engine, turned and saw a bright-yellow single-engine plane above the stubble field northwest of the house. The plane glided down slowly, the barn hiding it from Bugsy's view.

Forgetting about the doctor, Bugsy bounded up the hill and climbed through the barbed wire separating the pasture from the wheat stubble, looking all the time for the plane. He saw it, upright, intact on its wheels. A man carrying a black bag was climbing out of the left door.

It was the doctor from town.

Bugsy walked with him to the house, explaining as best he could his mother's symptoms. Then he ran back for a closer look at the plane. He'd no more than climbed into the cockpit when neighbors started arriving, brought there by curiosity. They had seen the plane drop below the tree line to the north and thought it might have crashed.

"I could just visualize that thing crashing into your barn," one of the nearby farmers told Bugsy, who had taken on an air of importance that surpassed his true value. But, after all, it wasn't just any farm around Heltonville that had an airplane parked out by the barn.

No one left. They wanted to see the plane take off back through the wheat stubble.

"Wonder what he'd have done a week ago before the wheat was combined?" somebody asked.

Nobody answered. The doctor was walking back toward the plane, looking like it was the type of house call he made every day.

"Your mom will be fine," the doctor told Bugsy. "I've given her some medicine. In a few days she'll be as good as new."

Bugsy looked relieved.

The doctor climbed into the plane—motioning the crowd off to either side—started the engine and taxied northwest before lifting off the ground. A few hundred feet in the air, he banked for a left turn and aimed the plane toward Bedford.

Zeb watched with the others.

Sharm, one of the neighbors who like to razz him, asked, "He give you a bill?"

Zeb said, "No, but I'm sure I'll get one."

"Probably be about $200. He's got to pay for that plane, somehow," Sharm said.

Zeb just smiled and said, "If he does, I'll charge him $180 for using my field for a landing strip."

Everybody laughed.

Then Zeb said, "Even if he does charge me $200, it'll be worth it. Don't find a wife like mine every day."

Bugsy added, "Or a mom like mine."

Comings, Goings, Doin's

Mr. and Mrs. Hiram Hoots motored to Bedford last Tuesday to pay their taxes.

* * *

Joe Hammer bought Elmer Glutz's Hereford bull one day last week but it got loose as he was taking it home and it tore up Clem Clapsaddle's garden a mite before Elmer got control of it again.

* * *

Ellie Hermon baked her first rhubarb pie of the season Monday. Her husband has been feeling poorly the last few days.

* * *

"Items." That's what farm folks called the personal paragraphs that appeared in the *Bedford Times-Mail* and other county-seat papers in the 1930s and 1940s.

They were news items grouped under geographical areas—places like Popcorn, Lick Skillet, Pinhook, Fishing Creek, Flatwoods, Buddha, Tunnelton, Springville and Heltonville.

"Items" usually appeared once a week and women usually looked for them before they did anything else when the rural carrier delivered the mail. Occasionally, you'd get some of the men to admit they sneaked a look before checking the sports pages or grain tables.

The news was usually gathered by a housewife in the community, written in long hand on scratch paper and dropped in the mail. There was little if any money involved for the report-

ers, except a free copy of the paper, but the prestige of having a byline on the items was a reward in itself. That, plus the fact people figured the writers were in the know, even if they did snitch a few lines from eavesdropping on the party line.

Almost all the "items" read alike. The church report was always first: "Attendance at Sunday School 57. Attendance at worship 38. Everyone enjoyed Pastor Parson's sermon."

Nobody ever drove anywhere in the items. They always motored. The farther folks went from home, the better the placement they got in the list of a dozen or so items. The more times a name was mentioned, the higher a person rose in the social pecking order.

Some people said they didn't want their names in the "items," but that was usually because they didn't do anything to deserve mention.

Nothing bad ever happened in the communities. If it did, the correspondents would leave that story for the reporter on the police beat, who could get the information from the sheriff. The country correspondents may have tipped the editor to a "bad news" development from time to time, but you'd never get them to admit it.

Quite the contrary. The correspondents were community boosters, cheerleaders of sorts.

Evadna Cummings, who wrote the "News From Norman," once devoted most of her column to a complaint about newspapers giving the town a bad name because they often referred to some culprits as being from Norman, when actually they lived out on the rural routes.

"We want the readers of the *Times-Mail* to know that the people in Norman are fine upstanding citizens. Nothing bad ever happens here. It is the people who live outside town who often give our town a black eye," she wrote.

Her complaint made the papers in Indianapolis and other big cities throughout the Midwest and brought a lot of attention to Norman it might not otherwise have received.

But from time to time you'd hear one of the teen-age boys say, "Ain't no point in goin' to Norman. Nothing exciting ever happens there."

"Items" don't appear much in county seat papers any more. That may or may not be one for the better.

This House Could Tell a Thousand Stories

If houses could talk, the big white one up on Todd Hill south of Heltonville could tell a hundred stories. Nay, a thousand stories.

It is abandoned now. Abandoned but unvacant. The memories of two caring parents and their ten children dwell within. The walls that once echoed with the joy of life are quiet, clutching silently the sounds of laughter and weeping, triumph and defeat, praise and discipline.

It's like that in any home that becomes an empty house. It's more so in the house up on Todd Hill. It was into that house that Leona and Will Todd moved in 1921. It was the house they turned into a home for the rest of their lives. It was the house where they were the happiest when their kids were happiest.

Will had met Leona—or maybe Leona met Will—years before. She was Leona Mark at the time, riding horseback from Mundell to teach school up on Henderson Creek. She had finished the eighth grade, then become a certified teacher at State Normal in Mitchell.

Will was one of her fourth-grade students. He wasn't younger than she. Back then a boy, even a young one, had to work on the farm. That came first. Schooling, as parents called it, came second. That's why he was older than most fourth graders would have been.

Romance blossomed in the one-room school. Will and Leona married and moved onto a farm on Henderson Creek, where their first eight children were born.

If they had one goal for their children, it was that all graduate from high school. That may have been one reason they decided to leave Henderson Creek for the farm atop the hill a half-mile. or so from Heltonville. It was a lot easier to get to school from there.

In years to come, friends and neighbors would say all ten of the Todd kids had each gone twelve years to school without ever missing a day. That was an exaggeration. But not much of one. All of them graduated. Few ever missed many days. It was a remarkable achievement for their parents, who had youngsters in school for 32 consecutive years.

Earl was the oldest. He graduated

the year the family moved. Olin graduated in 1924, Ralph in 1925, Howard in 1928.

In an era when many rural youngsters quit school, it was becoming obvious the Todd boys and girls were more ambitious, an ambition fostered by Will and encouraged by Leona.

Two girls graduated next, Bèssie in 1930, Pearl in 1931. Frank graduated in 1936, Kenneth in 1938.

That left Cora and Irvan, who were born in the house on the hill. Cora graduated in 1939, Irvan, whom everyone called Harry, in 1941. **The score: Graduates 10, Dropouts 0**.

Will and Leona were proud of that. They had a right to be. Nobody had ever raised a family like that around Heltonville.

They set the standard of respect for others. Their conduct was exemplary —or if it wasn't it was so much better than the norm it seemed that way.

Will and Leona were just as proud of the kids in the years to come.

Leona and Will are gone now. Seven of the children are still alive, all successes as their parents had intended them to be.

It is to them the house on Todd Hill has the most meaning.

So Sorry To See It Go

Tad Smith was maybe three years old when he became aware there was a school at Zelma. Zelma was just a wide spot in the road between Heltonville and Norman where Ind. 58 made a ninety-degree wrap around two sides of Jimmy Cummings' garden. The school was one-story, frame with white weatherboarding. Inside there was only one room. The building doubled as a church and a lot of folks said it was hard to tell who was the most feared—the teacher or the preacher.

Teachers and preachers came and went, but people all said one thing never changed. You could always count on some Smiths being there. Tad didn't think it ever would be any different.

He became old enough to understand about the school in the mid-'30s. That's when he began to wait for his older brother and two older sisters to arrive home from school.

It was impossible to have any secrets in a one-room school, even though the three were in different grades. Tad's brother, Tyke, didn't have any secrets. Neither did his sisters.

Tyke told Tad, "The only privacy I get around here is when I do the chores and then the cows look at me like they know everything I've done."

His two sisters would start ribbing Tyke as soon as they all got off the school bus. "Didn't know what eleven times twelve was, did you?" one taunted him.

Tyke always had a retort, "I saw you staring at Tommy when you wuz supposed to be studyin' jogerphy," he replied.

It was always fun at first, but by the time the three got to the house they'd be downright fussing at each other. Their ma would have to settle them down. Once she said, "I think I may move tomorrow while you're at school and leave no forwardin' address." But she didn't.

When Tad could, he'd ask Tyke about school and Tyke would tell him what it was like, about how the teacher would have to sorta conduct six classes at once because the twenty-five or so students were scattered in six grades.

Tyke said, "If you pay attention when you're in the first grade to what Mr. Johnson teaches the sixth graders, shucks, you can be as smart as any eleven-year-old by the time you're seven. I'm tellin' you, Tad, you hear the multiplication tables over and over again so much you 'member them better than you do your birthday."

He also told Tad he could make some points by offering to bring in coal from the shed out beside the school and to offer to clean the blackboard once in a while.

Tad also picked up some helpful hints about school at church each Sunday night. He never paid much attention to the parson, but he did let his eyes move ever constantly . . . from the blackboard . . . to the walls . . . to the windows. He'd always smile when he saw some paper done by Tad or the girls or some decoration they had made for Valentine's Day on the window. He noticed the sentences and

figures on the blackboard and thought it must be nice to know what it all meant.

By the time he was five, Tad was eager for school. What he had learned from Tyke and his sisters left him with little fear of the unknown. He figured he and Mr. Johnson would get along just fine.

But things weren't to be. In January before Tad was to enter school, the trustee decided he'd close the school and all students in Pleasant Run Township would have to go to Heltonville. Tad didn't like that at all, even though his parents tried to explain why he'd be better off at a bigger school.

Later in the school year, the principal at Heltonville invited the kids from Zelma and their brothers and sisters who would be first graders to spend a day to see how the bigger school operated. Miss Lively, who would be Tad's first-grade teacher, told him, "I'll be looking forward to seeing you in September."

Tad hung his head and said, "I'd rather be goin' to Zelma."

Miss Lively put her arm around him and said, "You're going to like it here just fine."

He did. But he always sort of felt sad about missing out on at least a year at a one-room school.

Memorials for Those Who Cared

Most of the farmers who lived around Heltonville worked on Decoration Day. There was corn to be cultivated and hay to be harvested and stock to be tended.

The men usually stopped work early, though, to help their wives place flowers on graves at Mundell and Gilgal cemeteries. They didn't say much on those occasions, keeping their thoughts to themselves, too reserved to put into words their feelings.

Those men are gone now, leaving others to decorate their graves on what is now known as Memorial Day.

In a group, they sometimes were loud and boisterous. Away from their friends, in the company of youngsters, they were quiet, thoughtful, and self-effacing.

Some of the land they farmed was flat and fertile, made that way by years of crop rotation, fertilization, and conservation. Some fields were hilly and rolling, scenery more suitable for viewing than for cultivation.

The men sat in the back rows at church, looking uncomfortable in Sunday shirts and ties drawn too snug against bronzed necks unaccustomed to confinement. They put hard-earned, crumpled $1 or $5 bills in the collection basket, figuring salvation would yield more profit than investment in seed corn or fertilizer.

There was Clyde, a man who never saw a stranger. He could turn a chance encounter into a friendship. And often did. He had a knack for making a boy forget his troubles and expect brighter tomorrows.

There was Ben, who had no children, but who befriended others. Hours under the sun had left the felt hat he always wore dust-covered, limp, and faded. Ben was old enough to have seen things when they were new and to appreciate the progress he witnessed. Maybe that is why he kept a Model T longer than any of his neighbors.

There was Jimmy, who never accumulated much wealth or land, but toiled for others as laboriously as he would have for himself. He wore overalls, faded from dozens of boilings, in a soapy kettle, sometimes using a No. 6 nail to hold galluses to bid.

There was George, who lived in a big house a quarter-mile off the road and who seemed a bit distant to youngsters until they found the softness beneath a thin outer shell. George had learned that conversation, like sugar, was more savory when used sparingly.

There was Jake, who lived even farther off the road. There was an aura of dignity about him. He was a craftsman as well as a farmer, able to turn rough cherry lumber into fine furniture.

There were Wes and Clarence, who farmed and worked at the stone mill and always put their families' needs before their own. Like most neighbors, they sometimes disagreed. But their friendship outlived any differences they may have had.

There were others, men like Roy, Joe, Oval, Jasper, Nolan, Stanley, Lawrence, Jim. Men like Johnny, Tom and Homer—men still remembered by the boys they steered down the road of life.

It is a memorial that would have pleased each of them.

Seventh Wonder— Self-Serve Shopping

Tad didn't pay much attention when his parents started talking about an A & P store that was to open in Bedford.

He should have. The store was to be a model for the future.

It must have been just before January 1939 when his folks started discussing the new store, which was to be between "H" and "I" Streets on 16th Street in Bedford.

Tad couldn't understand what all the fuss was about. He figured one store was like another. But then he was only nine years old.

He was familiar with C.E. Cummings' general store in Norman, Roberts' general store in Heltonville and the Jay C store on Ind. 58 at the northeast side of Bedford. His folks shopped at all three places from time to time when they wanted something not carried on the huckster truck.

Most of the time, though, they shopped at Norman or Heltonville because they knew and liked the owners and employees. And, probably, too, because the stores offered credit.

Shopping was the same at each store. Some customers read from a list of things they wanted and a clerk located the item, placed it in a box and wrote down the price on a three-by-five order form. Other customers just handed the clerk the lists which had been scribbled on scrap paper.

Tad thought that was the way shopping would be at the A & P store. It wasn't the case.

The store opened a few days later and the word spread quickly that it wasn't like any other store most of the rural residents around Heltonville had seen.

A & P had closed two stores in other parts of town, creating what would later become known as a supermarket. Clerks no longer gathered items for shoppers. Instead, customers were permitted to walk through the aisles, placing the items they needed into baskets they had picked up at the front. Once they were finished, they carried the baskets to a gate where a cashier waited.

Tad tagged along to help his mother the first time she shopped at the store. She would have been happier if he had helped his dad do whatever he was going to do at the Courthouse.

The boy picked up everything his mom had on her list, plus a lot of things she didn't. When the cashier finished adding up the items, the total took her grocery allowance, plus half her egg-and-butter money.

On the way home, Tad gave his dad a full report on the store. "Don't think that kind of store will last. People want to be waited on. They don't want to have to run up and down aisles looking for what they need," his dad said.

Tad replied, "Well, I helped Ma."

His mom sighed and said, "That's not the kind of help your dad's talking about."

In the years to come she continued to do most of her shopping with the peddler truck driver or at Norman and Heltonville. The only time she went to the A & P store was when Tad wasn't around to help her.

Pair's Life Passes Under the Gavel

The handbills told much of the story: *"Having sold our farm because of poor health, we will offer at public auction the following items."*

A farm sale was both an end and a beginning, a time of sadness and a time of high expectations. It was usually held in early spring when winter died and the earth burst forth with new life. It was a time when one family passed on the stewardship of the land to another.

It was that way when Ez looked back on his life, added up the years and the toil that had gone into them and decided to hang up his overalls for the last time about 1940.

He did so only after long talks with his wife, Minnie, who had shared almost fifty years of quiet contentedness with him on the farm they loved near the Lawrence-Jackson County line.

Minnie hated to leave the farm even more than Ez did. But she knew they must. As long as they stayed and there was work to be done, Ez would do it, despite an aging body that stooped more each day from years of hard work.

The decision to sell the farm did not come easy. Ez would have preferred to give the land to a son or a son-in-law, but none was interested in farming. Life was easier in town, they thought.

Ez and Minnie lived a few miles from Pokey's folks and Pokey knew

Illustration by Gary Varvel

Ez as well as any ten-year-old boy can know a neighbor. Pokey read the sale bill all the way to ". . . and other items too numerous to mention" and noted the sale would be "10:30 a.m. sharp" on a Saturday, when he'd be home from school.

"You goin'?" he asked his dad.

"Sure am. Want to go along?"

It was a question that needed no answer.

The day of the sale was warm and clear. Pokey and his dad drove up to Ez's place about 10:15 a.m. and saw cars already lining each side of the gravel road that went past his place. The barnlot was full of cars of all kinds. "Looks like a lot of people are interested in what Ez has offered for sale," Pokey said.

"Either that or they're just curious," his dad said.

"We interested or curious?" Pokey asked.

His dad said, "Don't have no extry money to buy anything and I've seen everything he's got to sell. We're here as friends. At a time like this, a man needs all the friends he can get."

Ez and the auctioneer were checking over the tools and implements one last time. Pokey and his dad helped them straighten out a harrow and set a breaking plow upright, then move a corn shelter so it could be seen more easily.

The auctioneer started first with the smaller items, giving a sales pitch each time before he opened the bidding. If no one nodded at the price the auctioneer suggested, Pokey's dad would do so.

After he did that three or four times, Pokey said, "Thought you weren't going to buy anything."

"Don't plan to. Just getting other people interested. If they see I want it, they'll figure it must be worth tryin' to get themselves," his dad said.

The items sold almost as fast as the clerk could keep track on his clipboard of who was paying how much for what.

Once in a while Minnie came out to watch, then stopped by the food stand to see how the women from the church were doing selling barbecue sandwiches, pie and coffee. Most of the time she stayed inside alone with her thoughts.

The time passed quickly for Pokey. He bummed thirty-five cents from his dad, twenty cents for a sandwich, ten cents for a piece of apple pie and a nickel for a Royal Crown Cola.

The auctioneer waited until last to sell Ez's team of horses. He knew that, next to Minnie, Ez loved the horses more than anything else on the farm.

Before the bidding started, Pokey's dad testified how good the big sorrels were. Ez had harnessed the horses and drove them around the barnlot for all to see.

The bidding was spirited before a farmer who lived nearby bought them. Ez looked pleased that it was someone he knew.

The buyers quickly paid for what they had bought and loaded it on trucks or wagons.

Pokey and his dad waited around, helping however they could. It was almost dark when there was nothing left to do.

Ez thanked them as they drove away. Pokey looked back to see Ez pull the big blue handkerchief out of the bib pocket of his overalls and dab at his eyes as he walked into the house.

People Drift Off, but Autumn Is Unaltered

Some of the names on the mailboxes are different now. The roads in Pleasant Run Township are now marked with impersonal numbers like 950E, not names like Powerline, Possum Hollow, Dutch Ridge and Goat Run, by which they are really known.

The chuckholes are the same, except they have moved to new locations on the county roads to torment motorists. Some of the old two-story frame farm houses have been replaced by ranch-style bricks. The barns are smaller, the grain bins bigger. The fence rows cleaner. The fields larger. The crops better.

The older generation is gone now. Gone, for the most part, to manicured cemeteries beside neat little churches. Those who remain are the sons and daughters who loved the land enough to stay, those who missed it enough to move back and those who liked it well enough to buy parcels of it and build homes.

For those who left for good, fall is the best time to go home. The sugar maples are taking on the first tinge of yellow. The sassafras is becoming embarrassed red. The beeches, the ash, the oaks, the poplars are forming a kaleidoscope of color. The corn and soybeans look relaxed, rustling softly in the gentle breezes, unfearful of the harvester yet to come. The pumpkins rest at the end of wilted vines, awaiting invitations to become pies and jack-o-lanterns.

Out in the pastures, the cows rip the last threads of green grass, savoring its flavor, knowing there will be no more until spring. The squirrels are at work, gathering a winter's supply of food. The chipmunks do likewise. Animals and pets have taken on heavier coats. Just in case.

Farm wives look over their gardens once more, picking the last of the tomatoes, even the green ones, rescuing them from Old Man Winter. The turnips are about ready to be pulled, the beans dried and ripe for shelling. Walnuts and hickory nuts have fallen and so have the persimmons. They remain along the roads, treasures waiting to be picked up.

Drive out Ind. 58 east from Heltonville and you see the men at Lloyd White's sawmill at work in shirt-sleeves, mindful of the cold weather ahead, days when the weather will keep them from their jobs.

Farther east, the old garage where Abe Martin once repaired cars, tractors and washing machine engines, still stands like a painting amid a grove of trees. Abe is gone. Someone else must fix cars that won't start on cold mornings.

Elmer George's place looks different. The railroad has been abandoned, the tracks removed and the cut in the grade leveled off. The sumac bushes that once lined the railroad have been uprooted, but there are more in the distance.

Off to the left, the old brick house where Ivan Hunter lives looks durable enough to withstand its 120th or so winter.

Turn south off Ind. 58 on 950E and Everett Hunter waves from his self-propelled combine. He's running for Lawrence County commissioner, but he knows you can't vote. He's just friendly by nature. If he's lucky he'll finish the harvest about the same day he's elected.

The barn down the road is filled with hay as it always is in October. It'll all be gone by spring if the winter is long.

Nature's mural grows more colorful after the road passes the junction with 350N. The hills grow steeper and trees thicker, the colors sharper.

Saul Barrett's house still sits at the bottom of the first hill. The fragrance from the wood stoves he and his wife used for cooking and heating is gone, and so are the Barretts. The little house sits forlorn.

It's hard to drive past without expecting them to come out and talk. Off on the hill to the west, the sulphur water still runs into a little basin Saul chipped out of the limestone, just like it has for seventy-five or so years.

Eventually the road connects with U.S. 50. The scenery remains the same east toward Brownstown or west toward Bedford.

It has always been this way in the fall in Lawrence County. Like Brown County without traffic. But it is a beauty, a serenity, that is wasted on youth, whose chores and interest in sports, cars, girls and good times block out the scenes nature paints before them.

Everybody's Life Got a Little Brighter

Each new year in the late 1930s brought a promise of a brighter future for farm families. It would be, they hoped, the year the lights came on in the country.

Congress voted in 1935 to create the Rural Electric Administration, an agency that would loan money to cooperatives to string power lines to farms. That was good news for folks around Heltonville, where fewer than ten percent of the farms were linked to electric lines.

Some of the more prosperous farmers went to work immediately to form a cooperative in Lawrence County, hoping to borrow enough money to build three hundred miles of lines. They were foiled in their efforts.

That was the second of many disappointments for Zeke and his family.

They lived east of Heltonville on a farm that was crossed by transmission lines that carried electricity from the Williams generating station to Clearspring and towns to the east.

Zeke's first disappointment had come years earlier when he tried to convince the Indiana Public Service Co. to install a transformer on the transmission lines and extend a line to his rambling farm house. The power company declined, citing a number of reasons, none of which made much sense to Zeke.

When 1936 arrived, Zeke told his wife, Mollie, "Maybe this will be the year we get electricity." Nothing was done.

He said the same thing at the start of 1937. There was no progress that year, either.

He repeated his hope in 1938. "This surely will be the year," he said.

It seemed at first like he was right. He and some farmers in the eastern part of the county petitioned the Public Service Commission to let the Jackson County REMC extend its lines into their area. County agent John Armstrong added his support.

The petition was granted, but Zeke was told not to be too excited. "These things take time, you know."

At the start of 1939, he had grown disillusioned. No longer did he build up Millie's hopes. He learned later the Jackson County REMC had moved into Guthrie Township to the south. He was disappointed when the lines didn't reach into Pleasant Run Township.

Another year passed. In 1940, the REA released $100,000 to permit REMCs to string lines into all areas of the county.

"It looks good," Zeke told Millie.

The work went slowly. The year ended and 1941 began. Electric lines reached more homes in the county, but not near where Zeke lived.

Gradually, the threat of war became more pressing than the extension of electrical power. The Japanese bombed Pearl Harbor later that year and Zeke's dream of electric lights and other conveniences was shelved.

He and Millie read at night by the light of an Aladdin lamp. The kids grew up. The older ones moved to town where the lights were brighter. The younger ones studied next to coal-oil lamps and listened to a battery-powered radio.

The war ended in 1945. It was another six months or so before an effort to extend the power lines was renewed.

Nothing happened in 1946. Zeke waited for 1947 to arrive to announce: "Millie, I got some good news for you."

Millie shrugged. "Don't tell me this is the year we get electricity."

Zeke grinned. "Yes, but it won't be until the end of the year. I've decided to build you a new house. No sense in wiring this old place. We'll just have the wiring put in the new house when it's built."

The house was built as he promised.

When 1948 arrived, they moved in . . . . and turned on the electricity.

A Barn Full of Memories

If barns could talk, one east of Heltonville could tell a dozen stories. It went up in 1946, when materials were still short because of World War II. It was erected with something old, something new, something borrowed and ended up painted red.

Wes, who owned the farm where it was built, spent hours designing it and accumulating what was needed to build it.

It replaced a fifty-year-old barn that had served well but was almost past repairing, though it did have huge timbers, free of damage, that could no longer be duplicated.

Wes took great pains to salvage a dozen eight-by-eight-inch beams, each 48 feet long, that had been hewn in the 1800s from giant poplar trees.

The braces and the wooden pegs that held them in place were set aside and covered to be used in the new barn. The floor of the barnloft was saved, too. Some of its boards were two inches thick and three feet wide.

Galvanized roofing still was in short supply. The roof off the old barn was removed and carefully stacked, to be used later despite remarks by farmers that it would leak because all the old nail holes couldn't be covered.

Wes scoured nearby farms for poplar trees and ended up buying a dozen from Grant. He and his sons felled the trees and a sawmill cut them into lumber, which was stacked to cure.

It was late summer when Pete came to lay concrete blocks on the firm foundation that had been poured into trenches. He was a skilled craftsman, who preferred masonry to carpentry, but he agreed to help finish the barn at Wes' insistence after the blocks were laid three feet high. The work went well; the quality was excellent.

That is, until Pete and his partner began to nail the sheeting onto the rafters that formed a pattern for the hip roof. Pete reached for a board, thinking it was nailed down, and toppled twenty-five feet to the ground. He got up, fell back, his back broken.

Another carpenter came in and the barn was finished before the winter became too severe.

The rains came the next spring and Wes went up to the loft. He smiled as the rain pelted the tin and ran off the roof without a drop falling through onto the hay.

Pete recovered, came back to look over the barn and agreed it was a job well done. He refused when Wes offered to pay him for some of the time he had lost. "You didn't fall, I did," Pete said, reflecting the manner of man he was.

Later, "Jap" came to paint the roof, and Wes assigned one of his sons to help. "Jap" put a ladder on the roof, tossed a long hay rope over the opposite side and tied it to a steel-tired wagon. The son's job was to move the wagon and retie the rope each time "Jap" got to the peak of the barn on the rungs of the ladder.

Once after the rope had been tied, "Jap" screamed. The boy ran to the opposite side, fearing the painter had fallen, but "Jap" was still on the roof, hanging tightly to the ladder.

"Hey, kid, you put too much slack in the rope and ladder dropped down two feet. I thought the barn was going to have its second broken back."

The boy watched his rope-tying from then on.

The barn is still standing, the holes in the roof still there, the old poplar beams still in place.

The memories are still there, too, of basketball games in the loft, of wrestling matches on the feed floor, of hay being hauled to the barn.

Index

Advertising, 5–6, 12, 28, 30, 149
Agricultural Adjustment Act, 26, 32
Air transportation, airplanes, 145, 146–147, 153–154
Allis Chalmers, 118
Ambrosia artemisia folia (ragweed), 109–110
A & P, 160
Armistice Day (Veterans Day), 45
Armstrong, Jack, 1, 20, 28–29
Artificial sweetener, 36
Atomic bomb, 37–38
Auctions, 161–162
Austin, Ind., 140
Automaking, 30–31, 149
Automobiles & automobile travel, 3–4, 8–9, 27–28, 30–31, 41, 42–43, 46–47, 73–74, 78–79, 87–88, 90, 105–106, 108–109, 120, 124–125, 132–133, 133–134, 145, 149, 150–151, 155; starting, 78–79
Back Creek, 22, 89, 97, 105–106
Bailey, Cladie, 70–71
"Backsliders Brought Back," 90
Baler, stationary, 13
Baling hay, 13
Baltimore & Ohio R.R., 146
Banking and banks, 92, 93–94
Baptism, 105–106
Baptist church, Heltonville, 128
Barber shop, 48–49
Barns, 40, 43, 64, 86, 125–126, 130, 131, 165–166
Barrett, Saul, 164
Bartlettsville, Ind., 8
Baseball, 121–122, 126, 138–139
Basketball, high school, 14, 51, 65–75; referees, 67–68, 111
Beauty aids, 14
Bedford, Ind., 3–4, 5, 12, 14–15, 16, 26–27, 32, 55–56, 65–66, 68–69, 70–71, 74–75, 87, 92–93, 96, 113, 116, 120, 122, 128, 133, 134, 148, 150, 151–152, 153, 160, 164
Bedford Daily Mail, 25, 44, 62, 70
Bedford Stonecutters, 65, 70–71
Bedford Times, 52, 122
Bedford Times-Mail, 68, 74–75, 124–125, 149, 155–156
Beer, 9–10, 14–15, 113–114, 123
Bird, Larry, 65
Bloomers, 20
Bloomington, Ind., 47, 65, 108, 132
"Blue buzzard," 18
Bowman, Doris, 15; Jasper, 125–126
"Breakfast of Champions," 28
Brewster, Al, 74–75
Bridges, 31, 82, 147
Broom-sage, 4, 121
Brown County, 18, 46–47, 164; State Park, 46–47
Brownstown, Ind., 27, 92, 112, 140, 164
"Buckshot," 71–72
Buddha, Ind., 155
Buffalo nickels, 21
Buick autos, 4, 133–134
Bull Durham tobacco, 7, 35
Bundy Bros. elevators, 43
Burns City, Ind., 32
Buses, school, 19, 49–50, 60, 73, 80, 82, 84–85, 97, 130–131, 139–140, 141, 157
Byrne, James, 34
CCC (Civilian Conservation Corps), 32, 52
Cabin builders, 115
Cain, Ed, 70
Cain, Jasper, Dr., 61, 118
Camel cigarettes, 35
Canning, 51–52, 112
Captain Marvel, 5
Carpentry, 125–126, 135–136, 165–166
Catalogs, 12, 51
Cats, 130
Cattle, 41, 50, 64, 103, 109–110
Caves, 113–114
Cedar trees, 51, 53, 115
Cellars, 9–10, 51–52
Cemeteries, 94–95, 98–99, 159, 163
Charlestown (powder plant), 31, 32
Chase, Paul, 44
Cheerleaders, 74
Cherry phosphate, 14
Chesterfield cigarettes, 6, 35
Chevrolet autos, 5, 46, 112, 131, 153
Chicago Cubs, 138
Chicago, Milwaukee & St. Paul R.R., 48, 99–100, 103, 148
Chocks, 129
Christmas, 24, 25, 37, 53, 54–55, 55–56
Chromium, 36
Chuckholes, 79, 163
Church (see Religion, rural)
Cigarettes, 6–7, 35–36
Civil Defense, 32
Civil War, 31
Clampitt, Thornt, 73
Clark, Gen. George Rogers, 30
Clark, Miss., 34–35, 139–140
Clearspring, Ind., 21, 111; Road, 49
Clifty Falls State Park, 139–140
Coal oil, 33
Coca-Cola, Coke, 65, 150
Columbus, Christopher, 85
Combine, 63, 118, 154, 164
Comforters, 59
Comic books, 5
Compass, 5, 28
Conscription (draft), 32
Contour farming, 26–27
Copper, 36
Corn, 26, 39–40, 101–102, 129–130; crib, 41, detasseling, 37; shucking, 43–44
Corncob pipe, 6–7
Country Gentleman, 83
Cox, Pastor, 63
Crane, Hayden, 75
Cream separator, 28, 54, 56, 109
Crime, 22–23, 113, 150–151, 155–156
Crowe, Rep. E.B., 44
Cultivating, 101–102
Cummings, C.E., store, 21, 111, 112, 160; Evadna, 155–156; Laura, 15; Mildred, 15
Daisy Manufacturing Co., 5–6
Dancing, 28
Days Work chewing tobacco, 7
Dean, Dizzy, 138–139
Death and dying, 94–95, 98–99, 128, 159, 163–164
Decoration Day (see Memorial Day)
Dentyne, 3–4
Depression, 18–29, 30, 32, 48, 60, 112, 116, 121
Devil's Backbone, 145–146
Di Maggio, Joe, 138
Dickey, Bill, 138
Dr. Pepper, 103, 111
Doctors, country, 61, 118, 153
Draft, 32
Drinking (alcohol), 9–10, 27–28, 51, 113–114, 123, 139–140
Drought (Depression), 18
Dudleytown, Ind., 31
Dunbar, Sheriff Lincoln (Curly), 25
Dust storm, 18–19
Dutch Ridge, 163
Economic Stabilization, 34
Elliott, Dave, 66, 69
Electricity, 53, 69, 164–165
English, Ind., 34–35, 133–134
Erosion, soil, 26–27
Ethiopia, 18
Farmall tractors, 10–11, 80–81
Farm Journal, 83
Farmers Guide, 12
Farmer's guide, 17
Fallen Timbers, Battle of, 30
Farming, 4, 7, 10–11, 13, 21, 26–27, 39–40, 42–43, 49–50, 51–52, 54–55, 62–63, 79–80, 82, 83–84, 86, 88–89, 99–100, 101–102, 104, 111, 116, 118, 120–121, 127, 129–130, 159, 161–162, 164–165, 165–166
Fashion, dress, 20, 34, 80, 86, 89–90, 93–94, 140–141, 144
Father's Day, 93
Faubion, Mrs., 45, 77
Fayetteville, Ind., 67, 74
Feed sacks, 20
Feller, Bob, 13, 90
Fertilizer, 81, 87–88, 127
52-20 Club, 139
Firearms, 5–6, 71
Fishing, 76, 97–98
Fishing Creek, 155
Flatwoods, 106, 133–134, 140–141, 155
Foch, Marshall Ferdinand, 45
Food and foods, 24, 28, 51–52, 56–57, 59, 80–81, 106–108, 109–110, 112
Ford autos, 4, 21, 78–79, 86, 90, 149, 150–151, 159
Franklin, Benjamin, 86
Freeman Field, 147
Freetown, Ind., 21, 46, 99
Frogs, 96–97, 146
Funeral homes, 128
Furnace, 58–59
Gambling (see poker, pool, slot machines)
Gardens and gardening, 40, 76, 80–81, 163
Gasoline stations, 148
Gehrig, Lou, 138
General Mills, 28
Geodes, 11, 49, 82, 88–89
George, Elmer, 163; Horace, store, 111
Gilgal cemetery, 159; Drive, 80
Gilstrap, Lester, 74–75; Wilbert, 66–67, 68–69, 74–75

Goat Run, 9, 13, 163
Grable, Betty, 152
Granary, 11, 40
Granny White House, 113
Grant, Cary, 97
Gravedigging, 98
Graves, Jim, 66, 69
Great Plains, 18–19, 111
Green, Joe, 88
Greenville, Ohio, 149
Greyhound bus, 149
Grit, 62
Grocery stores, 160
Groundhog Hill, 9; Road, 49, 82, 147
Guthrie, James, 28
Guthrie Township, 141, 165
Halloween, 48–49
Hames, 143
Harness, 143–144
Harrell, Clarence, 50; Florence Anna, 15
Harrow and harrowing, 81, 162
Harvard University, 115
Harvest, 7, 40, 42–43, 51–52, 63, 111, 118, 120, 129–130, 132, 154
Hay, 13
Hayden, Ind., 74
Heating, 58–59, 60, 64
Heltonville, Ind., 6, 9, 9–10, 12, 15, 16, 21, 22–23, 24, 25, 26, 27, 28, 30–31, 33, 35, 38, 39, 42, 43, 46, 48–49, 51, 53, 55, 56, 61, 64, 70–71, 78, 80–81, 83, 88–89, 91, 94–95, 96–97, 99, 101, 103, 105, 106, 111, 112, 113, 116–117, 121–122, 124–125, 125–126, 127, 132, 133–134, 138, 140, 142, 145, 147–148, 153, 155, 156, 157, 159, 160, 165; basketball team, 66–75; 400s, 121
Heltonville Limestone Co., 93
Henderson Creek, 8, 89
Hickory Grove, Ind., 21
Hiroshima, 38
Hirscher's crossroads, 134
Hitchhiking, 87–88, 111
Hodges, John, 66
Hogweed (ragweed), 109
Holidays, 15–16, 24, 25, 37, 40, 45, 48, 53, 54–55, 55–56, 91, 93, 94–95, 98–99
Holt, Walter (Dutch), 121–122
Holy Rollers, 8
"Home brew," 9
Homes and houses, 52, 140, 156–157, 163, 164–165
"Hookers," 119
Hoosiers, 1, 18, 30, 39, 46, 65, 101, 115, 145
Horses, 10–11, 54, 64, 80, 102, 143–144, 161–162
Housekeeping, homemaking, 20, 33, 76–78, 130–131, 136–137
Houston, Ind., 21
Hudson Motor Co., 149
Humpback bridge, 82, 147
Hunter, Miss, 62, 64, 141
Hunter Everett, 163–164; George, 50; Grover, 49; Ivan, 15; Stanley, 50
Hunter's Creek, 80, 89
Hunting, duck, 118
Huron, Ind., 74

Ice cream, 56, 107, 109–110, 139
Illness, 13, 61, 104, 116, 118, 153–154, 166
Indiana High School Athletic Association, 67
Indiana Public Service Co., 164–165
Indianapolis, 101, 108–109, 120, 147
Indianapolis News, 1
Industry, 30–31, 32, 133, 147, 149
International trucks, 101, 108–109
Items, 155
J.C. Penney store, 55, 120
Jackson, Bob, 66, 69
Jackson County, 46, 111, 143–144; REMC, 165
Jails, prison, 23, 25
Japan, 37–38
Jay C Store, 160
Jello, 24
Jobs, occupations, 13, 32, 55, 58, 93, 99–100, 111, 112, 118, 119, 121, 122–123, 125–126, 127, 128, 149, 159, 163–164, 165–166
Johnson, Floyd, 147
Jones, "Indiana," 3; Leston, 128
Karo syrup, 36
Katis, John, pool parlor, 16–17, 66–67, 152
Kool cigarettes, 35
Kool candy bars, 21
Kurtz, Ind., 21, 99
LS/MFT, 35
Labor Day, 40
Lampblack, 143
Lawrence County, 1, 16, 25, 26, 31, 43, 65–66, 74–75, 88–89, 111, 116, 122, 124, 146, 164
Lawrence Theater, 150, 151
Leatherwood Creek, 26, 49, 82, 89, 96, 108, 113, 117, 121, 147
Leesville, 113–114, 125, 146
Leonard's confectionary, 14
Lick Skillet, Ind., 155
"Light in the Kitchen," 51
Lightning rods, 86
Little Salt Creek, 89
Lively, Miss, 18–19, 158
"Lorenzo Jones," 28
Louis, Joe, 78
Lucky Strike cigarettes, 6, 35–36
Mackinaw jacket, 53, 54, 56
Madison, Ind., 65, 139–140; State Hospital, 117
Maher, Fred, 20
Mail order catalogs, 12
Marshall Township, 108
Martin County, 32
Marvel cigarettes, 6, 35
"Mary Foster, the Editor's Daughter," 28
Masonic Temple, 66
Matthews, Harry, 44
Maumee, Ind., 21
Maple trees, 50, 51
Mark, Charlie, 50; Miss, 61
Martin, Abe, 49
Marty, Joe, 139
Mash sack, 107
Mayapples, 84
Measles, 61
Medicine, 61, 104, 108–109, 153–154
Medora, Ind., 52, 43, 107; junction, 88
Melons, 42–43

Memorial Day, 94–95, 98–99, 159
Merit Shoe Store, 56
Methodist church, Heltonville, 50
Military service, U.S., 32, 36, 45, 99, 108, 139–140
Milk separator, 28, 54, 56, 109
Milkhouse, 109
Milking, 62
Miller, Cecil, 147
Mincemeat, 24
Ministers (see Religion, rural)
Mitchell, Ind., 43–44, 134
Model A (Ford), 21
Model T (Ford), 4, 78–79, 86, 159
Monroe County, 89
Montgomery Ward, 12
Moonshine, 22
Moore, Ralph, 43–44
Morel mushrooms, 84–85
Morgan, Gen. John Hunt, 30
Morgan Packing Co., 100, 112
Motels, 27–28
Mother's Day, 91
Mount Pleasant Church, 122
Mourer, H.H., 43–44
Movies, 1, 5, 21, 96–97, 151–152
Mowing, mowing machines, 102, 104
Mud, 79–80
Mumblety-peg, 146
Mundell cemetery, 95, 98–99, 159; church, 15, 50, 101, 138
Mushrooms, 84–85
National Geographic, 101
National Recovery Administration, 18
Neat's foot oil, 143
Needmore, Ind., 67, 73, 108
New Deal, 18, 25, 26–27, 32, 121
New York Yankees, 138
Newhouse, Dr., E.A., 43–44
Newhouser, Hal, 13
Newkirk, Jeptha, 128
Newspapers, 5, 44, 74–75, 124–125, 155–156
Nichols, Harry, 50
Norman, Ind., 21, 46, 49, 50, 56, 112, 122, 155–156, 157, 160
Odd Fellows, 113, 128
Oertel's 92 (beer), 123
Office of Price Administration, 36
Ohio River, 139
Old Gold cigarettes, 35
"Old Rugged Cross," 8
"One-armed bandit," 27
Oolitic, Ind., 66
Orange County, 89; courthouse, 134
Orleans, Ind., 134
Outhouses, 48
Owensburg, Ind., 74
P-80 Lockheed jet, 147
PT-26s, 147
Paoli, Ind., 134
Pasture, 4, 62–63
Pearl Harbor, 34
Pedometer, 28–29
Persimmons, 163
Petrolatum, 143
Phillip Morris cigarettes, 6, 35
Picker, mechanical corn, 129
Picnics, 113
Pigs, 54, 57, 83–84; ringing, 83–84
Pinhook, Ind., 155
Pioneer Seed Co., 37

Planting, 62–63, 76, 80–81
Pleasant Run Township, 14, 41, 43, 105, 108, 118, 120, 121, 163, 165; trustee, 118
Plows and plowing, 10–11, 76, 80–81, 88–89, 131
Plymouth, Michigan, 5
Poison ivy, 104–105
Poker, 113–114
Politics, rural, 116, 116–117, 118, 164
Police and law enforcement, 150–151, 155
Pollution, 56, 146
Pontiac autos, 46
Pool, pool halls, 16–17 (see also Katis)
Popcorn, Ind., 155
Possum Hollow Road, 94, 163
Potatoes, planting, 81–82
Poultry, 54–55, 92, 116
Powerline Road, 49, 80, 86, 94, 134, 147, 163
Pranks, 48–49, 89–90, 119
Prince, Ronnie, 88
Prince Albert tobacco, 7
Prohibition, 4, 22
"Quarry, The," 65–66
Quilting, 20
Radio programs, radio, 1, 20, 28, 68–69, 126
Ragweed, 109–110
Railroad, 48, 99, 142
Rationing, 34–35, 36–37, 73
Recreation, 6–7, 16–17, 21, 27–28, 42–43, 46–48, 48–49, 51, 53, 61, 76, 84–85, 89–90, 96–97, 97–98, 101, 103, 108–109, 113–114, 117, 123, 127, 138–139, 139–140, 145, 150–151, 151–152, 155
Raines, Loren, 45, 73, 135–136
Referees, basketball, 67–68
Religion, rural (beliefs, churches, preachers), 8, 14–15, 15–16, 29, 58–59, 63, 90, 101, 105, 106–108, 122–123, 135, 138–139, 155, 159
Resorcin, 96
Retail business, 21, 55–56, 103, 132–133, 148, 160
Revenue agents, federal, 22
Rheumatism, 13
Riverside Park, 108–109
Roadhouses, 27
Roads and highways, rural, 8–9, 27, 34–35, 46–48, 73–74, 79–80, 82–83, 105–106, 108–109, 123, 133–134, 139–140, 146, 163–164; named roads—Ind. 37, 133–134; Ind. 46, 46–47; Ind. 58, 46, 50, 82, 87, 94, 103, 111, 115, 116, 120, 124, 126, 128, 134, 157, 158, 163; Ind. 252, 31; US 50, 27, 42, 87, 89, 146, 164
Roberts, W.C., 115–116
Roberts & Sons general store, 6, 103, 115–116, 122, 133, 160
Robertson, Oscar, 65
Roosevelt, Franklin D., 18, 25, 26 30–31, 32, 48, 121
Royal Crown Cola, 162
Ruffing, Red, 138
Rugbeater, 77–78
Rural Electric Administration, 164
Ryder, Red, and carbine, 5–6

St. Louis Cardinals, 139
Salt Creek, 8
"San Antone," 140
Sassafras, 21, 163
Saturday Evening Post, 30
Schools, rural, and education (see also Basketball), 18–19, 24, 34–35, 38, 39–40, 40–41, 45, 49–50, 59–60, 61, 80, 84–85, 101, 115–116, 135–136, 139–140, 140–141, 142–143, 156–157, 157–158
Scythe, 104
Sears, Roebuck & Co., 12
Seymour, Ind., 65, 111, 147
Sex, 27–28, 87, 96–97, 142, 151–152
"Shall We Gather at the River," 106
Shawswick, 73, 147; basketball team, 66–67, 68–69
Shawswick Township, 122
Sherrill, George, 49
Shooting Star, 147
Shredder, corn, 129–130
"Sioux City Sue," 140
Slot machines, 27, 41
Smithville, Ind., 8, 9, 68
Smoking, 6–7, 35–36
Soapstone, 90
South Bend, Ind., 30–31
Spiegel, 12
Spinning, 20
Sports (see also Basketball), 121–122, 138–139
Spring Mill State Park, 113–114
Springhouse, 84, 107
Springville, Ind., 102, 122, 155
Spur station, 148
Stafford, D.F., 120
Still, 22–23
Stimson, Henry, 38
Stone Belt, 119
Stone City National Bank, 92, 93–94, 120
Stonecutters, Bedford, 14, 103
Stonecutting and stonecutters, 93, 119, 122, 127
Story, Ind., 46
Stoves, 33, 54, 59, 131
Straw boss, 122
Strip farming, 26–27
Studebaker auto, 30–31
Suckers, 76, 98
Sunday School, 15–16
Supermarkets, 51, 160
Swimming, 89–90
Tack, 143–144
Taverns, 14–15
Taxi, 150–151
Tenderloin, 24, 51, 57, 59
Terraplane autos, 26
Terrell, Dee, grocery, 6, 21
Thanksgiving, 25
Thresher, 129
Thurman Funeral Home, 128
Thurman, Tom, 128
Tobacco, 6–7, 35–36
Todd, Leona and Will, family, 156–157
Todd Hill, 156; Road, 82
Tomatoes, growing, 100, 112
Tourist cabins, 27–28
Townsend, Gov. Clifford, 44
Tractors, 10–11, 62–63, 79–80, 104, 118, 129, 143

"Trail of the Lonesome Pine," 53
Travelers, 103, 119
Trogdon, Wendell, 1, 39, 51
Trucks, 87–88, 101, 108–109, 112, 120
Truman, Harry S, 38
Tunnelton, Ind., 67, 74–75, 115, 155
Turtle, 90
Twain, Mark, 41
U.S. Congress, 25, 32
Uniontown, Ind., 140
V-J Day, 38
Vallonia, Ind., 42, 107
Velvet tobacco, 7
Veterans Day, 45
Victrola, 53
Vincennes, Ind., 30, 65
Von Ritz theater, 96, 151
WBIW Radio, 69, 73
WHAS Radio, 33
Wagons, 102, 130, 133–134
Walton, Ike, 44
War Between the States, 30
War Production Board, 34
Washing clothes, 136–137
Washington, Ind., 65; County, 89
Washington Redskins, 112
Watermelons, 42–43
Waverly, Ind., 108–109
Weasel, 92
Westerns, 5, 150, 151
Whale, 142
Wheat, 26, 40, 62, 111, 118, 154
Whiskey, 22–23, 139
White, Lloyd, sawmill, 39, 163
White, Lobie (Shorty), 60, 73–74, 82, 85, 130, 141
White lightning, 22
White River, 26, 42, 107, 134, 146
Wills, Jan, 51
Wings cigarettes, 35
Winklepleck, E.O., 45, 128, 142–143
Women, and rural life, 12, 20, 28, 76–78, 80, 83–84, 91, 106–108, 130–131, 136–137, 140, 155–156, 160, 161–162, 163
Woodhouse, 55
Works Progress Administration (WPA), 60
World Series, 126, 138–139
World War I, 45
World War II, 14, 30–38, 55–56, 73, 132, 147, 165
Wray, Wes, 89, 98
Yarn, spinning, 20
Zelma, Ind., 21, 26, 89, 94, 157–158

The Author

Wendell Trogdon grew up on a farm near Heltonville in Southern Indiana and has retained his love of small towns and country life. That love is reflected in his award-winning column for *The Indianapolis News*, "Those Were the Days," which has appeared weekly since 1975.

A graduate of Franklin College and a U.S. Army veteran, the author began his career in journalism at the Logansport *Pharos-Tribune*. Since joining *The News* in 1957, he has been a reporter, suburban editor, city editor, news editor and assistant managing editor. He is also the author of "Quips," a front-page feature which has appeared daily in *The News* since 1974.

He and his wife, Fabian, live in Mooresville, Indiana. They have three grown daughters, Tamara, Deanna and Jenell.

Wendell Trogdon

The Artist

Gary Varvel was born the same year Wendell Trogdon began working at *The Indianapolis News*. The artist's own career at *The News* began in 1978. As the newspaper's chief artist, he has illustrated the daily "Quips" column and feature stories and has designed section covers.

A graduate of Danville (Indiana) High School, he attended The Herron School of Art while cartooning for the *Danville Gazette*. He later worked as production manager and editorial cartoonist at *The County Courier* in Brownsburg.

He lives near Avon, Indiana, with his wife, Carol, and their two small children, Ashley and Brett.

The Editor

A wide-ranging writer and journalist now based in Chicago, Martin Northway is former managing editor of *The Brown County Democrat* (Nashville, Indiana) and was a contributor to *Power Team*, the Cummins Engine Co. magazine. His numerous articles have been published in national and regional newspapers and magazines.

He is president of The Highlander Press and is the author of *Brown County Artists and Where To Find 'Em* (1979), scheduled to be republished by Highlander in a new, revised edition.

He and his children, Heather and Andy, live in Evanston, Illinois.